NINETY-TWO POEMS
AND HYMNS OF
YEHUDA HALEVI

Contents

GOD

SOUL

PEOPLE

No asterisk: *Sixty Hymns and Poems* (Konstanz: Verlag Oskar Wohrle, 1924).
Ninety-two Hymns and Poems (Berlin: Verlag Lambert Schneider, 1927).
**(1) labeled "Excusus" in 1924 volume (and 1927), making total 61.
***(2) labeled "Excursus" in 1927 volume, making total 95. Rosenzweig uses the term "Excursus" to indicate that Halevi's authorship of these poems (6, 58, 86) has been considered doubtful.

EDITOR'S NOTE

This volume has the virtue of reproducing the contents of the 1927 book, *Jehuda Halevi, Zweiundneunzig Hymnen und Dedichte*, that Franz Rosenzweig saw into print. Although Rosenzweig entitled that book *Ninety-Two Poems and Hymns by Yehuda Halevi*, there were actually ninety-five poems translated and commented upon. Rosenzweig's first edition, entitled *Sixty Hymns and Poems of Yehuda Halevi*, actually contained sixty-one poems. For precise details regarding the "extra" poems, and to see which poems appeared in which books, see the editor's note at the bottom of the Table of Contents in this volume. The order of the poems in this volume has the additional virtue of conforming to the same in *F. Rosenzweig: Der mench un sein Werk, Part IV, I. Band—Hymnen und Dedichte des Jehuda Halevi* (The Hague, Martinus Nijhoff, 1983), held in copyright by Kluwer Academic Publishers, which, unlike the earlier editions, is still in print. In both the 1924 and 1927 books, the whole set of Rosenzweig's translations of Halevi's poems and the whole set of Rosenzweig's commentaries upon those poems appeared in two separate sections, one after the other. In this volume, each poem appears together with its commentary.

Bible translations are for the most part from *The Holy Scriptures: According to the Masoretic Text*, published by the Jewish Publication Society of America, Philadelphia, Pennsylvania. *The Holy Scriptures* (also known as *The Jerusalem Bible*), published by Koren Publishers Ltd., Jerusalem, Israel, also has been consulted. Occasionally changes have been made to suit the text to Rosenzweig's translation.

Footnotes by Rosenzweig are labeled "FR," by Kovach "TK," by Jospe "EJ," and by myself, unlabeled. Where I have thought it useful, I have provided in footnotes some of the biblical passages to which Rosenzweig refers.

Thomas Kovach translated Rosenzweig's preface by himself. The co-translation of Rosenzweig's commentaries proceeded as follows: Eva Jospe produced a first draft that was reworked by Thomas Kovach for final publication. Gily Gerda Schmidt translated the poems by herself.

The editor, Richard A. Cohen, is presently Isaac Swift Distinguished Professor of Judaic Studies at the University of North Carolina at Charlotte, author of *Elevations: The Height of the Good in Rosenzweig and Levinas* (Chicago, 1994), translator of several books by Emmanuel Levinas, and editor of several volumes of philosphy. Eve Jospe, who formerly taught at Georgetown University and George Washington University, has also translated Moses Mendelssohn, Hermann Cohen and Martin Buber.

Thomas Kovach is presently Head of the Department of German Studies at the University of Arizona. Gilya Gerda Schmidt is Chair of the Fern and Manfred Steinfeld Program in Judaic Studies at the University of Tennessee, Knoxville. She is author and editor of several volumes on Martin Buber.

INTRODUCTION

ROSENZWEIG'S REBBE HALEVI:
FROM THE ACADEMY TO THE YESHIVA

Richard A. Cohen

To those who knew him, or to those who read his works or read about him, Rosenzweig's short life has always meant more than a chronology of dates, facts, or publications.[1] Indeed, his life is often discussed in hagiographic tones. The seven final bedridden years of almost total paralysis, during which Rosenzweig maintained and even enriched an unflagging and productive commitment to Judaism, completing his translations of Halevi and working with Buber, are certainly the stuff of legend. My purpose, however, is to pursue his intellectual and spiritual growth, which together make sense of a life's most concrete movements, decisions, and relations.

For Rosenzweig, as for many of the twentieth century's Western religious seekers, it was education that guided his spiritual development. This meant moving from the demanding intellectual and spiritual commitments of university education, to the no less demanding commitments of life within a religious community. To learn the meaning of Jewish religious life meant turning to Yehudah Halevi, the great medieval Jewish poet and thinker. Rosenzweig's study, translation, and commentary upon the religious poems and hymns of Halevi (born c. 1080) represent the culmination of his impressive European education and the final stage of his self-education as a religiously observant Jew.

There is no topic to which Franz Rosenzweig devoted more attention, as a person or in his writings, than that of education and Jewish

---

1. The outline of Rosenzweig's life is easy to trace: 1886, birth in Cassel, Germany; 1886–1905, assimilated upper middle-class upbringing; 1905–1914, university study of medicine, history, philosophy, law; 1914–1918, WWI military service; 1920, publication of doctoral dissertation, *Hegel and the State;* 1921, publication of *The Star of Redemption* (translation by William W. Hallo, Notre Dame: University of Notre Dame Press, 1985); 1920, marriage, director of Lehrhaus (Jewish adult education) in Frankfort; 1922, birth of a son; 1922–1929, paralysis and home confinement with amyotrophic lateral sclerosis (Lou Gehrig's disease), Bible translations with Buber; 1924, 1927, two volumes of translations of and commentaries upon ninety-five selected poems by Yehudah Halevi; 1929, death at the age of forty-three.

education. Like many of his privileged compatriots in the German Jewish bourgeoisie, he was a student of Germany's gymnasium and university system. After completing his doctoral dissertation in 1912 on the development of Hegel's political thought, published as *Hegel and the State* in 1920, Rosenzweig could easily have embarked on the university career that beckoned to him. Instead, as we know, he chose another path: a career in Jewish adult education.[2]

In writing the narrative of Rosenzweig's life and thought, scholars (especially Nahum Glatzer) have highlighted two closely related events of 1913, both central to his relation to Christianity. I want to add a third no less decisive event: Rosenzweig's rejection of a promising university career and his acceptance of an appointment as director of the *Lehrhaus*, the Free House of Jewish Learning in Frankfort. This third turning point led him away from the work of the Western university, encapsulated in *Hegel and the State*, but also in the essentially apologetic work of leave-taking, *The Star of Redemption* (1921), to the fuller Jewish life that produced his two volumes of Halevi translations and commentaries (1924, 1927). This work was the result of his complete engagement in Jewish learning and communal life.

Conversations with Rosenstock: From Relativism to Christianity

First there is the famous conversation of July 7, 1913, with Eugen Rosenstock, the culmination of several conversations with Rosenstock on the topic of truth, philosophy and religion. What is decisive about this conversation has two dimensions, one negative, the other positive, though they are two sides of a single new appreciation for the subordination of philosophy to religion. On the negative side, Rosenstock persuades Rosenzweig of the untenability of his or any skeptical relativism.[3] On the positive side, Rosenstock does so in the name of a religious absolute, more specifically, in the name of Christian faith. Persuaded to give up his skeptical relativism, and under the influence of Rosenstock's (himself a convert) commitment to Christianity, Rosenzweig believes that he too, like

---

2. As early as 1917, Rosenzweig published "It Is Time" ("Zeit ists"), written as an open letter to Hermann Cohen, on the topic of Jewish education in Germany; in 1920 he wrote and published another open letter, this time addressed to Eduard Strauss, again on Jewish education in Germany, in English called "Towards a Renaissance of Jewish Learning" (*"Bildung und kein Ende"*). (In Franz Rosenzweig, *On Jewish Learning*, edited by Nahum N. Glatzer [New York: Schocken Books, 1965]. Henceforth JL.)

3. See *Franz Rosenzweig: His Life and Thought*, edited by Nahum N. Glatzer (New York: Schocken, 1967), pp. 23–24. Henceforth FRLT.

Rosenstock, and like his cousins Hans and Rudolf Ehrenberg before him, can only make good on his new found appreciation for religion by converting to the Christian faith.

Rosenzweig was no doubt influenced by Hegel's reading of history. His decision to convert to Christianity depended not only on the logic and faith of Rosenstock but also on his own conviction, shored up by Hegelian philosophy, that the *zeitgeist* of all of modern Europe was essentially Christian, regardless whether one identifies with the *ecclesia* (like Rosenstock and Ehrenberg); or with the *seculum,* through the sciences, humanities or arts (as he himself had done); or through the power of the State, as did many others. After studying Hegel for a little more than a year with Professor Heinrich Rickert at Freiburg, and four years before his own decision to convert in 1913, Rosenzweig had supported his cousin Hans Ehrenberg's decision to convert to Christianity. Explaining his reasoning to his parents, who opposed this decision, Rosenzweig writes on November 6, 1909: "We are Christian in everything. We live in a Christian state, attend Christian school, read Christian books, in short, our whole 'culture' rests entirely on a Christian foundation; consequently a man who has nothing holding him back needs only a very slight push . . . to make him accept Christianity."[4]

With "nothing holding him back," conversion to Christianity would be a forthright acknowledgment of the implicit truth that Hegelian philosophy had already made objectively explicit a century earlier, namely, that modern Europe, and hence modern Europeans, regardless of overt profession, are essentially Christian.

This Hegelian reading of European history is based on a philosophical appropriation and conceptual reinterpretation of Judaism into mainstream Christian historical self-understanding. This version of Christianity understood itself not simply as a new and different religion from Judaism, indebted to Judaism for various forms and ideas, to be sure, but rather as a further and higher development of Judaism itself. It was the new Israel. Such supersessionism was a development, furthermore, which, this argument insisted, historical Judaism to its eternal discredit and shame had shirked in the first centuries of the common era and on up to the present day: the spiritual validity of Judaism would be only that of a preparation for Christianity. Hence all the vast literature of rabbinic Judaism would count for nothing, would be an empty and stubborn casuistry. Judaism after Christianity would be essentially obsolete. Jews would be walking relics. Thus when Rosenzweig gave up his skeptical relativism for the sake of the absolute truth of religion, he could only become a Christian, and

---

4. FRLT, p. 19.

not at all because of the contingency that Rosenstock happened to be Christian (and could have been Confucian, say, or a Muslim). Rosenzweig must become a Christian because the absolute truth of religion, which alone overturns skeptical relativism, is found in Christianity and in Christianity alone. The doctrine of the absolute or exclusive historical superiority of Christianity, the penultimate vision of truth in Hegelian philosophy, is the apex of Christian theology.

It was thus as an almost good Hegelian ("almost" because contra-Hegel Rosenzweig was convinced of the superiority of religion to philosophy), and as a completely good Christian, that Rosenzweig intended to convert to Christianity. Rosenzweig's conversion would be less a conversion, a radical overturning, transformation, metamorphosis, or rebirth of the self, than a realization, actualization, or "explication" of a latent but already operative Christian essence. For both Christian and Hegelian reasons, Rosenzweig decided to convert to Christianity not as a pagan or as a philosopher, but, replicating the Hegelian dialectic and the Christian drama, as a Jew.

Obscured from even Rosenzweig's brilliant self-consciousness, however, the ambivalence evident in his justification was not merely between Hegelianism and Christianity, but pivoted on the difference between a vilified Judaism, as it was understood by both Hegelian philosophy and Christian theology, on the one side, and a verified Judaism, as it was (or had been) understood and lived by the Jewish community. This deeper ambivalence—which allows enough space or time for what Emmanuel Levinas calls "the miracle of Jewish destiny, produced at the last hour, at the last instant, in an 'almost' as wide as a needle point, but wide enough to allow time for a voice to arrest the arms stretched toward the irreparable"[5]—must always be kept in mind when we understand Rosenzweig's insistence that he convert to Christianity as a *Jew*.[6] As everyone knows, Rosenzweig did not convert. Not only did he remain a Jew, but Jews and Judaism became the center of his life and thought.

Rosenzweig, the Hegelian, meant to replicate in his own person, by means of his conversion, the movement from the alleged anachronistic abstract particularity of Judaism to the historically situated universalism of Christianity—with "nothing holding him back." But Rosenzweig, the Jew, ended up with much more than he had originally bargained for. What he discovered was that Hegel, Christianity, Ehrenberg, Rosenstock, and he himself were all mistaken about the true meaning of Judaism, and hence

---

5. Emmanuel Levinas, "Franz Rosenzweig," translated by Richard A. Cohen, in *Midstream*, November 1983, Volume 39, No. 9, p. 33.

6. See FRLT, p. 25.

were also mistaken about the true relations that bound Judaism to itself, and Christianity to Judaism. Judaism, he discovered, was not merely particular, abstract, exhausted, nor trapped in a limited partiality criticized and overcome by Christianity and Hegelian philosophy.

Rather Judaism was neither abstract nor concrete, neither particular nor universal, according to the resources of a Hegelian or Christian appropriation. Instead it offered another path entirely, one whose contours were prior to and otherwise than the various conundrums or dialectical resolutions necessitated by the oppositions invoked by Christian theology and Hegelian philosophy. Judaism offered a path where the apparent disjunction (and hence the always abstract conjunction) of these oppositions was undercut in the ongoing material and spiritual life of a living community—in the daily, weekly, annual, and life cycles wherein temporality and eternity met and interpenetrated. Fully turning the tables, Rosenzweig discovered that it was upon the unbroken and indissoluble union of body and spirit lived by the Jewish community that Christianity itself, not to mention the redemption of the entire world,[7] had always been and would always be hitched and guided.

Yom Kippur Services:
From Hegel and Christianity to Judaism

The second great event of Rosenzweig's spiritual biography, just three months after the culminating conversation with Rosenstock: the now famous Yom Kippur experience in a small orthodox shul in Berlin, on October 11, 1913. Rosenzweig intended to convert to Christianity as a Jew. He attended Rosh Hashana services on October 2 and 3 in Cassel, his hometown, and afterwards informed his mother of his intention to convert. Glatzer's account of this encounter shows that though Rosenzweig's family was assimilated, like many upper-class German Jewish families of the time, for them, or for Rosenzweig's mother in any event, conversion to Christianity was still going too far:

A day or two later [after Rosh Hashana], after a night spent in discussion with a friend, he came down from his study into the living room and said to his mother: "I want to talk to you." His mother, guessing what was on his mind, said excitedly: "You want to be baptized!" Franz pointed to the *New Testament* in his hand: "Mother, here is everything, here is the truth. There

---

7. Nachman Krockhmal had the same grandiose vision of Judaism; see *Guide for the Perplexed of the Time* (Lemberg, 1851, posthumously published).

is only one way, Jesus." His mother asked him: "Were you not in the synagogue on the New Year's Day?" Franz answered: "Yes, and I will go to the synagogue on the Day of Atonement, too. I am still a Jew." His mother said: "When I come in I will ask them to turn you away. In our synagogue there is no room for an apostate.[8]

What happened to Rosenzweig just a few days later in Berlin? As Glatzer points out, in all Rosenzweig's writings and in all the conversations that have been reported, neither Rosenzweig nor his interlocutors relate the details, the unique circumstances, of that Yom Kippur experience in Berlin in 1913. What we do know is that from that day on Rosenzweig never again considered conversion. More importantly, from that day on he fundamentally reoriented his life to center on Judaism. If it is exaggeration and misnomer to say that Rosenzweig converted to Judaism on that Yom Kippur, we can certainly say that he atoned. The transformation and its consequences are so pronounced, in any event, that one would be correct to think of Rosenzweig thenceforth as a *ba'al teshuvah,* a returnee. He had returned to Judaism; he became a Jew returning from the periphery of Judaism to its center. Unlike the classical *ba'al teshuvah* of Jewish tradition who, brought up in an authentic Judaism, left it behind to later return, Rosenzweig is a modern *ba'al teshuvah,* one who returns to a Judaism that had never been his own. Since Rosenzweig had gone so far first into the non-Jewish periphery and then into the Jewish center, first into the heights of Western culture and then into the heart of Jewish life, his life remains to this day exemplary for the *ba'al teshuvah* disengaging from modernity. On that Yom Kippur day in Berlin, Rosenzweig discovered that Judaism was neither a relic nor a preparation, but that it was very much alive.

He had discovered that Judaism was the true cure for the skeptical relativism that he now came to see as a spiritual sickness.[9] As such it was neither a theology, a religion, nor a culture, but rather a comprehensive way of life. What Rosenzweig understood on that Yom Kippur day was that not only did he have a real and living option in Judaism, but that to appropriate this option he would have to educate himself into what he now thankfully recognized as his true inheritance. Glatzer perceptively captures the fundamental life-significance of Rosenzweig's new orienta-

---

8. FRLT, p. 25. Glatzer learned the details of this encounter directly from Franz's mother, who also informed Glatzer that she immediately recognized Franz's change of heart after his Yom Kippur experience in Berlin.

9. See Franz Rosenzweig, *Understanding the Sick and the Healthy: A View of World, Man, and God,* translated by Nahum N. Glatzer (ed.) and T. Luckman (New York: Noonday Press, 1954).

tion in a sentence from the later commentaries on Judah Halevi, from a poem Rosenzweig entitles "Return" (*"Umkehr"*): "To have found God is not an ending but a beginning." (105)[10] After that Yom Kippur day, Rosenzweig began the arduous task of becoming not the Jew who would convert to Christianity—the Jew of Christianity and Hegelianism, the Christian or Hegelian "Jew"—but rather the Jew of Judaism, a Jewish Jew, a Jew neither in theory nor in practice but fully engaged in Jewish life.

Letter to Meinecke: From Scholarship to Learning

These two events, the conversation with Rosenstock and the experience on Yom Kippur, were decisive in Rosenzweig's intellectual and spiritual development. First was the rejection of the intellectually attractive but merely free-floating possibilities of skeptical relativism, for the sake of an absolute and concrete grounding in religion. Second was the rejection of the Christian faith, including its Hegelian formulation, as the desired religious solution, for the sake of a comprehensive life and learning within his own Jewish heritage. These two profound transformations determined the path of Rosenzweig's subsequent life and work. But to trace Rosenzweig's route to Halevi, one must turn to a third event. This was Rosenzweig's decision, during the summer of 1920, to turn away from a successful academic career, whose future was assured not only by the scholarly work he had already done on Hegel (and Schelling), but more immediately and practically by the offer of a university lectureship made by his mentor, Friedrich Meinecke, Professor of History at the University of Berlin.

Like the earlier events, there were two sides to Rosenzweig's third decision. Rosenzweig was obviously rejecting the university career of an academic scholar, at the same time, however, he began a career as Jewish educator, accepting in August an appointment as director of the *Lehrhaus* in Frankfort. Jewish adult education now takes central place in Rosenzweig's spiritual and practical development. It is within this context, too, that we must understand his decision to translate and comment upon Halevi's hymns and poems.

Turning from secular relativism to religious nonrelativism, and then turning from Christianity to Judaism, meant turning away from the brilliance of academic scholarship and toward the wisdom and piety of life in the Jewish community. One might suppose that this turn is properly represented by the difference between Rosenzweig's scholarly dissertation *Hegel and the State* (1920), which he was to retrospectively call "dues paid

---

10. FRLT, p. xviii.

to the German nation," and the "Jewish book" that he recognized as the "work of his life," *The Star of Redemption* (1921). But the difference between these two works, profound though it is, does not cut deeply enough into Rosenzweig's *teshuvah*. The true depth of Rosenzweig's turn separates both *Hegel and the State* and *The Star of Redemption* from what Rosenzweig called "life beyond the book," life in the Jewish community. No doubt the *The Star of Redemption* points to this life, but its pointing is at the same time always looking back over its shoulder.

As he noted in a letter to his teacher Professor Meinecke: "The man who wrote *The Star of Redemption* to be published shortly by Kauffmann in Frankfort—is of a very different caliber from the author of *Hegel and the State*. Yet when all is said and done, the new book is only —a *book*. I don't attach any undue importance to it."[11]

Rosenzweig's assessment of his progress from his Hegel studies to the *Star of Redemption,* and more to the point, his expression of *distance* from the *Star of Redemption,* should not be confused with a false modesty, or controverted by the rightful pride that he expresses elsewhere in having completed so great a task.[12] Rosenzweig was well aware of how much he accomplished in the *Star of Redemption,* which indeed was a great deal. What Rosenzweig wrote to Meinecke, nonetheless, was that he was no longer especially interested in books that measured themselves by the scientific standards of European higher education, whether directly as in a *Hegel and the State,* or apologetically as in a *Star of Redemption.* Rather, Rosenzweig wanted now to learn and enter into the prescribed activities and goals of religious communal life, Jewish in his case (Christian for others), which requires an intense learning in sacred texts respected as sacred texts, and not merely as scholarly source materials.

Rosenzweig certainly never turned against books and book learning, which would have been contrary not only to his character but to Judaism as well. Not at all. In the early 1920s, Rosenzweig was a regular member of a daily morning Talmud study group, led by Rabbi Nehemiah Nobel. He was also director of the Lehrhaus, where text study and Hebrew language were central to the curriculum. Rosenzweig did not turn from books but turned instead from secular to sacred literature, and from a secular to a sacred approach to sacred literature. In this turn from the secular to the sacred one can see the significance of Rosenzweig's new appreciation for Halevi. It was not a turn to Halevi's apologetic work, the *Kuzari,* a book which like Rosenzweig's own *Star of Redemption* points Jewish readers from

---

11. FRLT, p. 96.
12. See FRLT, pp. 103–104.

Athens to Jerusalem,[13] but rather an appreciation for Halevi's hymns and
poems, which belong to the living "religious" community toward which
the *Star of Redemption* and the *Kuzari* are themselves turned. Halevi the
liturgical poet, the "sweet singer of Zion," stands at the Jewish center
toward which the Jew at the periphery aims. Here precisely lay his great
significance as a guide in Rosenzweig's quest for Jewish authenticity.

We must understand, too, that Rosenzweig's work on Halevi was
intended to take its place as an integral part of Jewish communal life. The
Halevi volume was not meant to be "only a book" in the sense that *Hegel
and the State* and *The Star of Redemption* are "only" books, still enthralled
with theorizing, whether for or against. These two books are not on the
same plane as a *siddur* (prayer book), for example, where one finds several
of Halevi's hymns. Rosenzweig aims instead to produce a commentary that
could find a place alongside the many works[14] which constitute the life
blood of the living tradition of rabbinic Judaism into which he was now
entering ever more deeply. The Halevi volume was meant neither as a
contribution to disinterested scholarship nor as a bridge from science to
religion or religion to science, but rather as an integral part of Jewish
learning, at once inquiry and worship, which Rosenzweig then under-
stood to be inseparable from authentic Jewish life.

Rosenzweig's letter to Professor Meinecke was written on August 30,
1920—not long after an earlier unsuccessful conversation with Meinecke
in Berlin—and one month after Rosenzweig had accepted his appoint-
ment as director of the Lehrhaus in Frankfort. The decision to leave the
university for Jewish adult education no doubt appeared to Meinecke and
to Rosenzweig's assimilated family and peers (and doubtlessly also to the
younger scholarly incarnation of Rosenzweig himself) as an inexplicable
step down, a loss not only of prestige but perhaps even a lapse of good
sense and objectivity, not to mention a great risk professionally and peda-
gogically. Rosenzweig tried to explain (it is the "duty of the disciple toward
his master"[15]) to Meinecke his new Jewish life in terms of the difference
between university education and Jewish learning. The meaning and role
of learning in Jewish life is in fact central to Rosenzweig's thoughts on the
modern "return" to Judaism, a project he engaged in not only for himself,
but in whose service he had clearly found his vocation.

---

13. See Michael S. Berger, "Toward a New Understanding of Judah Halevi's *Kuzari*," in
The Journal of Religion, April 1992, Vol. 72, No. 2, pp. 210–28.

14. Such as the Bible commentary of Rabbi Samson Raphael Hirsch (1808–1888), *Der
Pentateuch ubersetzt und erlauter*, published in Frankfort-am-Main between 1867 and 1878.

15. FRLT, p. 98.

The letter to Meinecke reveals several of the fundamental tensions, which will determine Rosenzweig's subsequent life and thought about the relationship between Jews and Judaism, and between Jewishly awakened Jews and the larger non-Jewish (Christian) culture within which Jews live. The key to what Rosenzweig now reveals to Meinecke is the central place of Judaism in the whole of Rosenzweig's life and thought. Indeed, the expression "central place" is not even adequate to capture its importance. Judaism is the whole place, the very essence and wholeness of Rosenzweig's being and his becoming. "The one thing I wish to make clear," he writes, "is that scholarship no longer holds the center of my attention, and that my life has fallen under the rule of a 'dark drive' which I'm aware that I merely name by calling it 'my Judaism.'" For the sake of his professor, Rosenzweig describes his own personal transformation as the "conversion of the historian into a philosopher."[16] What is really at stake, however, to use the proper names that a residual formality, or perhaps a student's reticence, still withholds from expression, and about which he himself still retains certain ambiguities, is the conversion not of a *historian* into a *philosopher*, but of the historian and philosopher Rosenzweig, who happened in some undetermined sense to be Jewish in his private life ("of the Israelite persuasion," his peers would have said), into the *Jew* Rosenzweig, who happened to be a loyal citizen of Germany.

It is as a Jew, in his new-found appreciation for the all-embracing character of an authentic Judaism, that Rosenzweig turned away from the academy. Because his reorientation was fundamental, Rosenzweig found it difficult, even impossible to *explain* himself to Meinecke. No longer apologetic, his "reasoning" now finds its roots and nourishment in a different climate. Rosenzweig did not give up his academic career for academic reasons, as the result of a feeling of intellectual inadequacy or a failing of creative or critical talent (which he certainly did not have, and which Meinecke did not attribute to him). Instead, Rosenzweig is attempting (and once again failing) to explain his new resolution, even though it lives and breathes, as he is increasingly aware, within a different atmospheric pressure than that of academic explanation. Despite Rosenzweig's efforts, Meinecke could only see his star pupil's discontent as motivated by the more general malaise of postwar disillusionment.[17]

That Rosenzweig was discontented with what he takes to be the limitations of scientific objectivity is obvious. But this discontent he shared with most nineteenth- and twentieth-century academic rebels. With few exceptions, however, their rebellion found solace not in reli-

---

16. FRLT, p. 96.
17. See FRLT, p. 98.

gion but in various permutations of aesthetic individualism and social-
ist politics. Rosenzweig, in contrast, turned from scientific study to a
whole hearted commitment to the concrete historical exigencies of daily
life in the Frankfort Jewish community. In his letter to Meinecke, di-
rectly after minimizing the significance of his Hegel book and the *Star
of Redemption*, Rosenzweig writes:

> The small—at time exceedingly small—thing called [by Goethe] "demand
> of the day" which is made upon me in my position [as director of the
> *Lehrhaus*] at Frankfort, I mean the nerve-wracking, picayune, and at the
> same time very necessary struggle with people and conditions, have now
> become the real core of my existence—and I love this form of existence,
> despite the inevitable annoyance that goes with it. Cognition [*Erkennen*] no
> longer appears to me as an end in itself. It has turned into service, a service
> to human beings (not, I assure you, tendencies).[18]

Commitment to Judaism for an educated man such as Rosenzweig, accus-
tomed to the meditative quiet of home study and university library, who
now wants nothing more than to become a learned Jew, and to teach other
Jews, meant that the core of his existence would be taken up by the appar-
ently bothersome but "necessary struggles with people and conditions,"
rather than with the abstractions of an academic cognition removed from
direct community service. Whether the immediate and local spark for his
new appreciation for real life came as a response to war experiences in the
Balkans, or from an encounter with the vibrant hustle and bustle of eastern
European Jewry in Warsaw, or from maturation and marriage, or from
something else entirely, is not the issue. A deeper undercurrent was drawing
Rosenzweig into a more turbulent ocean, making demands that could no
longer be met with intellectual abstractions alone. That ocean was Jewish
life in the Jewish community. Rosenzweig's attachment to Judaism now and
for the rest of his life would mean—would demand—wholehearted engage-
ment, without a hint of condescension, in the everyday life and needs of the
Frankfort Jewish community, especially (given Rosenzweig's training and
proclivities) an engagement in Jewish education.

From within the embrace of the exigencies of his time, place, and
people, Rosenzweig now understands something that he would earlier
have understood as heresy from the scholar's cognitive concern for free-
floating possibilities. Taking a Schleirmachean direction, Rosenzweig hence-
forth denounces "possibility" in the name of Jewish (and Christian) actuality.
In his letter to Meinecke, he writes:

---

18. FR, pp. 96–97.

Cognition is autonomous; it refuses to have any *answers* foisted on it from the outside. Yet it suffers without protest having certain *questions* prescribed to it from the outside (and it is here that my heresy regarding the unwritten law of the university originates). Not every question seems to me worth asking. Scientific curiosity and omnivorous aesthetic appetite mean equally little to me today, though I was once under the spell of both, particularly the latter. Now I only inquire when I find myself *inquired of.* Inquired of, that is, by *men* rather than by scholars. There is a man in each scholar, a man who inquires and stands in need of answers. I am anxious to answer the scholar *qua* man but not the representative of a certain discipline, that insatiable, ever inquisitive phantom which like a vampire drains him whom it possesses of his humanity.[19]

The "unwritten law of the university" is that any and all questions have equal right to command scholarly attention. Kinship rules of New Guinea aborigines, agricultural habits of pre-Columbian Aztecs, the precise dating of Schelling's "Systematic Program for German Idealism" are of no less importance in an academic context than the fate of twentieth-century German Jewry, the laws of *kashrut,* or the story told at the Passover seder. But, and this "but" is important—*no longer for Rosenzweig.* For the scholar, yes, but not for the man Rosenzweig, the Jew Rosenzweig. Attentive to the real needs of a real Jewish community, to what, after Goethe, he calls the "demand of the day," Rosenzweig is no longer tempted by the unlimited openness of the university, no longer tantalized by its forever uncommitted freedom.

Rosenzweig at the same time grasped the limitations of what Meinecke had valued in the potential colleague to whom he offered a university post. Rosenzweig's talents were considerable and his excellent scholarly abilities had been proven very early on. But Rosenzweig had already called these into question in the course of the two earlier events of 1913. In the letter to Meinecke, written several years after those first awakenings, Rosenzweig is still grateful for his talents, but only when they are put in the service of his true Jewish self, hence of the Jewish community too, and not when they only encourage the detachment and ghostlike existence of the scholar. Recalling his earlier experience, he now writes:

In 1913 something happened to me for which *collapse* is the only fitting name. I suddenly found myself on a heap of wreckage, or rather I realized

---

19. FRLT, p. 97. In his comments on Halevi's poem (#18) "The Remote-and-Near-One," Rosenzweig makes this same point, namely "that you should make no statement about anything that does not concern you or that is not concerned with you." (p. 57).

that the road I was then pursuing was flanked by unrealities. Yet this was the very road defined for me by my talent, and my talent only! I began to sense how meaningless such a subjection to the rule of one's talents was and what abject servitude of the self it involved. . . . Amidst the shreds of my talents I began to search for my self, amidst the manifold for the One. It was then (one can speak of such matters in metaphors only) that I descended into the vaults of my being, to a place whither talents could not follow me; that I approached the ancient treasure chest. . . . These, indeed, were my own treasures, my most personal possessions, things inherited not borrowed! By owning them and ruling over them I had gained something entirely new, namely the right to live—and even to have talents; for now it was *I* who had the talents, not they who had me.[20]

In discovering Judaism Rosenzweig discovers his true self. The rich heritage, the "treasure chest," of his Jewish self can only be expressed in metaphor for the same reason Rosenzweig's earlier attempt at an "objective" explanation to Meinecke in Berlin failed. And doubtlessly too for the same reason that his letter also fails: without being merely personal, merely subjective, Judaism is too deeply personal. It is no longer about "one" that Rosenzweig is concerned, but about his own self *qua* Jewish self: "The error I made in Berlin arose precisely from the fact that I tried to explain the personal element—decisive in my case—through the objective, while actually the latter was nothing more than the visible confirmation of something I had long since felt to be right. . . . It was a kind of moral cowardice that made me expound myself to you in objective terms."[21]

In the Meinecke letter, then, we find the fundamental dichotomies that structure all of Rosenzweig's subsequent understanding of Judaism, Jewish education, and the hymns and poems of Judah Halevi: between the objective and the personal; between the objective resources of historiography and an ineffable but rich inheritance; between the autonomy of cognition, its open questioning and possibilities, and the specific demands of and hence services required by time, place and person; between the abstraction and tentativeness of history and philosophy *and* the immediacy and commitment of Judaism; between the fashions and tendencies of scholarship and the real demands of flesh and blood persons. Rosenzweig will always understand the proper significance of his own Judaism, the purpose of Jewish education, and the worth of Judah Halevi in terms of a living tradition of Jewish communal life, where the past lives in a present

---

20. FRLT, pp. 95–96.
21. FRLT, pp. 94–95.

that orients a future. Here thinking is not a *thinking about* but an *undergoing*, an engagement in the always *particular exigencies* of the differences that separate human beings from one other and from God, as those differences manifest God's creation, revelation, and redemption.

Escape from Assimilation: Learning from Halevi

Erich Fromm (who taught at the Frankfort *Lehrhaus* in 1924) distinguishes the empty possibilities of "freedom from" from the rich actuality of "freedom for." In his arduous journey from the abstract but empty freedom of German culture and the university, to the rich treasures of concrete Jewish life, Rosenzweig longed for a trustworthy guide. He longed for the vision of a post-biblical Judaism pure in heart and soul, unlike the corrupted Judaisms he saw around him. He longed to learn a thoroughly Jewish Judaism, a Judaism pledged to the unlimited resources of Jewish tradition. Rosenzweig longed for the vision of a whole Jew. And thus spoke Halevi—to Rosenzweig's thirsty ears. More and more he would heed the purifying call of Halevi, who in "Reply" writes: "And do not be led astray by the wisdom of the Greeks, which never bore fruit, only blossoms" (238); and in "Wise Teachings": "Wait for His advice and do not trust the academic wisdom of the scholars." (122) In Halevi, Rosenzweig found the teacher for whom he yearned, a teacher whose Judaism could be trusted without qualification, condition, or hesitation. From Halevi, Rosenzweig would learn what his own emancipated upbringing had denied to him, an authentically Jewish Judaism. He would learn, we see from his Halevi commentaries, the Jewish meaning of messiah, sabbath, love of Israel, longing for God, service to God, prayer, holiness, Yom Kippur, Rosh Hashana, Hanukkah, Torah, exodus, and so on. He would learn the far-stretched, four corners of the Jewish world: God, Soul, People, Zion.

What Rosenzweig wanted was to return to a Judaism purified of the "corruptions" of the very return to Judaism; he wanted a de-Christianized, de-Europeanized, and de-academicized Judaism. Halevi had negotiated these dangerous waters in medieval Spain, keeping his sights unwavering on Zion within a larger world of contending Islam and Christianity. It matters not whether we today judge Rosenzweig's desire and its object to be fact or fiction, living reality or romantic fantasy. Rosenzweig could not and did not find what he wanted in Hegel's dialectic, Meinecke's ideational historiography, Leopold Zunz's historical science, Hermann Cohen's[22] rational reconstruction, or his own *Star of Redemption*. His holy grail, an intact, whole Judaism, he found in Halevi.

---

22. Rosenzweig met Hermann Cohen in Berlin in 1913.

... and so Rosenzweig "edited out" personal, passionat, emotional humane "non-religious" poems from the Halevi Corpus?

In this same spirit, Rosenzweig was also dissatisfied with the renowned Rabbi Nehemiah A. Nobel of Frankfort. Though they mutually admired one another, and though Rosenzweig recommended Nobel's sermons, and though he participated in Nobel's morning Talmud classes, Rosenzweig remained dissatisfied and critical. His dissatisfaction is instructive, however, showing us what he truly longed for and could not find in Nobel. Shortly after Nobel's death on January 22, 1922, we find Rosenzweig writing to his friend, Dr. Joseph Prager: "I respected only the talmudic Jew, not the humanist, only the poet, not the scholar, only the prophet, not the philosopher. I rejected the qualities I did reject because in the form in which he had them, they were deeply un-Jewish."[23]

What was wrong with Rabbi Nobel, beyond all the great virtues Rosenzweig appreciated and respected, was precisely his assimilation of non-Jewish ideas, his infatuation, indeed his infection, "with Christian and pagan ideas."[24] In a later letter to Buber, Rosenzweig sums up his criticism, writing disparagingly that Nobel "still believed in the university."[25]

Let us note at this juncture that Rosenzweig harbored no ill will against Christianity. Quite the reverse is true. Just as Jews should be Jews, he thought Christians *should be* Christians, both for the sake of the world's redemption. The problem with the Christian and humanist influence on Rabbi Nobel, then, had nothing to do with a problem with Christianity *per se*. Rather the problem was the impurity, adulteration, corruption, as Rosenzweig saw it, which Nobel's assimilation of Christian and humanist ideas and values produced upon his Judaism.

> All my veneration and love never blinded me to his [Nobel's] toying with Christian and pagan ideas. True, it couldn't do me any harm, since I am armored against this kind of temptation as perhaps no Jew in *galut* [exile] has been before me. But in the effect he had on others I was always aware of the poison mixed with the medicine. I always tried to steer people away from his mostly horrid lectures to his sermons, where at the decisive moments the Jew in him came to the fore. Only there did he believe himself able to manage without loans from the Christian and pagan cultural spheres, and even *there* one was never sure one wouldn't be handed a quotation from "the master" [Goethe]. Also in the *shiur* [lecture] he made the most of its weaknesses, i.e., the silly quibbles of philological criticism (the original *mishnah*, first, second, second-and-a-half, etc. strata), while he often seemed to present genuinely Jewish matters almost reluctantly or with the cool,

---

23. FRLT, p. 106.
24. Ibid.
25. FRLT, p. 126.

ironic remark, "As they say in the Yeshivas" (what followed was always par-
ticularly good).[26]

These are very telling remarks, especially the last, with its parenthetical
praise.

In contrast to the *Star of Redemption*, Nobel, and even an "orthodox"
thinker such as Samson Raphael Hirsch,[27] Judah Halevi would represent
an assured and untarnished Judaism, resistant to Christianity, humanism,
critical philology, philosophy, and so on. Rosenzweig was no longer inter-
ested in the "silly quibbles of philological criticism." In the epilogue to his
Halevi book, he singles out the most eminent philologist of his day, the
famous "Professor Wilamowitz from Berlin" (44) for criticism. In a 1924
letter (when he is at work on the Halevi book) to several distinguished
Lehrhaus factulty, Rosenzweig writes tellingly, that "it is not at all that his-
torical and sociological explanations are false," but rather that "in the
light of the doing, of the right doing in which we experience the reality
of the law, the explanations are of superficial and subsidiary importance."[28]
University scholarship was not false, it was superficial and secondary. From
a detached reflection upon free-floating possibilities, Rosenzweig's world
now had weight and bearing. What Rosenzweig wanted more than any-
thing else was to find out—without reluctance, coolness, or irony—what
"they say in the Yeshivas."

Retrospectively, then, we can grasp what Rosenzweig came to see as
the limitation of both the *Star of Redemption* and the *Lehrhaus*. Their virtue
is the same: movement from the outside, from a non-Jewish "periphery,"
into the core of Judaism. But this virtue is at the same time their vice: they
are only vehicles, arrows but not destinations or targets. After being led into
Judaism from the outside, the Jew disenchanted with Western enlighten-
ment would no longer tolerate the *taint* of non-Jewish intrusions. What
Rosenzweig wrote in a letter to Eugen Rosenstock in 1924 about his pam-
phlet on education, "The Builders," is also true of the *Star of Redemption* and
the program of the *Lehrhaus:* "The problem of 'The Builders' is . . . the
problem of a generation, or possibly of a century: how 'Christian' Jews,
national Jews, religious Jews, Jews from self- defense, sentimentality, loyalty,
in short, 'hyphenated' Jews such as the nineteenth century has produced,
can once again, without danger to themselves or Judaism, become *Jews*. . . .
It is addressed only to the 'hyphenated' Jews who want to return."[29]

---

26. FRLT, pp. 106–107.
27. See JL, pp. 62, 78.
28. FRLT, p. 245.
29. FRLT, p. 135.

We find Rosenzweig expressing the same thought, the same longing to overcome transitional "hyphenated" Judaisms, even when the hyphen means a *Lehrhaus*-Judaism, in a long letter to his successor at the *Lehrhaus*, Rudolf Hallo. He advises that precisely the *best* students must be encouraged to *leave* the school: "For those who are still Jewish, or once again Jewish, the *Lehrhaus* is only qualifiedly necessary, that is, as introduction and stimulation. There is even a real and typical danger of restricting their Jewish activities and studies to attendance at the *Lehrhaus,* since their work there readily bears fruit. It is one of the tasks of the director to help those who have really gone through the *Lehrhaus* to get out of it again and to stand on their own Jewish legs in doing and learning."[30]

The school, like the *Star of Redemption,* was only a crutch, necessary, to be sure, to escape a crippling assimilation, but only for a time. Its real aim was to get Jews "to stand on their own Jewish legs in doing and learning."[31]

Inside Jewish life one would still read and discuss, of course, since reading and discussion are integral to Jewish life. But one would dwell on texts as an integral part of Jewish religious tradition, dwell on the Talmud and its commentaries, the siddur and hence Halevi, as holy *sefarim*—holy books, books of Jewish wholeness. Torah (written and oral) and life would be inseparable, as they always had been in Jewish tradition. This is the point he makes in a letter of July 12, 1921, to his wife, Edith, almost accidentally bringing all these themes to a head. Rosenzweig had been asked to contribute a scholarly piece to a festschrift honoring Meinecke on his sixtieth birthday. As early as 1921, however, this task had become impossible for Rosenzweig—not because he lacked the "talent," but because he no longer had the desire. Scholarship, knowledge for its own sake, no longer interested Rosenzweig; it was too thin, arid, without passion, "of superficial and subsidiary importance."

> I'm still laboring over the piece for Meinecke. Or, rather, I realized this morning that it won't work. I'm too far removed from these things. I hope I can find something to substitute, as I should like to contribute to the volume. Perhaps I can find a short unpublished ms. In order to carry out my original plan I would need much time and energy. And I have time and energy at present for those books you are jealous of, the *Sefarim.* The only thing that gives me pleasure these days is to have learned a few folios of Gemara. I have now reached page 6a in *Megillah;* I'm getting more and more into the spirit of it.[32]

---

30. FRLT, p. 118.
31. Ibid.

"[T]here is no getting away from it," he wrote to Martin Buber five months later about the Halevi work, "one's time is better spent in translating ten lines than writing the longest disquisition 'about.'"[33] Unfortunately for Rosenzweig, illness slowed his learning, just as limitations in Hebrew language skills made his Halevi translations difficult.[34] What is clear, however, beyond what he did or did not accomplish (and he did accomplish a lot) is his motivating desire, his quest for and dedication to an unvarnished, unadulterated, unhyphenated core of Jewish "doing and learning." It is this quest and dedication that separates the scholarly and apologetic efforts of his Hegel book and his *Star of Redemption* from his Halevi translations and commentaries.

The Nostalgia for Wholeness

Rosenzweig's quest for the unhyphenated Jew must be set within a larger context of Jewish and European nostalgia for wholeness. For European civilization, the onset, pursuit, and conclusion of the horrors, mass deaths, and massive disruptions of the First World War made a nostalgia for a lost wholeness, a wistful remembrance of things past, a common thread of its spiritual and cultural life. The diminution and tarnishing of an original enthusiasm for the ultimate worth of enlightenment and the value of assimilation were painfully accelerated for Western European Jews by the Dreyfus affair at the turn of the century, and for Eastern European Jews by the pogroms of the 1880s that culminated in the Kishinev pogroms of 1903. In the aftermath of the shock of the First World War, everyone, so it seemed, Jews and non-Jews, sensed the loss of some intangible but invaluable ingredient of European social harmony and community spirit, a loss of optimism now replaced with a hesitation, a malaise before the hitherto enticing vision of progress through science.

Of course, there were precursors. A hundred years earlier the Romantics responded to an incipient mechanization, industrialization, and urbanization by escape into a fantasized medievalism. Wagner revived the Teutonic pagan gods. Ferdinand Tonnies' influential work, *Community and Society* [*Gemeinschaft und Gesellschaft*], published in 1887, idealized the wholeness and integrity of traditional folk community, *Gemeinschaft*, in contrast to the atomistic individualism and rationalism of modern society,

---

32. FRLT, pp. 102–103.
33. FRLT, p. 122.
34. See FRLT, p. 134.

Gesellschaft. Friedrich Nietzsche's writings, published in the 1870s and 1880s, immensely popular throughout Europe by the end of the century, attacked science along with religion, and bemoaned the belittling fragmentation, the "democratization," which he saw as the very definition of modernity. Against its motley pastiches, Nietzsche called for the grandeur and nobility of "unity of style." This he found in both a distant barbarian past and a distant unforeseeable future "surpassing man."[35]

Everywhere in Europe, within and without the Jewish world, the culture, sociology, economics, and spirit of the modern world were criticized as products and conduits to fragmentation, disintegration, atomization, alienation. Tonnies' fragmented world, *Gesellschaft*, was the modern world. In contrast stood *Gemeinschaft*, organic community, where individuals—persons, architecture, places, meaning, as so on—found their sense and worth, not in themselves by themselves, but as integral parts of larger organic wholes, participating in an extra-rational transpersonal unity.

It was precisely an organic whole and transpersonal unity beyond rationality that Rosenzweig found in a Judaism connected to and growing out of its own independent tradition. Rosenzweig, like many others of his generation, was no doubt influenced by Martin Buber's *Tales of Rabbi Nachman* (1906) and *The Legend of the Baal-Shem* (1907), which introduced Western European Jews to the fervor and pre-Enlightenment flavor of Eastern European hasidic Judaism. Unlike Buber, however, Rosenzweig understood that continued adherence to Jewish law, *halakha*, was a necessary and key ingredient to the wholistic Judaism he sought.

Rosenzweig's criticisms of the orthodox, liberal, and Zionist Judaisms of his day boil down to a single complaint: they are fragments, parts, pieces of Judaism, and as such, whether they will it or not, they depend for their completion on other fragments, parts, and pieces, whether ripped from Jewish tradition or, as was more likely, taken from the non-Jewish world. They could not produce or sustain the whole Jew that Rosenzweig sought, but only the hyphenated Jew he sought to overcome. In his pamphlet of early 1920, "Towards a Renaissance of Jewish Learning," Rosenzweig wrote:

---

35. After the Great War, in Rosenzweig's day, Martin Heidegger in Freiburg strove to renew and deepen Nietzsche's dark past and future, returning to the autochthonous wisdom of pre-Socratic Greece, while calling for a future beyond the technology which had enveloped and diminished the Western spirit. The Frankfort School at the same time argued against a modernity where only instrumental reasoning could make sense, defending an older, broader reason still in touch with the ends of man, concerned for higher truth and loving justice. Following this school, but also following Heidegger, Hans Georg Gadamer later argued against instrumental reason, but for the sake of the integrating but extra-logical wisdom of tradition. I thank Michael Platt for suggesting "surpassing man," rather than "super-man" or "over-man," to translate Nietzsche's *Ubermensch.*

It is necessary for him [the Jew seeking wholeness] to free himself from those stupid claims that would impose Juda-"ism" on him as a canon of definite, circumscribed "Jewish duties" (vulgar orthodoxy), or "Jewish tasks" (vulgar Zionism), or—God forbid—"Jewish ideas" (vulgar liberalism). If he has prepared himself quite simply to have everything that happens to him, inwardly and outwardly, happen to him in a *Jewish way*—his vocation, his nationality, his marriage, and even, if that has to be, his Juda-"ism"—then he may be certain that with the simple assumption of that infinite "pledge" he will become in reality "wholly Jewish."

And there is indeed no other way to become completely Jewish; the Jewish human being arises in no other way. All recipes, whether Zionist, orthodox, or liberal, produce caricatures of men, that become more ridiculous the more closely the recipes are followed. And a caricature of a man is also a caricature of a Jew; for as a Jew one cannot separate the one from the other. There is one recipe alone that can make a person Jewish and hence—because he is a Jew and destined to a Jewish life—a full human being. . . . Our fathers had a beautiful word for it that says everything: confidence.[36]

Against the artificial pomp of all "isms," Rosenzweig would instead reinstill the lost confidence of Jewish wholeness, Jews with Jewish arms and legs, Jewish eyes and ears, Jewish thoughts and feelings. By confidence he meant the Jew's trust that to be fully Jewish was at the same time to be fully human. The Zionism of Theodor Herzl's *Jewish State* (1896) and the several World Zionist Congresses, despite its apparent revival of an ancient Jewish nationalism, was still infatuated and infected with a Western universalism opposed to a truly Jewish humanism. Despite the disillusionment it shared with late modernity, Rosenzweig saw Zionism as still blinded by social and political optimism, still striving for a fantasized future where Jews and Judaism would be subordinated to the higher values of Western civilization. In contrast, Rosenzweig worked to expand the "Jewish adult education movement," despite its ultimate limitations, naming it the "most important movement among contemporary German Jews."[37] Even if the *Lehrhaus* was itself a manifestation of a hyphenated-Judaism, in contrast to the dominant Herzlian Zionism Rosenzweig rejected it at least led away from those hyphens and into a genuine Judaism.

If we ask from whence hyphenated-Judaisms arose, Rosenzweig's answer is clear and hardly original: enlightenment and emancipation. Enlightenment and emancipation lie at the root of the fragmentation of Jewish life, its loss of wholeness, its loss of confidence.

---

36. JL, p. 66.
37. JL, p. 67.

Emancipated Jewry lacks a platform of Jewish life upon which the bookless present can come into its own. Up to the time of emancipation, such a platform was provided by existence within the bounds of old Jewish law and in the Jewish home and synagogal service. Emancipation shattered this platform. True, all three parts exist still, but because they are now only parts, they are no longer what they were when they were joined together—the invisible platform of a real and contemporaneously lived life, which learning and education had but to serve and for which they drew their greatest strength.[38]

Orthodox, liberal, and Zionist Judaisms are inauthentic because they are fragments. Pre-emancipated Jewish life was built, Rosenzweig believed, on the harmony and integrity of Jewish law, home, and synagogue. In the modern world these once integral dimensions of a wholistic Jewish life had become fragments, pieces, that were contending, faltering, and retreating among themselves, vying unsuccessfully with external non-Jewish influences. "Today," Rosenzweig wrote, "law brings out more conspicuously the difference between Jew and Jew than between Jew and Gentile."[39] The home, for its part, "is no longer the heart from which the bloodstream of all Jewish life is pumped," but a place at best in defensive struggle against alternative cultural values.

In contrast to the complete fragmentation and partiality caused by the infiltration of non-Jewish values into modern Jewish approaches to law and home, Rosenzweig believed a remnant of wholeness had somehow survived in the synagogue. No doubt he was remembering his own Yom Kippur experience of 1913. He explicitly refers to Yom Kippur when he writes to Eduard Strauss about the residual Jewish vitality found in the synagogue.[40] But even in the synagogue, fragmentation had taken hold: "The synagogue has become," Rosenzweig writes, "quite in keeping with the spirit of the culture-obsessed, pigeonholing nineteenth century, a 'place of religious edification.'"[41] These fragmentations—of law, home, and synagogue—which in various reactive and compensatory permutations produce orthodox, liberal, and Zionist Judaisms, provide further proof for Rosenzweig of the danger represented by non-Jewish ways for a true Judaism. The Judaisms against which Rosenzweig wrestled, in his own person, in the *Star of Redemption,* and at the *Lehrhaus,* these hyphenated Judaisms were caricatures, the products and manifestations of a larger European enlightenment and Jewish emancipation.

---

38. JL, p. 61.
39. Ibid.
40. JL, p. 62.
41. JL, p. 63.

In conclusion, the decisive break in Rosenzweig's life and thought, between the scholar Rosenzweig and the Jew Rosenzweig, occurs not between *Hegel and the State* and *The Star of Redemption,* as is often imagined; but between, on the one side, a Rosenzweig educated in Western thought and values, as evidenced by his Hegel study and by his efforts to liberate himself apologetically in the *Star of Redemption,* that is to say, Rosenzweig up to 1920. And on the other side a Rosenzweig embedding himself—learning—within Jewish life and thought, re-educating himself in Jewish thought and values. This occurred first as director of the *Lehrhaus,* and then in the forced confinement of his illness, continuing through six years of taxing spiritual labor and personal growth in translating and commenting upon the poems and hymns of Yehuda Halevi, his Jewish teacher of a Judaism whole and intact.

I will let Rosenzweig conclude with his own words from a most remarkable letter, written to his mother on June 6th, 1929, just six months before his death on December 10th.

> . . . But now I have to tell you something embarrassing. R. says Cohen decided that in Hebrew translations of his works his surname Yeheskal should be used (with the name Hermann in parentheses). Now I know that I, a Levi, am named Louis. But this is really embarrassing since the whole *am-ha-aretz* [ignoramus] character of my background is expressed in it. Only Levites are called Louis. At my bris [ritual circumcision] probably the same thing happened that I saw happen ten years ago to poor Rudy Gotthelft. The mohel [ritual circumcizer] came to that part of the service when the name of the new born son was to be made public; he hurriedly asked while cleaning, "What is his name?" Uncle Richard turned around inquiringly and someone called to him "Ruben." So uncle Richard, enlightened, repeated "Ruben," whereupon the mohel broke out in resounding chanting about the so haphazardly found name of Ruben. But this is not the end of the tragi-comedy. The Hebrew name of Grandpa Louis, after whom I have been named, actually was not Levi, although I thoughtlessly had it put on father's tombstone without checking. As I later saw on Uncle Traugott's tombstone, he was called Yehuda (which also means Louis, like the lion Judah in Jacob's blessing). Correctly I should have been given the name Yehuda ben Shmuel, which is precisely the name of the great man, of whom I am a middling reincarnation returning to his people: Yehudah Halevi.[42]

42. Franz Rosenzweig, *Der Mench und sein Werk: Gesammelte Schriften,* Vol. 1, *Brief und Tagebucher* 2 Band, 1918–1929 (Haag: Martinus Nijhoff, 1979), pp. 1215–1216. Thanks to Professor Ephraim Meir of Bar Ilan University for pointing out this letter to me, and to Mr. Arjon Cohen of the University of Leiden for translating it.

POETRY TRANSLATOR'S NOTE

Gilya Gerda Schmidt

In 1910, Martin Buber (1878–1965) wrote about two kinds of human beings, the elemental soul and the problematic soul.[1] As an example of the former, Buber pointed to Theodor Herzl (1860–1904), the founder of the Zionist movement. As an example of the complex, dualistic, problematic soul, he cited himself.

Buber became Franz Rosenzweig's close friend, collaborator, and critic of the Yehuda Halevi poems. In working on Rosenzweig's poetry, I realized just how much he fit into Buber's category of the problematic human being, whose entire life consisted of the struggle to conquer his desperations so that he would be free to act. How much he must have admired Yehuda Halevi, whose zest for life, documented in his secular poetry, did not keep him from pursuing his real purpose in life—a return to Zion.

Yehuda Halevi was the rock upon which Spanish Jewry could found its direction. His goal did not change despite detours, and his spirit never wavered. Even though the word *Zionism* did not exist in the Middle Ages, nor the term *hibbat Zion*, Yehuda Halevi certainly was a lover of Zion. Even so, his life within Spanish Jewish culture, like Rosenzweig's within German Jewish culture, was complicated and problematic.

As a modern German Jew, Rosenzweig shared the medieval Andalusian Jew Yehuda Halevi's desire for messianic redemption. From his friend Buber, Rosenzweig understood the urgency of Zion for the Jewish people, but Rosenzweig's recent return to observant Judaism was attained through reflection upon and resolution of conflicts that had resulted from his assimilation into German culture. These struggles are still very much evident in the poems. Despite his own *Star of Redemption* (1921), Rosenzweig was still guided by an *"Unstern,"* an unlucky star ("Here I am"), embedded in Christian and German cultural imagery. Rosenzweig delighted in games of the mind and of language and in philosophical debates concerning Jewish topics.

---

1. Martin Buber, "Er und Wir," in *Die Welt*, XI/20, June 20, 1910. See my English translation in *The First Buber: Youthful Zionist Writings of Martin Buber* (Syracuse: Syracuse University Press, 1999).

One sees this in the brilliant commentary to the poems, whose sharp arguments and perceptive analyses reveal Rosenzweig's erudition. The translation of the poems was likewise undertaken for formalistic reasons— to prove that Hebrew poetry could be rendered into German rhyme, not to reform German Jewish thought on the Messiah and Zion. It is quite likely that Buber influenced Rosenzweig even indirectly in the selection process because Buber had already become an active Zionist in 1898, one year after the first Zionist Congress in Basel. Rosenzweig, on the other hand, was a *Nationaljude,* a national Jew, not a Zionist. He nevertheless dedicated the original volume of these poems to Martin Buber.

Translating Rosenzweig's Yehuda Halevi poems was a complicated process for me, both emotionally and technically, alternatively exhilarating and exasperating, gratifying and taxing, and sometimes both at the same time. When I began this work, I faced a moral dilemma. I wanted to be faithful to Yehuda Halevi, whose poetry shines like a beacon for today's Jew, but realized that my real task was to be faithful to Rosenzweig, the German *bàal tshuvah.* Although rhyming was of the utmost importance to Rosenzweig for polemical reasons, I felt no need to follow in his footsteps. Certain parts rhymed almost naturally, while others did not. More important to me was to render Rosenzweig's meaning as faithfully as possible. However, I have retained the visual images, the colophonic style, that Rosenzweig often, though not always, carried over from Halevi.

If the reader follows Rosenzweig's prefatory advice to throw away the translation and learn the original language (in our case two languages, German and, at one remove, Hebrew), the reader must have an understanding of the almost total immersion of twentieth-century German Jewry into German culture. Despite Rosenzweig's assurance that he does not want the reader to forget that he is reading Yehuda Halevi, there are instances when Rosenzweig makes it easy to forget Muslim Spain and the Jewish poet through his Christian imagery, Lutheranisms, Goetheisms, and images from German folklore. In the poems one encounters not only Luther German, as occasionally one does in the commentaries, but the entire pantheon of German Christian life and lore. Rafael Rosenzweig, in his introduction to the 1983 Nijhoff edition, acknowledges his father's great indebtedness to Luther German and documents his struggle to free himself from this religious influence by translating progressively more challenging Hebrew prayers, from the *Birkat Hamazon* to the *Kabbalat Shabbat* service to the central prayer of the *Kol Nidre* service. However, Rafael Rosenzweig does not comment on his father's deep subconscious immersion into secular German culture.

It was Islam in the Middle Ages that brought Greek thought back to the West via Spain. As Rosenzweig was influenced by German culture, so Halevi was greatly influenced by Islamic culture. We can see this in his personification of the world, which, counter to Western ideology, is oblivious to the passage of time in the world (see no. 15, "Your God"). Rosenzweig is aware of and points out the influence of Greek philosophy in Halevi's poems. For example, "The Universe," incorporates the zodiac, while in "Your God," Halevi admonishes his fellow Jews to follow the example of the heavenly spheres, the stars and the planets, which unquestioningly follow Divine law, while humans waver and do not.

If we look over Rosenzweig's shoulder while contemplating this collection, we find that he was an ingenious translator with a vivid imagination and a gift for the dramatic. Many interesting divergences between Halevi's Hebrew and Rosenzweig's German provided food for thought. These divergences fall into three categories: the weight Rosenzweig gave to rhyme; the influence of German culture on Rosenzweig's imagery; and the influence of Christian imagery and Lutheranisms on Rosenzweig.

Why the preoccupation with rhyming? Franz Rosenzweig states quite clearly that he was better at rhyming than previous translators, and that future translators would have no excuse for at least matching his efforts. This enthusiasm for rhyme often leads Rosenzweig far afield in his imagery, a factor that he readily acknowledges. Yet his insistence on rhyme, even at the expense of meaning, is astonishing and at times irritating, reminding the reader of the importance of formalism in the otherwise liberal Weimar Republic. Rosenzweig writes:

> This timidity about imitating the rhyme form has the same basis as that which, on closer examination, is shared by astonishingly many human affairs—laziness, laziness pure and simple. For the imitation of even the most complex rhyme forms is possible in German . . . In the worst case one can easily use a dictionary of rhyme; if one want to figure as a free renderer, one need not tell anyone about it. I, who want to be nothing other than a translator, hereby gladly confess that I owe much easing of my burden to the dictionary of Mr. Steputat, even if most of the time the best rhymes did not occur to him. (48–49)

The German cultural influence is also strong. The sections on God, the Soul, and the People are permeated with poetic metaphors quite alien to (and alienating in) Yehuda Halevi's poetry. At times the effect is comical, at other times jarring, producing a dissonance. It is obvious from these poems that being a German Jew in post-Emancipation Germany was a heavy yoke to bear. Rosenzweig's stylistic gymnastics mirror his existential agony and reflect the uncertainty caused by living in two worlds. Rosenzweig's protestations to the contrary notwithstanding, his translation is actually a recreation of Halevi within twentieth-century German culture. In our post-Holocaust period, however, Jewish symbiosis with German culture hardly seems the desired goal it once was. Hence, the many German cultural images that Rosenzweig merges with Halevi's reverence creates something of a *danse macabre.*

In general, Rosenzweig picked and chose what parts of a poem he wanted to accentuate or modify, and he modified liberally, as indicated by his own extensive comments on the translation. Sometimes he hits the mark, as with poem no. 35 on levirite marriage, "The World as Woman." Sometimes he adds, as for instance the spider's web in no. 25. Sometimes he omits, as for instance in no. 11, where only the *shofarot* (shofar blasts) are mentioned, while the *hoshanot* (salvations) and *zichronot* (remembrances) disappear. Elsewhere, he will reverse the order or at times alter the meaning.

In poem no. 1, "Praised!" we are faced with a new God, without the veil of the old, a German notion popularized by Schiller and Novalis, based on an image from the Egyptian Temple of Sais. This God is bedecked with the Greco-Germanic laurel wreath of victory, an association painful to the eye and ear that invokes the words of the *kaddish* as a refrain. How does one reconcile this image of God with the One reverently hallowed in Judaism's most exalted prayer?

While Halevi's language is usually simple and straightforward, Rosenzweig delights in philosophical formulations and complicated phrasings. These embellishments at times take him far afield, for example in the poems "Homecoming" and "The True One." Rosenzweig's language is often teutonic, conjuring up heathen images, as well as images and rhythms reminiscent of Goethe, especially of *Faust*. This is especially true of the poem "The Universe," which reminds of the witches' brew scene, and "This Soul Here," which recalls Faust's ascent to the *mater gloriosa*. At times Rosenzweig seems to capture the problematic of life better than did Halevi. This is the case in the poem "Delusion and Truth," where Rosenzweig expresses humanity's distrust of time and the world more clearly than did Halevi, possibly because Halevi did not feel this inner division as strongly as Rosenzweig. The poem "Home" echoes Schiller's *"Alpenjaeger"* poem, where God speaks of His herd's right to roam the earth freely. My favorite anachronism occurs in the poem, "To the Sabbath," a poem that greets *Shabbat*. Here Rosenzweig clothes Halevi's *"Shalom* to you, shalom, you seventh day," in the idiom of the German miner, who traditionally emerges from the pit with the greeting *"Glueck auf"* [hello]. Rosenzweig turns this greeting, popularized in a German folksong, into a rather irreverent and folksy version of *"Shabbat Shalom."*

Christian imagery and Lutheranisms abound in Rosenzweig's poems, an impossibility in Halevi's Islamic Spain. At times the German then current posed a true challenge to Rosenzweig's desire for Jewish expression. In the poems "Sabbath Morning," and "Your God," for example, the word choice for savior, no matter which available German word he chooses, is unmistakably Christian in character. (For example, for Lev. 25:26, Rosenzweig chooses *Heiland,* Rosenzweig and Buber in their Bible translation chose *Loeser* or *Einloeser,* while Moses Mendelssohn in his 1789 Bible translation chose *Wiedereinloeser.*) Rosenzweig conceived of creation as a one-time event, although for Halevi (and for Buber) it was ongoing. This view affects the translation of the poem "The Incomparable One." in "The Universe," Halevi did not speak of blood, while Rosenzweig's Luther-informed version does. Twice Rosenzweig blurs the religious boundaries between Passover and Easter. While in the poem "The Day at the Sea of Reeds," he does not name the actual holiday, in the commentary to this poem he names Easter when he, of course, means Passover. In the poem "The Pilgrim," he actually calls Passover "Eastertime" (*Osterzeiten*).

The only time I felt that Rosenzweig's existential burden as a German Jew, and consequently my burden as translator, were lifted was in the sea poems, in the section on Zion. Here the agonizing struggle over the possible journey to Zion had been resolved. These poems contain another reconciliation as well—between the very different agendas of these two Jews. In comparison to the other poems, Rosenzweig's translations here are less contrived, less artificed, and less stylistically complicated, allowing one to forget for a moment that his primary concern was formalistic, while Halevi's was poetic. In the sea poems one feels both men to be pious Jews who bow to the God of Abraham, Isaac, and Jacob. Perhaps Rosenzweig felt closet to Halevi in this set of poems because here Halevi revealed his personal fears regarding the perils of the journey, but at the same time his unerring faith in God. Rosenzweig succeeds in transmitting Halevi's anxiety as well as his inner peace because they parallel the existential *Angst* as well as the newly revived faith of his own spiritual journey.

In this particular endeavor, I was greatly aided by my learned colleague Rabbi Dr. Leon Weinberger, who patiently guided my uncertain footing in places where Rosenzweig's translation posed difficulties, leading me to Halevi's origins and sources. The credit for the felicity of my translation is largely his; any remaining errors or inaccuracies are mine.

As we know from Hillel, however, one cannot stand on one foot. If Leon helped me appreciate the richness of Halevi's world of faith and the certainty of Halevi's knowledge of Jewish sources, Richard Cohen aided me through his artistic bent and excellent command of poetic English. It was indeed a pleasure to have him seek out those passages that needed linguistic improvement and to free them from clumsiness and imprecision. I have enjoyed working with such knowledgeable colleagues.

I would like to dedicate this translation to them and to my other good friends in the Department of Religious Studies at the University of Alabama: Pat Green, Bill Doty, Betty Dickery, and Jan Moyer, whose encouragement and support have been a great inspiration during my tenure at the university. Thanks are also due to my present university, The University of Tennessee, and especially to the head of the Department of Religious Studies, Professor Charles Reynolds.

COMMENTARY TRANSLATOR'S NOTE

Eva Jospe

To translate the work of a master translator is a daunting task. But that task becomes truly awesome if the master translator's name is Franz Rosenzweig and the person charged with rendering his German into English grew up in an atmosphere in which something resembling sainthood was bestowed on the teacher of the *Lehrhaus* and author of the *Star of Redemption.*

Even so, it does seem necessary to abide by a few general principles guiding one's personal "philosophy" of translating. Foremost among those are the twin requirements of faithfulness to the original and readability in the "new" language. Unfortunately, these two are often in conflict with each other, especially when the original's language is frequently so "original" that to translate it literally would surely foreclose its readability. Yet to achieve the latter does not mean that one can falsify the "text" and do violence to it by taking unwarranted linguistic liberties. Still, though faithfulness to and respect for content and form, intent, and style of the original are imperatives, literalness of rendition into another language is in most cases undesirable; its result would merely alienate the reader and undercut or actually negate the very purpose of a translation: to introduce that reader to a "foreign" work that so far has been inaccessible to him or her.

To solve the dilemma of doing justice to the author's work as well as to the reader's needs, the translator must therefore strive for a balance that will satisfy both requirements without sacrificing either—an occasionally oxymoronic but in the end eminently worthwhile undertaking.

A few technical remarks: biblical quotes cited by Rosenzweig in German are here given in the 1955 Jewish Publication Society version. However, since he translated the biblical term *goyim* as *Heiden,* the translator tried to approximate it by rendering it as "pagans" rather than using the JPS chose of "peoples" or "nations." The author's use of *Osterwoche,* literally "Easter week," for the Passover week, is indicated with the bracketed German. It may be indicative of the general usage of his time and place.

The author's suggestions for alternative *German* renderings of Halevi's Hebrew, appended to quite a few of his commentaries, have been omitted. The same holds true for a very few passages referring to old German literature.

dedicated to
Martin Buber

PREFACE[*]

Franz Rosenzweig

> Dear reader, learn Greek and throw
> my translation into the fire!
>
> —Friedrich Leopold von Stolberg,
> From note on VI, 484 of
> his translation of Homer's *Iliad*

Yehuda Halevi was a great Jewish poet in the Hebrew language. The small selection presented here seeks to give the German reader a sense of this. Thus it was not my goal to promote the belief on the part of the reader that Yehuda Halevi wrote in the German language, nor that he wrote Christian hymns, nor that he was a poet of our day (even if only a poet of family albums)—for these, as far as I can see, were the approaches taken by the translators preceding me, especially the most recent. Rather, these translations want to be nothing other than translations. They do not want for one instant to conceal from the reader that he is reading not my poems, but Yehuda Halevi's, and that Yehuda Halevi was neither a German poet nor a contemporary of ours. In a word, this translation is not a free rendering,[1] and if in spite of itself it is that from time to time, this is only because of the necessities of rhyme. Fundamentally, it was my intention to translate literally, and with about five-sixths of the lines of verse presented here I believe I have succeeded in doing so. For the sixth sixth, where even I (although only to the most cautious extent) had to resort to free renderings, I must formally ask the reader's forgiveness.

The concept of free rendering is so generally accepted today as a standard for measuring the quality of translations that it demands for once to be examined more closely. If a great German poet declares his intention to render freely the work of a foreign poet, I cannot avoid a

---

* In the original 1927 edition this preface appeared as an "Afterword."

1. TK: I have translated the verb *nachdichten* here and elsewhere as "to render freely." The German verb also has the sense of "imitation."

quiet sense of astonishment that he does not prefer to compose something of his own. In any event, a *"Reinecke Fuchs"* by Goethe, rendered freely from the Middle Low German *"Reinecke Vos,"* will compel me to grant the respect due a work by Goethe, even if I cannot entirely suppress the suspicion that at the time the poet wrote it he did not have too many other ideas—a suspicion that Goethe scholars will confirm. But when Mr. Müller or Mr. Schulze or, more to the point, Mr. Cohn starts to render freely, the results will interest me as little as would the actual poems of Mr. Müller, Mr. Schulze, and so on. Anyone who cannot write poetry should leave "free renderings" be. He will not make the original more beautiful.

The patron of all free renderers today, the famous Professor Wilamowitz[2] from Berlin, who even in his first appearance before the public displayed the main characteristics of a capable philologist ("tact" and a sense for what is important) by discovering the greatest thinker, the (still) greatest artist, and the greatest philologist of his epoch, only to misappropriate their work—this same Wilamowitz has betrayed to us the goal of his generally beloved translations of Greek tragedians into a German fit for summer vacation reading: he wanted to make Aeschylus more comprehensible to the reader of today than the playwright was to his own Greek contemporaries. A most commendable confession! For in truth, it is such "making comprehensible" that is the result of the work of Messrs. Free Renderers. They are all too eager to lend a hand to the poor unfortunate original text. There is no getting around the fact that poetry is not quite as comprehensible as prose. Evidently, this is due to the fact that the poet did not entirely succeed in expressing himself, in the same way that the peculiar remoteness from nature of an Egyptian sculpture is due only to the fact that the artist just hadn't gotten the hang of it yet.[3] Nothing could be easier or more gratifying than to intervene in a corrective fashion and to fill in a few gaps. The fact that things that are strange to us may possibly be so for stylistic reasons is something that the free renderer just can't wrap his mind around—in fact, the whole idea of style is something for which he has no sympathy. His ambition is to clothe the monuments of the past and of foreign lands in the "clothes of today." But, one might ask, would the Apollo of Belvedere really gain that much by being clothed in cutaways and a standing collar?

---

2. Ulrich von Wilamowitz-Moellendorg (1848–1931) was a distinguished German classical scholar, editor and author of numerous critical articles and volumes on Greek history, literature and figures. Four years Nietzsche's junior, his first published work, *Future Philology* (1872), was a scathing critique of *The Birth of Tragedy* (1872).

3. FR: Fairness prevents me from concealing that the most important authority in the field of ancient history, Eduard Meyer, has discovered a different explanation for the trace of melancholy in the faces of Pharaohs from the centuries of the Middle Kingdom: the heavy burdens of governance. This may be found in his *History of Antiquity*.

In point of fact, the task of translating is totally misunderstood when it is seen as one of making something foreign into something German. This is the kind of translation I need when as a merchant I receive an order from Turkey and send it to a translation bureau. But even in the case of a letter from a Turkish friend, the bureau's translation would not do for me. Why not? Because it would not be sufficiently precise? It would be just as precise as their translation of a business letter. So it is not that. It will be German enough—but not Turkish enough. I will not hear the person, his tone, his opinion, his heartbeat. But is that possible? Are we not demanding the impossible of language when we make it our task to reproduce the foreign tone in its foreignness—rather than making the foreign German, to make the German foreign?

Not the impossible, but the necessary, and necessary not only in the case of translation. The creative accomplishment of a translation can lie nowhere else than there where lies the creative accomplishment of speech itself. The making German of what is foreign—thus, to cite a legitimate example, the bureau's translation of a business letter—happens within the German language as it already exists. That is the source of its comprehensibility and the popularity that only envy could deny to the translations of Müller, Schulze, Cohn, and Wilamowitz mentioned earlier. They translate just as someone speaks—someone who has nothing to say. Since he has nothing to say, he needs ask nothing of language, and a language whose speaker asks nothing of it becomes frozen into a tool for basic communication, whose reason for being may be called into question by every new kind of Esperanto. Anyone who has something to say will say it in a new way. He will become a creator of language. The language, after he speaks, will have a different face than it did before. The translator makes himself into a speech organ of a foreign voice, which he makes audible over the chasm of space or of time. When this foreign voice has something to say, then the language has to look different afterward than it did before. This success is the criterion for the dutifully executed accomplishment of the translator. It is completely impossible for a language into which Shakespeare or Isaiah or Dante has spoken to remain untouched by this event. The language will experience a rejuvenation, just as if a new speaker had arisen from within it. And more than this: for the foreign poet not only calls into the new language what he himself has to say, but he brings the heritage of the general spirit of his own language along with him to the new language, so that the rejuvenation that occurs here occurs not merely through a foreign individual but also through the general spirit of that foreign language itself.

That such a rejuvenation of one language by means of another is possible at all presupposes, to be sure, that, just as a language has given birth to each of its speakers, so also all human speech, all foreign languages that have ever been spoken and that ever will be spoken are contained, at least in embryo, within this same language. And such is the case. There is only One language. There is no peculiarity of one language that—even if only in dialects, childish speech, or idioms of a particular class—cannot be detected, at least in embryo, in every other language. This essential unity of all language, and based on it the commandment for all human beings to understand one another, is what creates the possibility and also the task of translating—the possibility, the permissibility, and the obligation to translate. It is possible to translate, because in every language every other is potentially present; it is permitted to translate if one can realize this potential by cultivating the fallow land of language; and there is an obligation to translate so that the day may come for that harmony of languages which can arise only in each individual language, not in the empty space "between" them.

An example may illustrate this. Luther was able to translate the Bible because in German it is possible to reproduce peculiarities of the Hebrew and of the "Hebrewisms" of New Testament Greek, for instance the coordinating rather than subordinating syntax of the sentences. If he had wanted in this instance to translate into the language of his own published works (which entirely betray the humanistically schooled master of language), then a Kautzsch-Weizsäcker[4] or something even worse would have resulted, but not the Luther Bible. But he had the courage to introduce the sentence structure of Hebrew, which even at that time was Cyclopic for the language consciousness of an educated German, into the German language, and in this way he created a work that outlived the language consciousness of his day. To add to the realm of the German language of his day, he conquered the new province of biblical German, which was now able to begin its own history within the history of the German language. And so this biblical German was not necessarily swept along without resistance by the further development of the total organism, but instead it intervened proactively in this development, and was thereby preserved in its distinctive character.

And Luther was permitted to translate because he possessed both the necessary courage and the necessary circumspection for this linguistic campaign of conquest. His renowned battle against the translating "asses" and their schoolmasterly literalness should not be understood as if he recommended a blind arbitrariness in opposition to them. For it is not indiscriminate literalness that lead to the goal that I describe here, and that Luther achieved. It is not the dictionary that must be the highest authority for a translator. Language is not made up of words [*Wörter*], but of ideas [*Worte*].[5] It is words [*Wörter*] that the pupil and the schoolmaster

---

4. FR: Bible Text of the Old and New Testament, edited by D. E. Kautzsch. The New Testament in the translation of Carl Weizsäcker.

5. TK: Rosenzweig is referring here to the two different plurals of the German *das Wort,* namely *"Wörter,"* which refers to words in the most literal sense, i.e., what is listed and defined in a dictionary or *Wörterbuch,* and *"Worte,"* suggesting larger units of meaning, even extending to the Greek *Logos.*

translate. It is words that are found in the dictionary. But it is words as ideas [*Worte*] that are found in a sentence. And it is misleading to speak of words "standing" in a sentence; this image does not do justice to the wavelike flow of word-ideas through the bed of the sentence. The contours with which the word positions itself in the sentence, and which cannot be found in a dictionary, since the latter is obligated by its nature to advance from the contours to the main emphasis or emphases of a word—these contours, and these alone, are what want to be and what must be translated. The example just given, of the coordinating and subordinating sentence structure, is such an instance of contours, only in this instance for the whole sentence, not for the word. How far this search for contours may penetrate into the elements of the linguistic configuration—whether as far as sentences or as far as words, or even as far as the word roots that may be excavated from underneath the word—is a question that can be answered only on a case-by-case basis. But always it is a question of contours. And when Luther, in one famous example, refused to translate the word of the angel's greeting as "Thou full of grace" [*du voller Gnaden*], he captured the contour of the word with his translation "sweet and lovely" [*holdselig*, an adjective formed from the words *hold* or "cherished" and *selig* or "blessed"] without giving up the root contained in the Greek word, which actually is conveyed far better by "cherished" [*hold*] than by the translation dictated by a school dictionary, namely "grace" [*Gnade*]. But the fact that he himself decided not to use in his translation the phrase that he came up with when carried away by the triumphant exuberance of his polemic—"You dear Maria"—is not due, as the asses of today would believe, to cowardly shrinking from the consequence of his logic, but is rather a proof of the authentic level-headedness of his work as translator. With the phrase "You dear Maria," he would have transformed the scene into a German folksong and thereby destroyed just that tension by means of which it was capable of becoming the basis for the folksong. Only respect for the distance involved makes it possible to leap over a ditch; he who starts by filling in the ditch cripples the powers of others to leap over it.

And Luther was compelled to translate because the German people at that time needed this influx from the spirit of a foreign language. The Bible is that book among all others whose destiny it is to be translated; therefore it is the earliest and the most translated. That which is the meaning of all translating, the coming of "that day," that is for the Bible with its unique amalgam of narrating, demanding, and promising virtually the ring that holds these elements together. Thus the entry of a people into world history is marked by the moment when it appropriates the Bible by translating. This entry demands at all times a sacrifice of that people's insularity, a sacrifice that is reflected in that recasting of the national language that is necessarily connected with a translation of the Bible. For whereas other translations always touch only on one part of life—for instance, a translation of Shakespeare affects only the theater—a Bible translation intervenes in all spheres of life; there is no such thing as a "religious sphere." The Heliand[6] was both a consequence and a symptom of the fact that the German people of that time were not yet ripe for world history; none of its accomplishments from the medieval period have been taken in by the rest of the world, whereas they themselves took in to the highest degree the accomplishments of other peoples in all fields. The Reformation is the first German event that had an impact on the rest of the world that did not disappear afterward. Since that time, Germany's destiny has been interwoven with that of the rest of the world. Luther's deed—his translation— marks this point. The so-called religious genius is never a world-historical personality as such alone—Meister Eckhart, for instance, was not. Another, worldly side is required in addition. Luther's other side was the Translator. It was this "worldliness" that completed his transformation into a world-historical figure.

But now let us return to Jewish poetry of the Middle Ages. The problem of translating here is first of all quite simply one of the external form. It is almost typical in the history of translation that those who come first shy away from the poetic form of the original. Homer was translated first into blank verse, alexandrines, ottava rima, before anyone dared the attempt to construct a modern hexameter. It remains true even so, even after Vofs,[7] that a German hexameter is not a Greek hexameter. But a German alexandrine is still less a Greek hexameter, and so in the long run the translator cannot avoid the task of producing a formation that is the closest possible equivalent to the form of the original. He will be forced at times to impose even stricter formal restrictions on his work than the original form imposed upon the poet—that is, when by means of such increased discipline of the language into which one translates, a closer approximation to the impression of the original can be achieved. An example of this is the necessary preference for monosyllabic words in the German translation of Shakespeare, which is natural for the poet due to his language, but which for the translator can only come from conscious discipline.

Of the previous translators of Yehuda Halevi, not one has recognized this essential responsibility with regard to meter; with regard to rhyme, only Heller has done so, who in general towers over all predecessors and successors and who naturally is described by common opinion as unpalatable (Heller, *The Authentic Hebrew Melodies*, Frankfurt a. M., 3d ed. 1908). This timidity about imitating the rhyme form has the same basis as that which, on closer examination, is shared by astonishingly many human affairs—laziness, laziness pure and simple. For the imitation of even the

---

6. TK: A ninth-century epic in Old Saxon depicting the life and teachings of Christ.
7. TK: The author of the first great German translation of Homer in hexameter.

most complex rhyme forms is possible in German, as Rückert[8] proves. In the worst case one can easily use a dictionary of rhyme; if one wants to figure as a free renderer, one need not tell anyone about it. I, who want to be nothing other than a translator, hereby gladly confess that I owe much easing of my burden to the dictionary of Mr. Steputat, even if most of the time the best rhymes did not occur to him. How important is the imitation of the rhyme form can be seen even from the fact that in the poems under discussion the rhyme is not merely the mortar that glues one stone to another, as in modern poetic forms, but almost throughout, at least in addition, it is its very building material, the unified tone of which determines the total impression given by the façade. Imagine an architect who —in an epoch when such commissions were given—had built a structure modeled after the Palazzo Pitti, with every floor made out of a different color of hewn rock. This is about how all these re-creations must appear to one coming from the original, these re-creations that ruthlessly tear asunder either the strictly uniform rhyme, or, in the strophic poems, the uniform rhyme of the last line of each strophe. What then remains of the beauty of these "belt songs," in which the rhymes of the individual stanzas are joined together by the precious seal of the system of circular rhyme, when one splits them up into the stanzas of German folk poetry? Nevertheless, this has happened almost every time, Heller being the sole exception.

The question regarding meter is more difficult. Here there exists in truth a powerfully alien element. To be sure, the rhyme too cannot without qualification be equated with that of European verse, which always begins with a vowel, whereas the rhyme in the poems translated here consistently draws a consonant into the rhyming element: thus, for example, not *ajich* but *rajich* is rhymed, not *im* but *bim*. Naturally, that cannot be imitated.[9] But the strangeness of the meter goes deeper than this.

It is customary to deal with the meter of Spanish Hebraists by calling it an imitation of Arabic metrics. This formulation is misleading in its brevity. The adoption of Arabic meters did not occur in blind imitation; this was precluded, although in and of itself it would have been quite possible, by the theory of the Hebrew syllable, which was dominant among

---

8. TK: Friedrich Rückert (1788–1866), German poet noted for his translations from Hindi and Persian and for his German verse in Oriental forms.

9. FR: An example of precise reproduction of the original rhythm indicated in the commentary to "Storm" is given. Only four syllables in each line in German constructed as double iams are virtually rhythmic, the others are dressing. (In the 1983 Nijhoff edition this note has been changed to read: "The translation of the poem ["Storm"] attempts such an imitation, while maintaining from the original the vowels preceding the rhyme. But it is inevitable the German reader experiences here not so much the sameness of the end syllable, but rather the rhymes of the pre-rhyme syllable that are scattered throughout and that from the standpoint of Hebrew rhyme-feeling are incident.")

the Hebrew philologists of the day. But the initiators of this new poetry in Hebrew seized with a bold grasp the peculiarity of the prose rhythm of their language, which distinguishes it from Arabic—the mute syllables, which sound something like the "Pa-" in "Pacific"[10]—and they gave to this sound the value of that type of syllable in Arabic which (according to the theory) was lacking in Hebrew. Thus arose the two elements of Hebrew metrics: a sort of iamb consisting of a mute syllable and an accented syllable, and an accented syllable that could be piled up in twos and threes and for all practical purposes, through the stringing together of feet of verse, in even greater numbers. The meter that arose in this way, to be sure, led far away from normal prose accentuation, both from the Sephardic accentuation of endings and from the Ashkenzic accentuation of the stem.[11] And herein lies the root of the difficulty for the translator as well. For in German starting in the seventeenth century, the principle arose that was firmly established in the classical literature around 1800, namely that the prose accentuation of words must be preserved in verse, a principle that only in recent decades, through the school of Stefan George[12] with its demand for uniformly hovering tone, has begun to experience some modification. But the reign of this principle is so absolute that it is hard for us today to grasp even the possibility of different principles in the past. The fact that Greco-Roman antiquity had an entirely different principle is accepted as a fact rather than experienced aesthetically. And yet the matter is not so difficult to grasp. Modern man needs only think of musical declamation, in which even he accepts an accentuation that is different from the standard for a particular word. The charm lies here—as it evidently did with the Homeric hexameter as well—in the constantly shifting tension between the prose tone and the verse tone, which flee one another and then find each other once more. Every Homeric hexameter thus has its own individual meter—a richness of which the metrics taught in school do not even dream, and which, by the way, is squandered in modern vocal music by the Wagnerian rules of accentuation with their one-sided predominance of the recitative style.

It is from here that the so-called unnatural quality of these Hebrew meters is to be understood. Anyone who wants to get a feel for these

---

10. TK: Rosenzweig's German examples are the *"Ge-"* in *"Gewand"* or the *"Be-"* in *"Bezug."*

11. FR: "Sephardic" (Spanish) and "Ashkenazic" (German) are the two most important systems of Hebrew pronunciation. The essential differences are found in the way of reading several vowels (e.g., *Aulom,* "world," is pronounced "Aulom" in Ashkenazic and "Olam" in Sephardic) and in the accentuation of the final syllable in Sephardic as opposed to the accentuation (in many cases) of the penultimate syllable in Ashkenazic.

12. TK: Stefan George (1868–1933) was the leading poet of German aestheticism. He and his circle cultivated an incantatory quality in their verse, and as the opponents of naturalism in all things, gravitated toward a poetic tone, which the general public would perceive as "unnatural."

meters would do well to read the verses in the fashion of Stefan George, thus with a uniformly hovering accentuation of all vocalic syllables, one that nevertheless must not allow the actual sound of the word (in this case Sephardic) to disappear entirely. But the task of the translator is now to create verse in German that will force the reader into such hovering accentuation and to overcome the natural tendency of the German language toward iambic, trochaic, possibly dactylic and at most anapestic rhythms, a tendency that in no way accommodates these Hebrew verses with their piling up of accented syllables.* Here is a case of the kind I referred to previously, a case where the translator must attempt by way of the artificial means of augmented ties [vermehrte Bindungen], to achieve an effect in the language of the translation that is as similar as possible to that of the original. The following paths present themselves: artificial evocation of hovering accentuation by destroying the iambic or trochaic tendency of a line of verse through the heavy use in close proximity of bisyllabic words consisting of syllables of equal accentuation, such as *heartthrob, ploughshare,*[13] and so on, the piling up of monosyllabic words of equal accentuation for the same purpose; and the artificial introduction of caesurae, which within the lines of verse permit the rhythm, which once more begins to tip [*verschlenden*] into an iambic or trochaic pattern, to right itself once more. But all these paths will work only with poems in strict meters; with the poems in freer meter—which as especially numerous among the cultic poems—in which only the accented syllables are counted and in which unaccented syllabes may be added, or not, among the accented ones, the task of imitating the meter precisely remains insoluble. For there are no means by which the German reader may be compelled to regard only a select few of those syllables constituting a line of spoken poetry (it is different with poetry sung to a familiar melody) as rhythmically significant. This is so because a difference of such magnitude as that between accented and unaccented syllables in Hebrew may be present in spoken German, but it is not metrically useful. The only remedy is the decision to limit oneself in German to the same number of syllables as in the Hebrew, thus a regulation of the stream of syllables that flows far more freely in Hebrew.[14] The only place where the freedom of the meter can (and so, according to my principles, must) be imitated even

---

* Regarding metrics: A verse "foot" is an integral sound unit (e.g. of two feet: "a red / red rose"); "iamb" is a bisyllabic foot with accent on the first syllable; "trochee" is a bisyllabic foot with accent on the second syllable; "dactyl" is a trisyllabic foot with accent on the first syllable; "anapest" is a trisyllabic foot with accent on the final syllable; "caesura" is a rhythmic pause in the center of a line. See Lewis Turco, *The Book of Forms* (New York: Dutton, 1968).

13. TK: Rosenzweig's examples in German are *Mißachs* and *Lichtstrahl*.

14. FR: An example of precise imitation of the original rhythm is given in the poem "Storm." Only four syllables in each line—constructed as a double iamb in German—are rhythmically essential; the others are mere filler.

in German is at the beginning of the line. But the syllable placed in front must not lose the character of an appoggiatura or grace note, specifically one that precedes a line more likely to be trochaic than iambic. It is the meter that also determines whether the rhyme in the translation is masculine or feminine, in those cases where the original has a masculine rhyme but the line ends with an even number of accented syllables, and as a result the translation has to have a feminine rhyme. Incidentally, this is no great misfortune, since the consonantal rhyme beginning makes even the masculine rhymes of the original poem sound to our ears like feminine ones. In the opposite case—a feminine rhyme and an odd number of syllables at the line's end—the feminine rhyme can be salvaged by placing it such that a strongly accented syllable precedes it.

The result of all these strategies will be an impression that at least lies in the direction of an introduction of the foreign rhythm into German. A third point to consider does not belong to the realm of form (as do rhyme and meter) but to that of content. This is what is called "mosaic style" and is considered to be as impossible to imitate as rhyme and meter. What is this?

All Jewish poetry in the Diaspora refuses to ignore this condition of being-in-exile. This would happen if it were to record the world in immediate fashion, as does other poetry. For the world surrounding this poetry is one of exile, and it must retain this character. And if it were to abandon this posture and open itself up to the streaming-in of this world, as soon as it did so, this world would become like home and would cease to be an exile. But this exiling of the environment is accomplished by means of the constant presence of the written word. With it, a different reality displaces that of the environment and demotes the latter to the status of an illusion, or more precisely, a simile. So it is not that the written word is adduced as an illustration (by way of simile) of life in the present; on the contrary, these events [of life in the present] serve to elucidate the written word and become a simile for it. The relationship here is thus precisely the opposite of what we imagine when we hear the expression *mosaic style.* This style is a phenomenon of those literary epochs that have not yet reached their age of maturity. When Einhard[15] describes Charlemagne with words from Suetonius's biography of Augustus, he intends to display him in the costume of Augustus, to illuminate him by means of Augustus, and not the other way around. When a Jewish poet refers to Christianity and Islam with the terms *Edom* and *Ishmael,* he is not commenting on the present by means of the written word; he is commenting on the word by means of the

---

15. TK: Biographer of Charlemagne, c. 770–840.

present. The basis of this is not literary immaturity [*Unreifheit*] but rather a quality of literary overripeness [*Überreifheit*]. One is not at a loss for a style of one's one; rather one is so much in possession of one's own style that one does not even consider the possibility of abandoning it for a form of writing that lacks all style [*Stillosigkeit*]. Such a relationship to the written word natually presupposes that this written word is classical, not only in form, but also in content, indeed that the classicism of the content and that of the form are considered to be inseparably interwoven with one another. A distant comparison with this phenomenon is presented by the way in which European peoples quote at present. Anyone who has heard Shakespeare quoted knows how much people quote him for the sake of "beautiful passages." Shakespeare quoted in the mouth of an Englishman gives an entirely "mosaic" effect. That is, he is quoted without any sense of real identification with him. The world view of the modern Englishman is rooted in Cromwell's century, not Shakespeare's. However, when an educated German quotes Goethe or Schiller, he is quoting Kant, Fichte, and Hegel at the same time. In other words, he believes in the spirit that he quotes; he does not quote it merely for social entertainment. To the extent one can speak of a superiority of the Germans vis-`a-vis the Western European nations, it lies in this historical stroke of luck: the connection between the most recent highpoints of their formal and their content-based culture. Among the older nations, only Italy with its Dante, and among the newer ones, perhaps the Russians with Dostoevsky have a similarly secure ground under their feet, allowing them to use the most beautiful words for the highest sentiments they have to express. Now it is this fortunate unity of speaking and thinking that is possessed to the highest degree—and, to be sure, in dearly purchased exclusivity—by the medieval Jew. With him it is not only the loftiest thoughts that find carefully shaped form; rather, every thought that wishes to legitimize itself as thought seeks such form. Here, a quotation is by no means a decorative appendage; rather, it is the label that announces the impact of speech.

But this presents another task for the translator. He is not permitted to suppress the allusive content of language. Not only has this task been considered insoluble, but it is so to some extent. For it would of course be no solution if, for example, one were to present the required biblical knowledge to the reader in footnotes. For the Hebrew reader, the connection with the written word is not *ex post facto*; rather, it is a sequence of momentary electric impulses that accompany one's reading, which precisely in their unbroken sequence bring about the fluorescence of that which is read. With this simile of the problem, the possibility of a solution is indicated at the same time. The succession of individual electric impulses cannot be as rapid in German as it is in Hebrew, for the simple reason that the quotability of the German Bible is less than that of the

Hebrew Bible. But in any event, there is a certain quotability here as well—thanks to the Luther Bible, thanks to several church hymns taken from the Bible, and thanks to a number of biblical passages that are known even to people today. And since a quote from the Bible is rarer in German, it has a much weightier effect in comparison, so even in its lesser frequency it still produces a certain fluorescence. So the translator has the task of bringing out every biblical quote that can in any way be brought to consciousness, in some circumstances even to replace a quotation unknown to today's reader with one that is more familiar to him. He need not fear committing the error criticized earlier of making a text more comprehensible than was the original; for someone today, the facts that the Arabs are descended from Ishmael and that Ishmael's mother was named Hagar are about as well known as were (for the readers of or listeners to a Halevi poem) the facts that Epher was a son of Ketura and that the latter is identified by tradition with Hagar. Incidentally, a further circumstance that comes to the aid of a modern reader is that precisely the books of the Bible most likely to be known to an educated reader today—the Psalms, the prophet Isaiah, the Song of Solomon—were also the ones most likely to be quoted by the Hebrew poet.

A fourth point I did not mention in the first edition since I thought it self-evident. However, as I have learned since, it is not so. So I will now speak also of my choice of words.

It is a bit awkward for a translator to touch on this point. Even more than the actual poet, he is vulnerable to the suspicion of making poetic virtues out of his technical necessities. His rhymes especially are always suspected of transforming themselves from the obedient servant into the master of the poetic thought. Since every servant does this, because this is the inherent way of making up for the condition of servitude, a poet may easily admit to this since the word is given into his service only so that it may gain power over him. But it is otherwise with the translator. He does not have the right to be borne by his own words; he must convey word after word, just as they are given to him. Thus every word places him before the question a conveying meaning, thus before what is in the broadest sense a scientific question. He and only he—not the poet— chooses his words. He must know the place of the poet's words within the field of vision of language in general and of the particular language of the poet. He must strive to know how close or how remote is the origin of the word whose trace he follows, whether it is at home in the center of the language or in its peripheries.

In the Hebrew of the Spanish poets, this determination is not at all difficult to make because of their limited—that is, their almost purely biblical—vocabulary. Working in mechanical fashion with dictionaries and concordances is excluded here as well; a word that appears in a daily prayer is familiar, even if the concordance describes it as *hapax legomenon*.[16] Nevertheless, awareness of these distinctions is anything but widespread (as I had the opportunity to learn between the first and second editions of this book). Yehuda Halevi in particular has the reputation of easy grace and remarkable smoothness. Evidently people are of the opinion that since they are entirely dependent, and in an entirely indiscriminate way, on the dictionary, Yehuda Halevi must have been so as well. But he knew more Hebrew, not only more than I, but—and may this be said in all the modesty that becomes the author—also more than my critics. He was a trusted servant in the whole great house of the holy language. And most likely he had a sense of whether a word belonged to the everyday tableware of language or whether it is preserved in a locked cupboard for use only on special occasions.

Here it is the translator's task to follow after the poet and as much as possible to imitate what is most unusual in the poet's vocabulary, if not word by word, then at least sentence by sentence—even at the risk that readers whose knowledge of the development of the German language reaches no further back than the *Book of Songs*[17] and who thus have yet to discover the *West-East Divan*[18] or Hölderlin's hymns, to say nothing of more recent work, might find his German incomprehensible.

Or is the poetry of Yehuda Halevi itself perhaps subject to conditions that allow him to use the smoothness for which he has been praised but forbid it to his translator? That in any case is the lesson that all these connoisseurs of Hebrew and nonconnoisseurs of German wish, with rare unanimity, to teach *him*. The scarcity of rhymes, which supposedly forced the translator to use his peculiar word formations—which, strangely enough, are to be found in the middle of lines as well, and even in the translator's entirely unrhymed prose writings!—allegedly did not exist for Yehuda Halevi. He, it is claimed, was able to string together rhyme on rhyme in a pleasing flow without giving it a second thought, and so he never needed to descend into the sublime.[19] As a justification for this opinion, the legend of the suffix rhyme is cited by all.

---

16. FR: Ancient Greek phrase designating an expression that appears only once in the sources (in this case the Bible).

17. TK: A much beloved book of poems by Heinrich Heine, many set to music by Schumann and other composers.

18. FR: Goethe's last collection of poems.

19. TK: Rosenzweig uses an ironic juxtaposition, *"ins Erhaben auszuarten."* *Das Erhabene* is the standard term for "the sublime," and the verb *ausarten* means to "degenerate into" or "to lose control." Applied to language, the verb would normally imply a descent into substandard speech.

Suffix rhymes are ending rhymes, such as (in English) the rhyme of *jubilation* with other verbs ending with *-ation*.[20] They really are more easily possible in Hebrew than in German. For that very reason, respectable poets shy away from them and use them only occasionally, as Goethe rhymed *Liebe* with *Triebe* ["love," "instinct(s)"] or *Sonne* with *Wonne* ["sun" with "bliss"]. But among connoisseurs, the legend is widespread that the Spanish-Hebrew poets made such extravagant use of this comfortable opportunity and rhymed through their monorhyme poems as contentedly as a German professor of philosophy easily fills a whole lecture with rhymes on *-ism.* This legend—a legend with respect to the Spanish-Jewish poets, but not to the German philosophy professor—has, like every self-respecting legend, some basis in reality, and my research in pursuit of this basis has been crowned with success. The expert writing in the *Vienna Morning News* instructs me in the following manner: "For example, when Yehuda Halevi uses the rhyme 'arich' (the ending meaning 'your' or 'thy') more than sixty times in his 'Zionide' ["To Zion"] it is surely a heavy burden for the translator who must find sixty German rhymes for the word 'questions' [*Fragen*]. In Hebrew, a suffix common to a variety of words is often rhymed, in German it is the word itself which is rhymed." This is about the same as if a Frenchman would maintain that the translation of "Zionide" in this book rhymes with [the French syllable] *en.* This expert has not understood that the rhyme in question is called "rajich" and thus is composed of a word element and an ending, just like the German rhyme for *-estions* [*-ragen*]. Obviously, he is unaware of the very trait that distinguishes this whole rhyming technique from our own, even though it was presented to him (redundantly!) in the Preface: the entirely consonantal rhyme beginnings. This sounds improbable. But whoever knows the almost fantastic ignorance that is the rule among us in all things which are scholarly rather than routine, and which makes it so difficult (in everything that can only be gained through routine) and yet incomparably easy (in everything that can be gained by a little understanding and scholarly instinct) to gain the title of an expert—anyone who knows this will not be surprised at this "expert's" ignorance. Years ago, I asked a friend, who was accustomed to reciting the "Zionide" from his childhood onward on the ninth of Av[*], what was the meter of that poem; he replied that he had often sought to find it, but that there was none present—the poem was written in free rhythms!

But it is precisely in the "Zionide" where it can be seen that even in Hebrew it is no child's play to find thirty-five (not sixty, to be sure) rhymes, which leads us to infer with certainty the very early appearance of rhyme

---

20. TK: Rosenzweig's German examples are *jubilieren* and other verbs ending with *-ieren*

[*] Jewish holiday of mourning commemorating the destruction of the first and second Temples in ancient Jerusalem.

dictionaries. For in addition to the requirement of the "arich" at the end of the word, there is the further restriction imposed by the meter, which allows only certain groups of words that comply with the requirements of rhyme. And in fact, the same rhyming word, with the same meaning, appears twice in the poem—in the sixth and in the twenty-sixth couplet. So rhyming in those days too—or rather, especially in those days—was just as hard as the believers in the legend of the suffix rhyme think it is today. And that means that writing poetry was just as hard. And among the thirty-five rhyming words of the "Zionide," there are two that appear only once in the whole Bible and another two that appear only two or three times. And on the other hand, for example in the hymn "My God," the rhyming possibilities of the word that appears in the title, and that from out of itself propels the whole poem in both its form and content, must be fully exploited[21]—precisely because the poet did not permit himself to use the suffix rhyme that would have been possible in this case, but in his honesty he made the stem rhyme as well, despite the difficulties. So this "pleasing smoothness" of the poet and his "effortless choice of words" is a myth, at least as far as the poet himself is concerned. The criteria named above may indeed apply to that which his translators have made out of him.

The selection of poems presented here was originally the product of chance. With each one of the first poems to be translated, I could have explained how I came to translating it, but the reasons would be personal and in part actually coincidental. However, it is no coincidence that the secular poetry, which occupies considerable space in the poet's *oeuvre* (though not nearly the space that the other German translators have sought to accord it in their selection), is absent in my selection. It wasn't exactly the timidity that S. D. Luzzatto*, the great and authentic philologist among those who have occupied themselves with Yehuda Halevi, cites as motivating his selection from the *Divan*—namely, that he didn't want to mix the holy with the profane. Rather, here too the reason is purely personal. In translating, there always comes a moment when the dividing line between poem and translation, if only for just a moment, falls away. But this moment is also the barrier that limits one in one's selection.

So what was coincidental in the selection was lost in the course of my labors. I began to notice that the poems I had translated wished as much as possible to grow into a complete portrait of the poet, both in form and content. At a certain stage of my work, I had more or less achieved this.

---

21. TK: Rosenzweig uses the German verb *auskaufen*, "to buy out."

* Samuel David Luzzato (1800–1865), often known by the acronym "Shadal," was a versatile Jewish Italian scholar, philosopher, philologist, translator, Bible commentator, and Jewish historian. He was a professor at the rabbinical college of Padua from 1829 to his death.

But this stage had barely been reached when it was already exceeded once more. And the condition that arrived at this point was, although less pleasing aesthetically than the previous condition, more faithful to the original (if such an expression may be permitted). For precisely the repetitions that now came in belong to the total picture.

It is not the case that entire sections of poems are repeated—though world literature offers examples of this, too—rather, what are repeated are the thoughts and images. Not merely the details but also and especially the entirety of each poem appears as a variation on a fixed type. And since this really is the case, this anthology would lack something if it did not give the reader a picture of this.

But it would be entirely misguided if this were to be attempted by grouping together poems of the same type—the *Meoroth, Ahavoth, Geuloth* [*Lights, Loves, Redemptions*] and the rest. This museumlike procedure would give the falsest impression of all. Where does what is typical come from here? Naturally, these poems are not intended to be read silently but—as is the case in all ages where poetry, or at least some of it, concerned the whole people—to be read aloud and listened to. Goethe's ineffectual wish, "Anything but reading—always sing!" (Ineffectual, because even in his day music, which with Goethe's house composers had humbly served poetry, began with Schubert, and under the pretense of serving it faithly, to gain mastery over poetry)—that wish, which even in Goethe's days was ineffectual, if fulfilled without any great fuss in such days [when poetry is the concern of the whole people] or among human circles in which the same condition holds. It all depends on the presence of a "circle," a "people," far more than it does on an "age." There is no cause for the usual sanctimonious (and in truth merely lazy) pretense at sadness over the "meaningless" or even "ungodly" present. Wherever poetry is composed for a particular human circle and is received by it in a natural fashion—in its throats, not only in spirit—the "age" is there. Thus it is in the evil present, for example in every army and in every Protestant congregation; but in the beautiful Middle Ages of Walther von der Vogelweide*, for example, it was not.

The poems of Yehuda Halevi and his contemporaries were thus, at least in large part, functional art of this nature. And to the extent they are not, they are still determined in their content and their form (even in the case of the entirely secular poems) by the laws governing that form of art. The particular use for which these poems aim is to be recited by the cantor and the congregation at certain points of the liturgical year in the synagogue. The stream of words known to all from

---

* Walther von der Vogelweide (1170–1230?) was a Middle High German lyric poet and minnesinger, probably born in Austria or Tirol, of noble family. He composed love songs, and political and religious songs in which he championed German independence and unity and opposed the pope.

ancient times, interrupted by these additions, is to be dammed up into lakes that offer to the eye new vistas of shores. They are the changing element among the eternally recurring, but since in their changing nature they are bound to what recurs eternally, they are by necessity forced into a certain uniformity. This is not noticeable as long as they stand in their natural context of usage; the various poems were after all separated by a full year of life in the synagogue, one genuinely full of events. In this context, repetitions were not perceived as such, or to the extent they were so perceived, this was only fitting. For it is just this recurrence in the course of the year that is the essence of the festival—just as in more recent times repetition is the great, and the only, form in which human beings express their innermost truth. For instance, one can object to the constantly renewed words in these poems expressing humility and devotion, despair and confidence in salavation, retreat from the world and longing for God, contrition for sin and confidence in God's mercy—one can object, but in doing so one does not abolish from the world the fact that the heart of the poet and the hearts of those for whom he wrote are full of such sentiments and seek expression for them. A lie can find many possible ways of expression, but truth has only a few, basically always only one. Its lasting power is demonstrated in the fact that it never tires of saying this One thing over and over again. The word of love does not grow old in the mouth of a lover—the same word that withers even the first time it is spoken from a mouth that only pretends to love.

But the practical problem of how one should conduct oneself as editor or reader of this collection is not solved thereby. One could say: like Yehuda Halevi, not at all—that is, he never collected his *Divan*. This happened only after his death but then several times in rapid succession. The practical implication for our age is that the authorized site, namely the synagogue, and especailly the Reform Synagogue of Central and Western Europe and of America, should be far more mindful of this poetry than it has been. What an opportunity for the cantors and the amateur composers among local synagogue choir directors! But above all, what an opportunity for the rabbis! Here, by making the simple interpretation of the day's poem the basis for their sermon, they could find their way back to the only genuinely Jewish style of preaching, the didactic, from which the admonitory and proclamatory may arise naturally, occasionally in the best sense of the word.

But what I have spun out above holds only for the original text. Nothing can be learned from this concerning the conduct of the translator. How could I prevent the reader of this anthology from behaving like a reader; in other words, how could I bring him to consume these poems not like cherries, but like peaches, that is, not to start on the next one when one has barely swallowed the previous one, but to consume each one nice and individually, with deliberation, and with the consciousness that there may not be another one any time soon?

The notes are intended to serve this purpose. Naturally not this purpose alone. Beyond this, they are intended to fulfill the normal obligation to annotate, thus to convey to the reader, while maintaining civilized manners (in casual fashion, as if he already knew all that), those things that are necessary for an understanding of the poem and that he most surely does not know. But the main goal is the former one: to cause the reader to take each poem as a thing in and of itself, just as the poet composed it as a thing in and of itself, and just as the singer and the listener at the site for which it was intended sung and heard it in the past, sing and hear it today, and will sing and hear it in the future. Thus, [the goal is] to transform the reader from a reader and consumer[22] into a guest and friend of the poem.

About Yehuda Halevi himself I do not wish to speak here. There will be better—that is, more immediate—opportunity for this in the notes to individual poems. The notes will also make good the excuse I gave at the beginning of this Preface for the fact that despite my best intention to be literal, I have had in places to resort to free rendering, by giving the text verbatim to supplement the translation.

If I may express a wish in conclusion, it is a double one: that the depth meter I have set up here with this small collection may soon be submerged under the rising waters, but that none of my successors in this field will have the nerve to be lazy and to fall short of the measure of exactness that has been achieved here. As of now, the excuse that "it can't be done" is no longer available.

---

22. TK: Rosenzweig uses the German word *Vertilger,* which can mean "exterminator," but in this context clearly refers back to te metaphor of eating cherries and peaches.

GOD

1. Praised!

Yes Lord, You
   You I praise;
Your Justice, may it shine far
   through me

   Listen, a sound—
   I already respond,
Query dissolves
    and conflict.

   And did it not
   resemble the raw material
demanding of the maker, "What
    are you making"?

   Him I desire,
   Him I receive,
as tower and defense
    and shelter:

   All-around glowing,
   Emanating light,
without veil
    without covering—

Praised be He,
   glorified be He,
    exalted be He,
     and hallowed.

Lord: to Your splendor,
   to the works of Your might—
the Heavens
    bear witness,

   Their rising and
   their setting and
when deeply they lower
    their face.

1] This hymn is an introduction to the Kaddish prayer. Its refrain is taken from the second stanza of the prayer, just as its overall rhythm is derived from that of this eulogy. Thus the refrain acts here, as it often does elsewhere, as the germ cell of the entire poem, the point toward which each stanza runs and which, as the point of reference, determines its course. This confluence with the familiar sound of the Kaddish (which in Jewish worship plays a role comparable to that of the Lord's Prayer in Christianity), this confluence—now in majestic breadth, now in sublime cascade, now in the wildness of rapids, and then again in mysterious roaring— determines the impact of the poem. (No accident, then, that both the earliest and the most recent translators simply omit the refrain, apparently because it is repeated five times and might therefore be "tiresome").[1]

The streams of the five stanzas, each flowing into the ocean of the "Praised be.á.á.," come from different directions. The first stanza starts out with the condition of the creature—that creature the expression of whose longing for the Creator's help is immediately rhymed with the assurance of his receiving that help. Thus confident of help, he sees the heavens open up; blinded, he falls to the ground.

In the second stanza, man dares to open his eyes again. The heavens are closed, and nature's expanse stretches out below. But the poem vaults from sphere to sphere, upward to nature's resting first Mover. Having arrived here, it sees the wonders of the divine throne (as described in Ezekiel's vision) and once more falls down, prostrate.

---

1. FR: The earliest German translator was Michael Sachs, *Die religiöse Poesie der Juden in Spanien* (Berlin, 1945); the most recent was Emil Bernhard (Cohn), *Ein Diwan von Jehuda Halevi* (Berlin, 1921).

And angels, who
walk among
walls of
    water and fire.

They acknowledge You
and name You,
You who created
    the sound that speaks

For You balance
with ease, and You carry,
And not on Your arm,
    nor on Your hands:

The deepest depth,
The Heavenly circle,
the throne seat and
    His attendants—[1]

Praised be He,
    gloried be He,
        exalted be He,
            and hallowed.

And whose mouth, whose,
    would be worthy of Him,
who creates clouds
    with His word,

Who lives forever
—creating mystery
in the height of heights
    around His place—

And yet He descended from
the throne to the tent
of the son,
    to live there.

---

1. The attendants are the four animal figures from Ezekiel 1.

Shaken by the tension between height and depth of which he is now aware, the poet now grasps the mystery of revelation: the tabernacle contains the Eternal One, whom the whole world cannot contain. The thinker knows that all our knowing, even that of the prophets, can see only a reflection. Yet he also knows that this "only" is not just an "only"; it is the form in which man can participate in the treasure of essence. But the thought of this "only" casts him down to the ground once more.

Assuredly He grants
the reflected splendor
of his refuge
to his prophets

But without form
and without norm
His spirit wanders,
aimlessly.

Only prophecy
saw Him as if
in royal garb's
majesty—

Praised be He,
glorified be He,
exalted be He,
and hallowed.

Great are the works,
unending the images—
who can delimit
the form of praise?

Blessed be the man
who early began
to see in Him
the All-powerful,

And bravely relies
on Him, who embraces
the universe
eternally,

Praises Him highly
with a lively spirit
and never called His Judgment
unjust

And freely admits
that always God's work
was also
his goal

And now as he looks around in the human world around him, he recognizes man's destiny in his dependence and his salvation in the free and joyful acceptance of that dependence, in the acknowledgment of Providence, and in the anticipation of God's judgment. This time the words of the prayer are merely the serene and natural result of wisdom's insights.

And that he brings
near the day, when
the world's judgment
will take place—

Praised be He,
glorified be He,
exalted be He,
and hallowed.

Thaw yourself,
renew yourself,
clearly see yourself
deeply within!

Comprehend, oh spirit,
what you are
and that you are
made from nothing.

Who gave you strength?
who knowledge?
who will someday call you?
do you know?

Behold God's
strength, and
let it kindle your heart's
sacred desire!

Know His work!
But remember,
to leave Him
untouched.

Seek at length
first things and last
wonderful and
concealed—

Praised be He,
glorified be He,
exalted be He,
and hallowed.

Yet the serenity of those insights does not last long. Man delves into his breast. He is not wise; he is—nothing. And out of this ultimate, this innermost experience of his nothingness, he looks up once again to the grandeur of his Lord. Trembling, he now pronounces the final thought that his mind has attained. It is only God's actions that he can know and perceive; upon God himself (here he uses the same words with which God withholds from the Adversary power over Job's life) he may not put forth his hand (Job 1:12[2]). And seized with awe at the feeling of this mystery above him, he stammers the words of the prayer that, though whispered by a solitary one, will carry farther than they had in the beginning, when they were accompanied by the choir of creation and of all created spirits.

---

2. "And the Lord said unto Satan: 'Behold, all that he hath is in thy power; only upon himself put not forth thy hand.'"

2. The All-Powerful One

Powerful One! Who would be   without Him!   Who would dispute His rank!
   Him, source of the universe   all around   which He created!
His shape   no eye   has seen, only the
   tender heart,   rushed towards Him,   gazing and apprehending.
His powerful splendor   envelops   the universe; He is "place"
   for the universe,   even though no   place contains Him.
The soul sees but is not   seen!   As He, who sees, is not seen;
   come to Him and bring   praise   and blessings to Him!

3. Longing

Him, the source of the true life, I desire.
   Therefore I despise the life which is dull and empty.
To behold my King's countenance—what else should I want!
   I do not acknowledge power and splendor other than Him.
If I could see Him, if only in my dream!
   Happily I would sleep eternal and never awaken.
And if I saw His countenance in the depth of my heart,
   I would not permit my eye to look outside.

2] What the preceding poem spreads over fire stanzas, this one crowds into eight overflowing lines, which, despite the poem's brevity, have the feel of a hymn, due to their heavily thundering rhythm. This enormous concentration is achieved in content by the means man has had throughout the ages for transmitting his perception of God for himself and to others from age to age: the dogmatic formula. Precisely because it is fixed, it will, if only it is given a true hearing, awaken in us an infinity of resonating sounds. The Incomparable! The Creator! The Invisible! The One revealed in our hearts! The all-encompassing One! The "Place," as the Talmud calls Him. And the One related in its essence to the human soul created in His image, which like him sees yet remains unseen. All of these words, familiar within the sphere of Bible and Talmud, are here joined together like building blocks of a gigantic monument.

3] A delicate interweaving of world weariness and longing for heaven. The focal point is the wish for "eternal sleep." For sleep and dream are to this poet the legitimate ways of reaching this goal since he, as forerunner of the great kabbalistic movements, felt that a vision of God was Israel's patrimony, one that has never been invalidated and that is to be actualized ever anew on its holy ground. But here the longing for a vision projects far beyond deep sleep and revelatory dream to the "sleep of eternity."

4. At Night

Recently thoughts of You awoke me
    and allowed me to behold the fullness [*Reigen*] of your Grace.
Clearly they demonstrated how Your image, the soul,
    is intertwined with me—neverending miracles!
And did my believing heart not see you, as if it had
    been there at Sinai?
You my visions sought. Your splendor
    entered me, to submerge in my dark clouds.
And then my meditating startled me up from my bed,
    to bow before Your Glory, Lord.

4] What was longed for has happened: a night vision has brought to the poet the experience of seeing God. In the state between dreaming and waking, which takes its individuality from dreaming and its validity from waking, pondering the linkage between body and soul, the poet looks upon God as if his heart "had been there at Sinai." Today's experience confirms and repeats historical revelation.

What is it that experience confirms and repeats? What is revealed? Just now, a problem occupying the poet's mind was mentioned. Does revelation offer a solution to the problem? Does it turn that miracle, never to be passed over in silence, into a handily practical dogma as conceived of, say, by Catholicism? Not a word is said about that, though there would have been ample reason to refer to it. So what is revealed?

What God reveals in a revelation is always only—that revelation. To put it differently: He always reveals only Himself to man, and man to himself. These direct and indirect objects constitute, in their linkage, the one and only content of revelation. Whatever does not follow immediately from the covenant established here between God and man, whatever cannot maintain its immediacy, has no part in it.

For the seer of the vision, the problem has not been solved—it has vanished. The wonder has lost its wonder; but his vision has given him the courage to bow down before the wonder's source. A problem for the mind has become a power of the heart.

5. EVENT

The spheres of heaven saw   Your splendor, then they tottered.
   The waves of the abyss quietly   descended when You departed.
And how shall the souls reside, there   where your secret lives,
   where fire rages through rocks,   so that in blazes they burst apart.
But their heart becomes strong through You,   if You will strengthen them,
   that they thank You, as   do the spirits who see Your Being.
Therefore, the praise of all souls   shall rise to You, oh Lord,
   for words of praise find You,   whom they splendidly envelop.

5] Revelation is both experience and event. It is a genuine experience only because and if it was also an event; it is a genuine event only because and if it can become an experience again and again. The present age shies away from this connection. It would like (in the most diverse forms, and by the most diverse means) to confine God to the "at night" of experience and to divert his path to the day of event. But God does not allow any of his paths to be diverted. For him the event is no more remote than the experience, and nature no more inaccessible than the soul. Nor will He be pulled down even in nature into a coarse objectivity, as the faint-hearted fear; He will surely take care of that.

Today it is no different, say, in the war that was such a revelatory event for mankind, than it was at Sinai. The Midrash relates that there, too, each of the assembled nations heard something different, and each responded in a different way. It is the response that matters—here, too.

Therefore, this powerful little poem, part of the liturgy of the festival of liberation (the first of the three festivals that celebrate a historical revelation[1]), plunges at once into the abyss of the question as to how any souls can withstand the fiery core of the mystery revealing itself. It realizes that it is from revelation itself that the strength to bear it must come, and does come. And thus in gratitude and praise man finds himself once more after the event, just as he did after the experience.

---

1. The "festival of liberation" is Passover, celebrating the Jews' exodus from Egypt and slavery. *Shavvot* (Pentacost) celebrates the "giving of our Torah" at Mount Sinai. Presumably Rosenzweig is thinking of *Sukkot* (Tabernacles) as the third of "the three festivals that celebrate a historical revelation," but its connection to a historical revelation is less obvious than the other two.

6. EXCURSUS: DAY OF REVELATION

Steep, oh mountains high,   you descend,   they do not
    contain You, before whose   force they burst apart   in trembling
If only my heart   had the strength to stand   before You by day,
    You who   scolds the stars   so they pale.
And the heavenly populace   who seeks Your name: they arrive;
    and the earthly populace   awaits your ancient   Truth.
The fiery Law   they received   from Your mouth,
    in it memory, action,   thought shall   govern
Enjoy hearing   the songs of those   who are near. Rejoice
    in the people, who themselves   rejoice, honoring   Your rule.

6] The collector of the "Divan"[1] (whose selections Luzatto used[2]) confessed just a few decades after the poet's death that he could not guarantee his volume contained only poems by Yehuda Halevi. He even names those that might be mistaken for Halevi's because they use the same acrostic. The poem translated above is one of those for which I should like to make use of the permission granted by the godfather of Yehuda Halevi philology to question their authorship.

A comparison with the poem "Event," which is very similar in content, shows precisely the quality of a "genuine" Halevi, which is lacking in this poem. It is not the specific linguistic features—the entire Spanish School handles language in much the same way, based on the biblical idiom, so that in general it would be difficult if not impossible to decide on the basis of such criteria which poem is and which is not Halevi's. Rather, it is the philosophical content and, even more, the manner in which a train of thought is pursued that distinguish one poet from another.

Yehuda Halevi's charisma lies in the terseness, I would even say slenderness, of his line of thought, which is quite peculiar to him. He knows exactly how much space a thought needs to take flight. And that is precisely what the author of the above poem—whoever he may have been—does not know. Each line makes a new start, and none follows through. This shortness of breath, in which the most magnificent biblical words and images, invoked in vain, must suffocate, contrasts sharply with the free-flowing words of "Event," which express the two ideas contained in the first two double lines of "Day of Revelation."

Nevertheless, these impressions may not give us sufficient grounds to say with certainty that this is not Yehuda Halevi's poem. Philology can never be sufficiently mindful of Homer's sleep. Especially with poets who, like Yehuda Halevi (especially in his verse poems), display a strongly personal, often even a confessional tendency, one must be prepared for surprising failures from time to time. (Among the poems of the mature Goethe there are some of an inferiority one would never encounter in Schiller, that virtuoso whom Goethe regarded to the very last with a kind of slightly horrified reverence because of his "command of poetry.")

---

1. FR: Rabbi Yeshuah. [Joshua Elijah bar-Levi, 14th c.]
2. Samuel David Luzzatto (ed.), Yehuda Halevi, *Betulat Bat Yehudah* (Prague, 1864).

7. All My Bones

My bones   all exclaim: Lord, who is like you!

   Yes body and life,   from You they come,
   When my heart begins to quake,   You refresh it,
   My poetic striving,   it is dedicated to You.
The meter of my   songs—approximates   Your abode, standardized in You.

   Breath, which I suck in;   from You it comes,
   Light, in my eye,   from You it alights,
   Advice which I follow,   it is grounded in You,
My spirit, no matter   what obstacles it encounters,   beholds You, yields.

   And if my pining   yearns for You,
   Deep in my bosom   embraces You,
   Those who have pondered You,   struggle unsuccessfully,
My winged thought,   no matter how fanciful,   does not satisfy You.

   But You increase the number
     of those   who pledge allegiance to You,
   And raise high the standard   for those who follow You,
   That you never abandon   those who beseech You—
Alas, my desire achieves   again that I   desert You.

   Oh see, You beheld   all my thoughts,
   Once, when You created   my beginning,
   You entrusted me   with this within:
My heart—down to   the slightest barrier—   nothing escapes You.

7] Between the—as it were—preliminary prayers and the central part of the Sabbath and holiday morning services, there is a hymn in which the worshiper pours out everything he has merely touched upon, as in an overview, during the preceding quick "saying" of numerous psalms. It is a very old hymn: the French Jews of the Middle Ages ascribed it in all seriousness to the Apostle Peter. It resonates with the language of the Psalms, augmented to monumental proportions. And the poets allowed their ivy tendrils to enwrap this monumental structure until it was completely covered.

One of its passages—traditionally fixed in the Jewish liturgy, comparable to passages in the text of the Catholic Mass on which the great movements of the musical masses have been built— one of the passages of this prayer (to which, since the re-awakening of our poetry after centuries dominated by the Talmud, terms such as *every mouth, every tongue, every knee,* and *every heart* have been added in messianic intensification) ends in the words of the Psalm "as it is written" (Psalms 35:10[1]). And it is in this passage, and for this one moment, that the individual, that the single worshiper calls out: "All my bones shall say: 'Lord, who is like unto Thee?'"

Yehuda Halevi's hymn immerses itself in this moment in which the "We," the "breath of all living things" (the prayer's opening words) becomes submerged in the "I." "My bones," "my song," "my spirit," "my winged thought," "my desire," "my heart"— over and over again the word *my.* It is man, the individual who speaks, but it is the individual standing before God. He does not look within himself; he spreads himself out; he says, "my," but only so that he may lay this "his" down at God's feet, over and over again. He says, "I," but only in order to forget his own self. Again and again, his words begin with "my," and again and again, they end with "You."

---

1. "All my bones shall say: 'Lord, who is like unto Thee, who deliverest the poor from him that is too strong for him, yea, the poor and the needy from him that spoileth him?'"

8. The Incomparable One

Who is like unto You, for whom the depths are luminous,
You who is surrounded by whispered praises, source of miracles!

   Suddenly He transformed nothing into something;
   He drew near to hearts, and His image escaped the eyes;
   Therefore do not ask, how and where!
The whole world is full of His presence.

   If you keep evil desire at a distance,
   You will find God in your bosom;
   You only need to stroll peacefully—
He raises and lowers the wave of life.

   And see the puzzle: the paths of the soul!
   Serenely bask in this wisdom—
   Therein you will find the grace of freedom:
You are a prisoner, your cell is the world.

   Send thought to unite with Him!
   Wipe out Your own will and do His!
   Where would His eye not reach?
His doings know no limits or threshold.

   At the very first He lives prior to the specks of the world dust.
   And He crated. And He keeps. Like a flower
   Which wilts, human fame passes:
As a wilted leaf, so it fades quickly.

8] God's uniqueness, which is sung by this poem (for the same prayer-passage as the preceding poem), will sometimes lead man to a thought-provoking comparison: next to the Incomparable One, what is he, he who is all too comparable, a "wilted leaf"? What is he, whose awareness of the Creator ultimately keeps him from asking any questions; he, who finds his life's divine anchorage in his commitment to human duty; he, for whom the bliss of freedom grows only from the mystery which he remains to himself; he, who can realize his own will only by subordinating it to God's? By varying this comparison in a contemplative manner, the poem circumscribes the omnipotence of the Incomparable.

9. NONE BUT YOU

Those who know my   wailing, increase my sorrow when they sneer at me,
"What sweeter bauble   can a friend give to friends?"
   Hymn and wisdom   should encircle His image,
   Beautiful ones—praise   surrounds him without end.
   I donned a robe   of wailing at His flight.
You want to have pity!   make him love me anew!
You want to console me!   How can I bear it: Loved—and He then vanished!

   Original fire locked up   in me—thus burns His
   Name, sealed   into my heart and bones.
   And stirred up,   those who spit at my Law,
Abuse and harass   me, who turned to serve Him
They dare to slander me,   who preserves the token of His honor.

   They threaten to extinguish   Your sacred discipline,
   I will choose disgrace and pain   before such desertion.
   Salve, Share with the heart   the fruit of your Law!
If I should forget   You, forget me, right hand.
If alien words   should suit me, may my tongue cleave to my mouth!

   To my ear came the   news of Your glory,
   The Sea of Reeds and Sinai   are full of your greatness.
   How could my mouth   possibly pay tribute to another?
Heart and eyes hesitate   to loosen the ties of my foot,
When I see Him tower,   the Only One. There is none but You.

9] The great German scholar Lagarde,[1] whose spleen was probably even greater than his erudition—and that is saying much—once remarked that to Jews monotheism means that there is only one edition of God. What the real truth is, that is, seen from the inside, can be learned (if one really does not know it) from this poem. It is one of those which enclose the saying of David from the morning prayer: "O Lord, there is none like You, neither is there any God beside You" (I Chronicles 17:20). (See also: Isaiah 45:5 and 21; Hosea 13:4; Psalms 18:32).

There is no God but You. This "none but You," "no one else," "no other"—this root word of faith in the One is here actually derived from the skeptical question put to the bride by her companions in the Song of Songs: "What is thy beloved more than another beloved, O thou fairest among women?" (Song of Songs 5:9). And the answer surges in on the crest of waves issuing from a song of praise, the destiny of having been called (Jeremiah 20:9[2]), the passion of martyrdom, and the ever-present sense of history, until it finally and gigantically rises above all of those. For God's uniqueness is the exclusiveness of love. There is only on edition of God.

---

1. Paul Anton de Lagarde (1827–1891), German orientalist, Bible scholar, and editor of the Italian works of Giordano Bruno.

2. "And if I say: 'I will not make mention of Him, nor speak any more in His name,' then there is in my heart as it were a burning fire shut up in my bones, and I weary myself to hold it in, but cannot."

10. THE LOVERS

His lovers entreat Him,   they question His loving,
   yet they dare to await   the ripe outpouring of His Grace.
Does not His Grace dwell nearby?   even though He dwells at once up high
                                       and towering
   His deeds are great,   and far-reaching.
And those would like to see His light,   with their eyes, hence they examine
   their heart; yet when they see His sublime   light, they are fearful.
But the word of His law,   His Kingdom—they accept,
   supported by His Glory,   and His Glory—they support.
All splendor, all majesty   they search and announce,
   and their voice proclaims   His greatness.

10] But it is difficult to love, even to love God. This is in fact the most difficult love. For that portion of unhappy love that is in every love, even the happiest—due to the tension between man's infinite desire to love, his compulsion to love, and his finite ability to do so—is here raised to the infinite. To love God is at the same time happy and unhappy love, the happiest and the unhappiest love. For He comes close—the closest of all—to man, only to withdraw from him once more into the remotest distance. He is the most ardently desired, yet also the most difficult to bear; man yearns passionately to take refuge in the eternal arms, yet no one may see the eternal countenance and live. Thus, the reciprocity of God's love will forever remain an open question for man who loves him, yet must entreat Him for His love ("entreating" and "asking" are the same word in Hebrew).

The solution to these anxieties and conflicts depends, though, as does the solution to all of love's anxieties and conflicts, on the lover. It depends on his inner strength to say "even so," the "even so" of bearing it, the "even so" of letting himself be borne. Thus, it depends here on man and his strength to desire of God—that He love him in return.

11. JUDGMENT DAY

Yes, innumerable ones come,
    they, the children of the earth,
And all of them are taken
    under the staff like a herd,
The sinners like the righteous,
    that all will be judged
Before the Lord, for He comes,
    yes He comes, to judge the earth.

Today destinies are decided
    and the world has to appear before the Judge.
The powers that once created it
    God today revealed for the first time.
Today He erected the steps to the throne,
    On high creating and destroying,
Yet beholding the farthest lands
    in the Heavens and on the earth.

Today the universe is encircled.
    The pillars of the world, they stood.
Barrenness disappeared today
    the Holy One delivered three women
Who felt the pressure of slave labor,
    today they heard freedom's tidings.
Someday these hours will bring
    a return home from foreign soil.

You people, singled out today! Acknowledge your
    "King!"—Your King drives away
Kings. That He becomes aware of you,
    shofarim, blow, wail, you!
To save you from death's grip,
    and that His countenance may shine upon you,
May He make you young like the eagle,
    and may He drench the earth like rain.

From a far land, oh dove,
    may your poor cooing resound.
You who are calling from a rush of waves,
    Your song rebounds to heaven!
May Your promise soon resonate with
    the rose in the mountain crevice:
Your people are the righteous,
    eternal heirs to the earth!

11] The idea of a Day of Judgment always awakens in men when times renew themselves and falls asleep again and again when times grow old again, and everything continues after all "in the same old way." But Judaism has kept this idea alive by assigning to it a place within the year, in spite of its implication of "the end of time." Thus, the New Year's Day in the fall has become "The Day of Judgment," bringing the individual every year face to face with the awesomeness of the last judgment. To be sure, it is a judgment only within the microcosm of the soul, of all souls whose fate will be decided on that day. However, it is in the nature of things that this inner awareness cannot become an external reality, since the end of the world can come but once, rather than occur annually.

Legend at least substitutes for this worldly reality by making this day, this "Today," into the symbol of the world's great days—the days of its beginning and its messianic perfection. So man can see each New Year's Day of his own life framed by the world's days of memory and hope.

Moreover, this day, which makes listening to the last trumpet[1] a duty within the sphere of Jewish duties and command Israel to be the first to acknowledge God's dominion over the world, also reflects the destiny of the patriarchs. For here is the point where man feels his dependence most intimately and at the same time very concretely, the point where the unbeliever believes as intensely as the believer does, where the believer can believe no more intensely than the unbeliever does.

Legend has it that it was on this day that the three barren women, Sarah, Rachel, and Hannah, were granted a special blessing. The fate of one of them, Hannah, has therefore become that portion of the Day of Judgment's Scripture reading interwoven with the most passionate and intimate prayers (I Samuel 1:1–28).

---

1. The *shofar,* usually a ram's horn, is blown several times during and at the end of *Rosh Hashanah,* New Year's Day.

12. HOMECOMING

'You support each one who errs. Spread out
    Your arm in welcome to the one who returns home!
I follow Your leadership,
    having to forego my own counsel.
May Your light spread over my eye!
    salvation turn the heart!
Prepare our return to you, Lord,
    that we may return home.'

    "Yes, your heart is precious property
    to me! My bosom burns for you.
Some day I will call you to account,
    since I warned you in your misery.
In the sanctuary you could hear
    my call, finally to repent.
Return home to me,
    and I will return home to you."

    'You taught us Your Law,
    which we did not exchange or change,
We only wanted Your service,
    and only knew Your name.
The men whom You treasure
    are like berries ripened by the heat!
Thrash the enemy like grain! Your sword,
    draw it on the one unnerved by fear.
They are not afraid of You,
    we are captivated!
A diamond pencil wrote
    Judah's rebellion.'

    "Hallow yourselves, be pure, flee
    from the smoldering corpses!
And approach, enter here
    as living souls.
Flesh, bone, will melt, so, too, those who
    devour those buried.
Like shards they will be consecrated
    to the silent secret of caves,

12] Does God take the first step, or does man? And can man take that step at all? This is a real question, not a foregone conclusion, as today's Protestant theologians would like to assume. Nor does it mark "the difference between Judaism and Christianity," as Jewish theologians, in their understandable need for harmless theories about this difference, would wish it. Rather, it is a genuine question of the human heart. For—to return to those neo-Protestant theologians—it makes a great difference whether one asserts the paradox of the "enslaved will" as a world-historical rebel, or whether one does so as a peaceful professor and writer of books. In the former case, theory is supplemented by lived experience and becomes truth. In the latter case, theory raises itself in life to become merely heightened—and therefore false—theory. Had Luther died on October 30, 1517,[1] all the audacities of his commentary on the "Epistle to the Romans" would have been no more than some latter-day scholastic's extravaganzas.

The real question arises because man, ever aware of his powerlessness as he stands before God, must of necessity wait for God, must implore God, to take the first step, though he cannot possibly avoid hearing God's demand that he, man, take that step. No theory can get around this question, whether it is man's perception of God's demanding voice or his sense of his own powerlessness, which he seeks to discredit as Satanic deception. And obviously it can still less be solved by a theory that tries to avoid this brutal alternative through a prudent distribution of roles assigned to God and man or by meting out the exact dosage of action to be taken by either. Thus, the matter remains an eternal discussion in which, as in every discussion, he who speaks last is "right"—and thus God must finally be right only because he has the last word—the very last!

The Midrash deals with this problem by showing man and God, the community of Israel and its Sovereign, having a conversation in which each requests—in words similar to those at the end of Lam-

---

1. Martin Luther's (1483–1546) ninety-five thesis regarding the ecclesiastical practice of indulgences were nailed to the door of the Wittenberg castle church on October 31, 1517.

The souls will be renewed, they will
   rise and become jewels of light.
Hurry! Forward! Do not moisten
   your eyes over fragments."

   'And can dark red turn white?
   Can purple take on the quality of wool?
Turn a stone heart—
   to tender flesh.
Can you discern in the son the glistening
   of real original sin?
Those whom You consider clay,
   what can they hope to achieve?
You can build up and tear down,
   but we can only pair words with words.
Can chaff and straw escape
   the hot flame?

   "How is it that the sons of God end
   buried in the pit of lust!
When angels send you bread,
   and the breasts of rocks nurse you!
Here is your work of repentance—which
   ought to reverse the sickness of souls:
God's magnificent bounties:
   Inspiration for commandment, Law.
Leave behind your prison walls!
   to the shores of furthest hopes!
Gird your loins,
   put on your shoes!"

   'Your spirit, Your power pours
   out the spirit, the power.
Yours is the universal Lordship!
   Do You lend it to someone so they can mock it?
From Your scales You can see
   a man's dealings.
Only the sap of your hope shoots
   into the shafts of earthly trunks.
The clasp of Your bolt closes
   the clasps of all bolts.
When You flee from me full of anger,
   whose favor shall I seek?'

entations (5:21[2]) and to those spoken by the prophet Malachi (3:7[3])—
that the other take the first step before it will take the second one.
And it is on this Midrash that Yehuda Halevi has built the great
conversation between man and God, a hymn of five and a half double
stanzas intended for the midday hours of the great Day of Atonement.

The poem's first double stanza, which is shorter than the ones
that follow, juxtaposes, mottolike, its two main themes in stark
opposition: human supplication and the divine necessity of denying
it. Then begins the dialogue proper, which is conducted in a man-
ner quite different from the numerous others between Israel and
God that Yehuda Halevi composed. For while in these cases the
participants are engaged in a real face-to-face talk, here they re-
main separated by a terrible distance, precisely the distance estab-
lished in the crucial first two stanzas. Man's voice—registering
disputatious desire, profound despair, determined humility, and
passionate imploration—remains a cry from the depths. God's
voice—demanding, exhorting, promising—remains a call from on
high. The tension between God and man appears—precisely on the
day whose entire concern is reconciliation—to be irreconcilable.

Moreover, the very thing that usually can resolve most easily this
tension here serves only to increase it. For while elsewhere God's way
and man's are far apart, here the path of Israel's God and the path
of his people meet at Sinai, shrouded in eternal smoke. Even today,
the day on which the Jew is entirely human and His God is entirely
the Judge of the world, the awareness of the bridge formed by the
Sinaitic event never leaves his consciousness. The bridge is even
entered on from both directions; yet the other side is not reached.

In the second stanza, when man as the bearer of Jewish land and
Jewish suffering addresses God, God replies with the strictest of all
requirements imposed on man, and on no one but man. And then in

---

2. "They have heard that I sigh, there is none to comfort me; All mine enemies have
heard of my trouble, and are glad, for thou hast done it; Thou wilt bring the day that Thou
hast proclaimed, and they shall be like unto me."

3. "From the days of your fathers ye have turned aside from Mine ordinances, and have
not kept them. Return unto Me, and I will return unto you, saith the Lord of Hosts. But ye
say: 'Wherein shall we return?' "

"The souls will be liberated
    from serving the dead.
Accept your inheritance,
    instead of wandering through the universe.
On the day of the new world order,
    when the graves open up
And in the body and spirit
    I insert the joints in bones:
Then, then you are surrounded by sanctity,
    to achieve crowns,—
When the signs of atrocities
    will be washed off of you."

'Alas, him who is nearest, You pushed far away,—
    Who shows him the stars of consolation?
Who helps him learn to stand—
    You left him and he fell!
When you do not spread salvation all around
    and have mercy on him,
Then enclose him in angelic flight
    and the walls of a castle,
To await the day which You promised,
    to lift him from the muddy cesspool—
Oh, do not be far from us,
    for destruction approaches!'

the third stanza when man, shatteringly conscious of being totally human and nothing but human, stammers a reply, God reminds him that as a Jew he is a son of God and recalls the miracle and the law bestowed on him. Thus, closeness itself becomes an element of distance on this awesome day. And the conversation continues across the infinite distance separating the two voices from which it arose.

But here it is man who has the last word. The concluding stanza is no longer a double stanza for God's voice is now silent. What does this silence signify? If one views the poem out of context, this cannot be determined—precisely because man's final outcry, that cry of utter distress, remains unanswered. However, it is just as impossible to remove the poem from the context of the day and hour for which it was intended as it would be, say, to remove an individual chorus from its context in a Greek tragedy. Halevi's hymn belongs in the noon hours of the "long day." And even if it were part of the concluding prayer (which one might surmise, given its beginning with the quote from that prayer: "Thy right hand is stretched out to receive the repentant"), all would still be tentative and no word final. A final word is possible only at the final moment. And if man were to speak it (which after all is God's task), this last word—of the day, of life, of history—can be only that word which stands behind all of God's speech. That is true, at any rate, for the way in which man can articulate this divine "I," namely in bearing witness to the "He."

With this bearing witness during the last moments of the day, the entire day finds its resolution at last, and so does our poem. In the sight of God, man himself finds the answer that grants him, for that one moment that anticipates the final one, the fulfillment of his prayer for homecoming; in this moment, he is as close to God, as near to His throne, as any human can ever be. In the ecstasy of this nearness, the "You" falls silent, not only the "You" to whom his agonized outcry had been directed, but also the "You" of his yearning and his love. Like the angel under God's throne, he turns around, acknowledging and confirming—"Him." And he is granted this anticipation of this final, highest moment, because just a few minutes later, when the trumpet blast of the Jubilee Year has brought the Holy Day to a close (Leviticus 25.9ff.), he will once more say, during the evening prayer, which ushers in the return to everyday life: "Forgive us, our Father, for we have sinned."

13. HEAR

Hear, those who dare
To prostrate themselves before you.
Father, will you close your ear
To the deed of Your children?

Yes from the depths they called,
They fled from many hardships.
Oh do not let them leave empty-handed
Today from your paths.

A wave of guilt wanted to stifle
The hotly upwelling heart,
Don't do it for their sake,
Do it for Your sake, oh my rock.

And today erase their errors.
Accept their simple prayers as
An offering. Turn their heart to you,
And lend them your ear.

Refresh those who are weary with tears,
Gather in the lost lamb,
Let their shepherd arise,
And attend to his herd tenderly.

Those who walk upright,
Show them forgiveness today!
When late in the day they beseech you,
May your blessing find them.

13] This reader's prayer is meant, as its ending shows, for the afternoon service of the Day of Atonement. In contrast to the hymnic dialogue of "Homecoming," which precedes it, its mode is one of entreaty. In its center stand the words from Ezekiel (36:22[1]), which appear in its middle stanza and re-appear throughout the day's liturgy. But while these words, in Ezekiel and in the Torah passages that anticipate their formulation (Genesis 32:12ff.; Numbers 14:13ff.; Deuteronomy 9:28), are based on God's relationship to His people, on this day, in accordance with the day's meaning, they are based only on the sin of mankind and God's forgiving mercy.

Some people have been horrified by these words, whose request for forgiveness they considered blasphemous, literally "for Heaven's sake"; in fact, some went so far as to excise the words from the prayers. And they surely are as malicious as is the psychological ploy of the sly child who says: "It serves my father right that my hands are frozen stiff. Why doesn't he buy me gloves?" But, after all, doesn't the ploy usually work?

---

1. "Therefore say unto the house of Israel: 'Thus saith the Lord God: "I do not this for your sake, oh house of Israel, but for My holy name, which you have profaned among the nations, wither ye came.'"

14. THE TRUE ONE

With all my heart, You Truth, with all my soul
   I love You, openly, and secretly.
Your Name is with me!—who would steal it from me?
   My most beloved He!—how could He not be with me?
My light is He! how could my wick lack oil?
   Could I doubt? when I put myself into the care of such authority!
Their scorn diminishes—Fools! Does not their abuse
   become my crown jewel in Your crown!
You, fountain of my life! May my life and song
   be to Your praise as long as there is breath in me.

14] This poem is an address to truth, or to the One who is true; the two are one and the same in the Hebrew language and in Jewish consciousness. That is, neither makes any conceptual distinction with regard to truth; whoever says "truth" knows that he speaks of God. Jeremiah puts it this way (Jeremiah 10:10[1]), and the daily liturgy follows him when it combines the last words of the "Shema," *the Lord your God,* and the first word of the prayer that follows it, *truth,* in one loud proclamation. Thus this poem almost naturally finds its beginning in that prayer's first words, the command to love God (Deuteronomy 6:5[2]). In this poem, love of God becomes love of truth, while yet retaining all the physical and metaphysical passion of the love of God. And anyone who understands this "yet" will know what "Jewish rationalism" really means, and that this rationalism, which may be very rational indeed, can never be as rational as it is— Jewish. Anyone who has known Hermann Cohen also knows that.

---

1. "But the Lord God is the true God."
2. "And thou shalt love the Lord thy God with all thy heart, and with all thy soul, and with all thy might."

15. YOUR GOD

Are you still sleeping? Enough of the rest!
  Abandon all nonsense!
Behold the route of the heavenly spheres,
  far from all human routine.
Direct your ways towards service to the eternal rock
  as does the fleet of stars.
But enough, henceforth no longer sleep,
  Get up! Call your God!

Arise, to see His heavens.
  His fingers created them.
And His canopy high in the sky,
  He held it in His arms.
And the stars—His seal—they marvel
  how He engraved His ring.
Tremble before His terror,
  awaiting the salvation which He brings,—
That the world may not affect you
  and spoil your heart.

And arise at midnight,
  to step into the footsteps of the great ones,
Who, with a plethora of psalms on their lips,
  with thoughtful steadfast feeling
Spent their day fasting
  and their night praying,
God is a shaft in their heart,
  and they the planets who encircle His throne—
May their way ascend powerfully
  to Him, Your God.

May tears stream from your eye continuously,
  so that your remorse washes away your sins.
And beseech your keeper in His place,
  to disabuse you of hatred of humanity.
And bow your pride this far,
  and choose the good: for it is beautiful.

15] For God is your God. If we were meant to know nothing about Him except that He is God—and this would actually be the most satisfactory answer to the question "What is He?"—it would be futile to call out to Him. Looking up to the stars would be merely an escape from the world. There would be no path leading up to His height (Hosea 14:2). Man's hope to be allowed once more to turn to Him and to prepare himself for Him on this earth would be in vain (Obadiah 1:21; Amos 4:12). The belief of Man, who is born of dust, that God may be found in the ecstatic heart-beats of vision, would be a delusion. And there would be no possible communion with Him, who is pure Being (Exodus 3:12), other than by posing those questions that the Talmud decries[1] about the Where and When, the Below and Above of His creation, thus excluding the one possibility that Scripture opposes to all such desire for "magical" knowledge—that of the whole and simple life (Deuteronomy 18:9–15).

---

1. FR: Mishna Hagiga 2: "Anyone looking for four things—What is above and below, before and thereafter—should not have come into this world."

Honor the Lord with your wealth,—
　　until some day saviors ascend to the heights
And from your multitude the word bursts forth:
　　Prepare yourself for your God!

The poor ones! Brood of the earth!
　　where shall there be wisdom?
Man's advantage
　　over the animals is negligible.
Only to behold the overarching radiance
　　—the vision of the heart! not of the eye—,
And the flood from hidden fountains
　　more delicious than wine.
In this way, flesh and blood,
　　you get closer to your God.

"I am who I am," so speaks He,
　　whose Will tests deeds,
Who sends death and life, side by side,
　　who lowers to the grave and lifts to heaven.
　　　Face His tribunal,
　　　　and live! Control your rage,
　　　the "when?" and "where?"
　　　　"what is below?" and "what is above"—
　　No, rather be completely and humbly
　　　with Him, with your God.

This is how things would be, if we really knew nothing else [about God]. But just as we must realize the limits of our knowledge, so (and no less) must we realize the limits of our ignorance. God dwells beyond all our knowledge. Yet before our ignorance begins, your God offers himself to you—to your call, to your ascent, to your readiness, to your vision, to your life.

16. His Peace

The hand of the living—may its shadow be your roof,
    if you focus on Him in truth and humility.
When you walk, He watches that your foot not falter.
    When you act,—He causes your arm to be strong.
Seek peace, pursue it! Confess
    that He is "the Lord of Peace," and the one "who makes peace"?

16] The main prayer,[1] recited three times a day, ends with a supplication for peace. Directed to the "Lord of peace" and followed by a concluding prayer and the Kaddish, it says: "May He who makes the harmony of the spheres make peace for us and for all Israel." The end of this prayer is also the end of all human wisdom. But in order to become the end of wisdom, it must be the beginning of action—of action, that is, not of activity.

---

1. Known as the "Standing" *(Amidah)* prayer or the "Eighteen" *(Shemonah Essay)* Benedictions, or very simply "the Prayer."

17. THE ALL

May the mouth rejoice
at everything you allow
this pupil of the eye
 to see in miracles!

He will sing,
as well as he can,—
even if he doesn't dare to do so
 before You.

Your path encompasses
the wheel of the spheres
and their structure
 never reaches you.

And that which lives,
how brazenly it rises up,
high above it all
 You reside in the skies.

The army of creatures
surrounds You,
Active One,
 bearing witness.

What do they witness?
Who created them.
The how resides far away,
 in the enigmatic sphere.

In the original chaos,
in the final decay
resounds the awed
 echo:

God only He
in the hall of the gods!
He, the Lord
 of all the lords.

Today and now
 always replaced,—
always irreplaceable
 His radiance shines.

He builds a zodiac,
 for the seven who
visit there,
 He carves out the path.

At His command
 the sun advances,
it moves on,
 goes to rest,

Through its kingdom it wanders,
 like a king,
from palace
 to palace;

The moonlight,
 pure but pale,
also is unable to circle
 in a celestial sphere;

Then, in the distance encircling,
 star on star,
innumerable,
 matching Him,

He clearly sees
 the flock of the pleiades:
seven around the
 stem of the candelabra;

The largest circle,
 which during the day
carries its burden
 westward,

17] This hymn takes a sentence from Deuteronomy (10:17[1]) and uses it "as is" for a quatrain that concludes each stanza. This sentence and the hymn that developed from it seem strange to us today. For the sentence takes the real existence of gods for granted, while today it is generally considered "an accomplishment of religious development" that mankind has learned there are no gods. Even an atheist looks with a certain benevolence upon "monotheism" as a developmentally necessary stage on the way from many gods to no God.

But the author of this hymn would have to refuse this benevolence. For him, the gods are real, and God is "merely" more real. And the truth of this has been concealed for us today by the delusion that monotheism is something self-evident. "Monotheism" may be self-evident; but belief in the One is not. Rather, this belief is clearly opposed by the experience of life, which would have all of us believe in a variety of powers. Their names change, but the variety remains. Culture and civilization, folk and state, nation and race, art and science, economy and class, ethos and religiosity—this is an overview, and surely not a complete one, of today's Pantheon. Who will deny the reality of these powers? Surely no "heathen" has ever served his gods much differently, or more piously and sacrificially, than we today serve those powers. And if the One encounters us, then a struggle with the many becomes unavoidable even today, and its outcome is uncertain, at least as far as we are concerned. The Talmud knows that if God wanted to destroy the gods—those powers man is tempted to idolize—once and for all, He would have to destroy no less than His World.[2] But it is His world coming from and returning to Him. It is His All.

---

1. "For the Lord your God, He is God of gods, and Lord of lords, the great God, the mighty, and the awful, who regardeth not persons, nor taketh reward."

2. FR: Mishna Avoda Zara, 7: "They asked the Elders in Rome: 'If God has no pleasure in idols, why does He not make an end of it?' They answered: 'If men worshiped a thing of which the world has no need, He would make an end of it; but lo!, they worship the sun and moon and the stars and the planets; shall God destroy His world because of fools?' They said to them: 'If so, let Him destroy that which the world does not need, and leave that which the world needs.' They answered: 'We should but confirm them that worship them, for they would say, "Know ye that these are gods, for they have not been brought to an end." ' "

Bows down,
  silently witnessing
the One who holds
    the boundless universe.

Exalted,
  but visible
to the eye that
    seizes upon His work.

God, only He
  in the hall of the gods!
He, the Lord
    of all the lords!

And all around
  He erects a tent,
to it He gave the
    earth to guard,

That it stands
  not on the ground,
but is suspended
    in the void;

Its force
  wants to flee downward,
Its desire aims
    for the lowest point;

The home fire burns,
  wherever its origin,
upward to
    Heaven's glow;

And to the two
  add in between
the blowing of the winds
    and the flooding of the waters.

Those who hate and
  those who love,
they all contain
    the elements in their blood.

From them blossomed
  the seedling,
such as the son of Adam
    and the brood of animals.

And the dew nourishes
  and is withheld,
following goodness,
    following anger;

For His arrow
  is aimed at the blasphemer;
the one He favors,
    is showered with Grace.

God, only He
  in the hall of the gods!
He, the Lord
    of all the lords!

Death is constant
  as is creation—
Only He continues
    forever.

Before all being—
  He alone,
and again in the end—
    only He.

Not the strength of the arm
  but of the spirit, produces
the creation which
    He commanded:

Many souls,
  wisdom's play,
and clever meaning,
    a beacon;

He shapes
  the magnificence of the vault,
and makes the stream
    of water stop before it;

And so this hymn, which is woven around this passage, sings of the All, of God's world. But once again, this seems strange to a child of the present; and the more contemporary he is, the stranger it will seem to him. For it is a new—not even 150 years old—doctrine of modern education, hence also of modern religious sensibility, that God may not be sought in nature. At the source of this prejudice is Kant with his refutation of the "physico-teleological proof of God's existence,"[3] which suddenly seemed to rule out as unwarranted the step from creation to Creator, a step that before then even the founders of modern natural science had regarded as self-evident. In truth, though, it only seemed unwarranted. No one knew that better than Kant himself, when he related how he had once, during a summer when insects were scarce, observed swallows pushing their own young out of their nest and concluded with the exclamation: "At that, my understanding was at an end, there was nothing left to do except to fall down and pray." What he had wanted to demolish with his scathing criticism was the proof, not the prayer.

But mankind certainly would not have let itself be dissuaded so easily from praying, had the world itself not become increasingly invisible to the human eye precisely during this past century. This must be blamed primarily on the indoctrination in, and the popularization of Copernican-Newtonian theory by elementary schools (which became a general institution only during that century). The fault cannot lie with the diffused light of our big cities since the senses of our farmers have become equally dulled. In this point, the entire nation consists of nothing but "educated" people. Today one finds among any ten persons at most one who knows that the stars, too, rise and set. The other nine, when asked, will answer that only the planets rise and set. And even the one will usually begin to waver.

---

3. See, Immanuel Kant, *Critique of Pure Reason*; Transcendental Dialectic, Book II, Chapter III, Section 5. "The Impossibility of the Physico-theological Proof."

The light of day
and bright stars
shine into
　　the valley of the earth;

And a frightful
and praising
voice sang
　　His praise;

And decked out with
diamonds they worship
Him with hymn,
　　with chorale;

　praising,
　circling,
flaming,
　　around Him a wall:

God, only He
in the hall of the gods!
He, the Lord
　　of all the lords!

Oh, He who thinks
and oh, He who directs
and, oh, he makes
　　known the future,

His glance meets
balsam and poison
and knows in advance
　　the outcome!

Oh, go and fetch them,
Your herd,
from within the throat
　　of the lion.

Tender sheep
Forced together
with strangers they
　　go round and round

You made them suffer,
You made them strong,
and submerged them
　　in hell's fire.
And even though You heap harm
　　　　　　　　　　on them—
their arm holds You,
and they trust
　　Your covenant.

From their mouth
Your name resounds
throughout Your world
　　far and wide.

Loudly they praise,—
as did the host
upholding Your
　　throne and

the ray of the
three-fold "holy"
falls onto the head of Him
　　who created them:

God, only He
in the hall of the gods!
He, the Lord
　　of all the Lords!

17] This hymn takes a sentence from Deuteronomy (10:17[1]) and uses i

It was the enormous advantage of the Ptolemaic system over the Copernican—an advantage we may freely admit today, now that neither one is valid—that in the former, the mind of those with common sense took at least its first steps in harmony with the view of the childlike soul. Thus, the understanding did not take from this soul the courage really to look around and therefore to "see" what one had merely "known." One saw, or thought one saw, the circle of the spheres, arranged within as well as above each other; and within them one saw the seven planets, the sun and the moon, included as the lowest, the one closest to the earth, swing around the earth, which floated at the lowest point of this funnel of the spheres; and one looked up to the outermost arch of the vaulted firmament, completing its once-a-day rotation. But whatever was beyond—was the Beyond. One's eyes could still follow the motions of the individual planets through the twelve signs of the zodiac. And one could still say in good conscience that below is really below and above is above, a certainty of which Copernicus was to rob mankind, incorrectly, as we also know today—Copernicus, whom Luther called a "fool" in an unknowing but somehow prescient statement. ("Where one stands is always below," a young child said to his sister who had asked why the Antipodes do not fall down). And because that was also known, it was now possible—once again—not only to know but to "see" elements of all things in whatever is below, whatever is above, and whatever is between below and above.

But when this "seeing" knowledge ended, people would (even then) interpose before the final cause a system of intermediate powers, exactly as we do today when we reach the limit of our computed knowledge. The angels of medieval Aristotelianism correspond precisely to the basic principles of modern physics; that is to say, all the world, here as well as there, believes in them, though most lay persons have no idea what they mean, and most experts' ideas about them are nonsense.

For the kind of intellectual honesty that can limit itself to simply speaking of what has been truly experienced, without letting the insights intuitively gained from the experience proliferate into

something mythological, always has been rare. The Talmud's angelology, for instance, recounts genuine and great experiences pertaining to God's workings. But these experiences always were all too easily suffocated by the excesses of a fantasizing mind bereft of experience, just as the genuine and great insights of science were suffocated by the excesses of an imagination remote from experience and obsessed with intellectual understanding.

However, to praise God based on nature presents a certain danger that becomes evident even in this hymn, in the last quatrains of the third stanza. The danger lies in the temptation to make a seamless transition from nature, not to man as such—which would be permissible—but to ourselves as individuals, and to drown out the seriousness of our own lot with a cheap "Halleluyah," one that has not been purchased with one's own body. The eternally necessary antidote against this danger is provided by the Jobs and Karamazoffs who do believe in God but will not acknowledge His world.

But Yehuda Halevi does not need this cure. He is a Jew, and therefore he is in no danger of singing "Halleluyah" rashly. This fact provides the very raison d'etre for the powerful central quatrains of the final stanza, which seem at first glance to interrupt the flow of the poem, further delaying its angelic conclusion, which has already been arrived at, only to take it up once more in an unbelievably concentrated form. In hardly any of the other poems devoted to this particular topic does the poet speak in a voice so audacious and hard-hitting, so proud of its suffering, so conscious of its righteousness. And it is this irrepressible consciousness of suffering that alone gives him the right to acknowledge God's world—despite everything. Only the sufferer is permitted to praise God as manifest in His works. But all human beings suffer, and therefore humankind has this right. Only one who denies his suffering, or wishes to forget it, does not have that right. For he who wants to belie his own self lies also when he speaks of Him who wishes to be praised only by the mouth of the righteous.

18. The Remote-and-Near-One

Lord, where will You be found,
  whose space is enveloped in ether.
And when would You not be found,
  whose hem covers the earth.

  The occupant, in the heart's depth is
    He, and He draws the boundaries of the earth.
  To the near ones He is a bastion of ore,
    to the far-off a ray of hope.
  You,—who presides over the angels!
    You,—who crowns the clouds!
You, decorated with battle hymns—
Blessed One, may You be praised.
You could burst the circle of the spheres—
  as once the walls of the Temple!

  And you elevated Yourself
    high in the cavernous dark *[Hoehle]*,
  You remain interwoven with them
    more than body, more than soul.
  Hear, what they vow:
    Only He shall command us.
When would You have freed from fear
  him who was chosen for Your yoke.
Even You would want to defer his pleading
  You must prepare his meal!

  Because of Your nearness
    my heart opened up and welled up to You.
  So it approached You—
    see! You are approaching me.
  With a shower of miracles,
    gushing forth as once, oh, you please me.
Who does not experience You!
  The heavens and the stars
striding silently
  have to acknowledge You.

18] This hymn—part of that portion of the morning prayer, already filled with hymns, that speaks of Ezekiel's vision of heavenly wheels and creatures—is animated by one single thought. But it is the ultimate thought ever to be surveyed by the human mind, and it is the primary thought that was grasped by the Jewish mind: the idea that the remote God is none other than the near One, the unknown God no other than the revealed One, and the Creator none other than the Redeemer. And of this the poem sings, expressing it in a short epigrammatically compressed introductory stanza, which is followed by four more that cause this idea to vault hymnically from the heavenly throne to the human heart and back again—this idea that is discovered ever anew within the circle of those concerned with revelation and ever anew forgotten within as well as outside of it, from Paul and Marcion to Harnack and Barth.[1]

Ever anew discovered; ever anew forgotten. For what men discover, theologians forget. And the better theologians they are, the more do they forget. The most correct theology is the most dangerous one. After a long dry spell, we have today a (mostly Protestant) theology whose correctness leaves nothing to be desired. We have thus determined by now that God is the Wholly-Other, that to speak of Him is to misspeak, that we can say only what he does to us. The consequence of this enormous correctness is that today all of us correct ones are standing around in a circle like children at play, the first one saying something that is right, but

---

1. Marcion (Second Century C.E.), from Asia Minor, taught in Rome a doctrine of two gods: the evil Creator God of the *Old Testament* and a pure but ineffable God. The latter sent Jesus Christ to save humans from their pollution in the created world. Marcion thus completely rejected the authority of the *Old Testament* and its Creator God. Adolf Harnack (1851–1930), was a leading German Protestant scholar, author of *The History of Dogma*, 3 vols. (1886–89), *The History of Ancient Christian Literature*, 3 vols. (1898–1904), and *What is Christianity?* (1900). He argued for an historical rather than a dogmatic understanding of early Christianity. Karl Barth (1886–1968), was a founder of the anti-Nazi "Confessing Church" in Germany during the Hitler period, and author of *The Epistle to the Romans* (1919), and *Church Dogmatics*, 4 vols. (1932–1967). He stressed the "wholly otherness" of God against anthropocentric readings. Presumably, the link that joins Paul, Marcion, Harnack, and Barth, together for Rosenzweig, is a gnostic other-worldly tendency.

Oh! will God share
　　His abode with the sons of Adam?
Can their spirit overtake Him?
　　Can they break away from the original dust?
Yes! where You will reside
　　there their song of praise shall crown You.
Animal figures stood
　　united to carry
Your hallowed throne. You
　　carry them, in Eternity.

his neighbor silencing him by saying something that is even more right—which makes the first one's rightness wrong. And so it goes around the circle, until it is the first one's turn once more. The whole is what we call "theology." We theologians cannot help it— we must turn what we know into a rule for God's conduct.

Having found out that God can be known only through His presence, we immediately establish a rule for Him that says that He must not let Himself be known during His absence. In truth, though, we assuredly may leave it to Him when and how and how much of Himself He wants to be known. All we have to do is say what we know with as much or as little equanimity as we can (and even that is not up to us), and to say it with as much precision as we can (and that is indeed up to us).

When God comes near us, all we can discern is what cannot be said. But we are not obliged to say it—nor do we deserve to, as we know in our heart of hearts, being such excellent modern theologians. Nevertheless, we can't help trying to say it; this is just because of His nearness. We therefore have not the slightest reason to cut each other off just because we attempt to say the unsayable. As long as it is and wishes to be unsayable, it will see to it on its own that we are unable to say it. So when we begin to say it, most likely this happens because it—no, because He, God Himself—enables us to do so, no matter how inadequately, by beginning to draw away from us, to distance Himself from us. By distancing Himself from us God makes Himself known to us as the Remote One. And when He is entirely remote, when He has distanced Himself totally from us, we can even—hand me over to the secular arm, you inquisitors of the new theology!—prove His existence.

That it is possible to prove God's existence is the simple consequence of His being, as you never tire of repeating, the "wholly Other." Or not even that. This "wholly other-ness" is itself the modern proof of God's existence; it is what remains of all the other proofs, diluted to the furthest remove of abstraction. But they too have their place before that last point in the distance, where each one, in a way suited to its distance, itself constitutes the precise expression of that

which is visible at that location. Hence, to be convinced that God is the most Perfect Being, or the Final Cause, or even the Ideal of Morality, is by no means an indication of being hopelessly lost. But to be so convinced, and to express this conviction as honest knowing, is only an indication that at the moment of this knowing, God really was very distant from him, the knower.

Yet what does "honest knowing" mean here? The same thing it always means: that you should make no statement about anything that does not concern you or that is not concerned with you. Without such concern, even research into fifteenth-century German agriculture would be worthless; and with it, statements such as *God is holy* or even *God is* are as true as are our fashionable pronouncements about God's nearness.

For nearness and distance as such tell us nothing about whether or not that mutual concern exists that alone makes all knowing true, thus, in this case whether man is of concern to God, and God is of concern to man. Even in the most terrifying proximity, man can look away, and then he will have no idea what has happened to him. And in the remotest distance, God's and man's glance can burn into each other to such a degree that the coldest abstractions become warm in the mouth of a Maimonides or a Hermann Cohen, warmer than any of our upset chit-chat. Nearness, remoteness—no matter! What does matter is that whatever is spoken, here as well as there, must be spoken before His countenance—with the "You" of the poem, who never turned away, not even for one moment.

19. THE NAME

Year in, year out   in Your house   the fortunate people
  settles down where   Your name   rests.
High, high up dwells   the Name, which   has being in
  the broken heart   and wherever someone   suffers in anguish.
And the highest heavens   cannot contain Him,   whether He descended
  onto Sinai,   or lived   in the burning bush.
For His   path is near   and also far,
  since He tied His creation   to the self and   to the other.
Only God I thank,   when my heart   forms thoughts,
  and only Him, when   my mouth is capable   of responding.

19] The contradiction that God is at once near and distant coalesces in the fact that He has a name. Anything having a name can be spoken about and spoken to, depending on whether it is absent or present. Since God is never absent, there can be no concept of God. (There can certainly be concepts of false gods, but not of the true One.) God is the only one whose name is also His concept, whose concept is also His name. One calls God merely God, and every other name given to Him has only this meaning.

God's distance and nearness even solves for our poet the problem of the world's purpose, with which the religious philosophy of his time was struggling. Everything that is created has a double relationship. On the one hand, it is simply there; it has being, self-being, and an intrinsic purpose. On the other hand, though, it exists also for the sake of something else and ultimately for the sake of everything else. In its selfhood it experiences the near God, in its connectedness with something other, the distant God. For the distant God is the God of the world, a world that as the whole and as a whole is composed entirely of the other; the near God is the God of man's heart, the heart that is never as much a self, and only a self, as when it is suffering.

It is noteworthy that in the second couplet, which states the poem's subject matter in the shortest and simplest form, the word used graphically to describe the world-high and world-distant being of God is *dwell,* a term usually designating the indwelling of His glory on earth, among His people, in His home. But for God's dwelling in man's contrite heart, the poem—diverging from the Bible verse (Isaiah 57:15[1]) on which it is based—uses the most abstract word imaginable: *being,* this true philosopher's term, which Western scholasticism appropriated by rendering it as "to exist,"— or *Dasein,* "to be there," as it should be translated, strictly speaking. This contradiction discloses the profundity of Jewish insight and

---

1. "For thus saith the High and Lofty One that inhabiteth eternity, whose name is Holy: 'I dwell in the high and holy place, with him also that is of a contrite and humble spirit, to revive the spirit of the humble, and to revive the heart of the contrite ones.'"

faith. Here, the *Bore' olam*, "the Creator of the universe," does not mean, as one might assume, something distant, which after all is what its content designates. It is rather a colloquial expression rich in feeling. As for the God of man's heart—it does not for one moment forget that God is He who "is." Here the spark does not merely fly back and forth between the poles of distance and nearness; instead, the poles themselves are charged with the two polar kinds of electricity, but in a different arrangement. The Creator exalted above all the world establishes His "dwelling," while the most abstract God of philosophy has his "being" in the contrite heart.

When Hermann Cohen was still living in Marburg, he explained the idea of God he had developed in his ethics to an old Jew, who listened respectfully. But when Cohen had finished, the old Jew asked: "But where does that leave the *Bore' olam?*" Cohen did not answer but broke into tears.

20. HALLOWED

Three time
  you call "Holy,"

           to hallow Him
             like the angels!

May jubilation ring out
  to the Creator, who

           kindly receives
             the creature's pleading.

A camp
  surrounds the throne

           and He
             encircles the camp.

May He be surrounded
  by a group of fiery servants,

           in which the thorny bush once
             was not consumed.

They seek His
countenance, wherein Grace

           and Truth
             coexist.

The glow of fire is
  mixed with water,

           and neither looses
             its power.

  "Here we are!"
    Your spirited army

           appears prepared
             for its mission.

They are the source
  of Your teaching

           that expands the circle
             of Your followers.

They proclaim
  Your sacred praise,

           which they quickly
             spread throughout the world.

They robe themselves
  in awe, crowning

           Your head with
             jewels.

And that they are
  Your work, they

           affirm with a whisper,
             never with a no.

And now, here I am,
  from misery's depths,

           a ship, surrounded by the
             blowing of the storm.

20] This hymn with its sparkling rhymes is meant (as is the one before the preceding one) to complement the passage in the morning prayer that depicts the "Threefold-Holy" of the heavenly hosts, as Isaiah had heard it (6:3[1]). For everything below has a correspondent "above." Thus Israel is supposed to echo the seraphim's "Threefold-Holy" on earth—Israel, whose city faces the heavenly city of God (or as it also can be expressed in memory of the prefiguration of this city during the wanderings in the desert: whose earthly camp faces the heavenly camp). The hymn is entirely filled with a vision of the divine, that dual sovereignty holding sway

---

1. "And one called unto another, and said: 'Holy, holy, holy, is the Lord of hosts, the whole earth is full of his glory.'"

Here, look at me,
  calling, "Holy,"

my circle resembles
  the highest circle.

Never my word escaped
  the circle,

which was compassionately
  formed by suffering;

There were also humbled
  before the maid's

sons, who
  once were the free.

They only await
  Your Grace

and never want to accuse
  You of injustice.

Even if oppression
  removed them

far from the beauty
  of the land,

They cried
  what one about to die

always cries out
  from the depths of suffering,

They found in You
  salvation's

sources, which
  never diminished.

Original knowledge
  of His name

goes from mouth to mouth
  collectively.

It emerges from the cry of the bosom:
  one hears I also

know Him—but oh,
  keep silent.

Your glory is known
  to all: for their

word tells how Your
  Grace rewards.

Clearly Your
  witness stresses that

it is Your work, which
  Your arm protects.

He who slaves for You
  summons the people,

which lives near
  Your counsel:

You shall
  sing songs anew, know

all this, and
  be brave.

Call out a
  threefold "Holy,"

to hallow Him
  like the angels!

in heaven and on earth. It is wondrous to behold, both in the way in which it unifies the angelic forces of mercy and truth (which ought to counteract each other like fire and water) and in the way in which it manifests itself once more to its messengers at the destination to which they had been sent. For God's dual reign is just as evident at the end as at the beginning of a mission. And it is no less wondrous in the way it steels the human powers of the people for infinite patience in suffering and an indefatigable bearing of witness—that people to whom the poet directs his admonition to emulate the angels.

21. YOUR DWELLINGS

Yes, lovely are Your dwellings
   and Your four courts.
The splendor of the lion and the strength of the bull
   are the supports of Your throne.
And Jacob's encampments
   are your new foliage on earth.
You assign them to banners, teach
   them the meanings of Your name.
To behold you, Holy One, and
   pronounce Your works—oh what rewards!

21] The burning glass of these few lines collects the rays of the preceding great hymn: the doubleness of the heavenly and earthly sanctuary, the "camp"—there, the animal-angels of Ezekiel's vision who bear the wagon throne (Ezekiel 1:10[1]), here Jacob's sons, the bearers of His Name, the witnesses to His works.

---

1. "When they moved, these moved, when they stood still, these stood still; and when they were raised from the earth, the wheels were raised with them; for the spirit of the living creature was in the wheels."

22. THE GOD OF THE SPIRITS

Every tongue gives praise   to God, the Lord of the spirits.

    Throne, surrounded by grace,
    Elevating those who elevate Him,
    Place, which silences all raging
He who is considered wise, who is an   orator, his success comes from there.

    And in the heart of Your servants
    There are tablets, true
    Witnesses; your right hand
Engraved therein the original   laws which never become tattered.

    The wheels of the chariot
    Approach the paths of the soul closely;
    For Your blessing spirit
Points them to the glorious   waters, Glorious One!

    Oh, the sounds of souls—Yours,
    The prostrations of bodies—Yours,
    The hope of all—all Yours,
Service to You, the master, consumes them   like the service of handmaids.

22] The spirit, his spirit, is man's proudest possession. This pride is shaken by the words *God of the spirits,* with which Moses addresses God (Numbers 16:22[1]) in one of his great intercessory pleadings.

This is a mild shock, one that leaves the spirit where it is, namely within "all flesh," and that nevertheless extirpates his pride. His wisdom remains undoubted, as does the brilliance of his word, but he owes both to the place at the heavenly throne from which they came. To be sure, the tablets of the Law do have a place in the human heart, but it was the finger of God that inscribed them. And the soul's path to heavenly bliss is short, but it is the spirit of God that must guide the soul on that path. In each case, there is just a little "but," yet it is a "but" on which the human spirit's self-satisfaction and sense of autonomy are based. Thus, in the last stanza, the artifice of the spiritual order, in which the soul has its legitimate place above the body, collapses into a great equalization and confusion of "all" bodies and souls. What we are left with in the last stanza is not the proud order of the spirit but the chaos of humility represented in the image of the prostrate maid-servants.

---

1. "And [Moses and Aaron] fell upon their faces, and said: 'Oh God, the God of the spirits of all flesh, shall one man sin, and wilt Thou be wroth with all the congregation?'"

23. HOLY

Armies of saints rejoice
And choirs of angels

'holy' they chant   for Him,
surround   Him above.

Great magnificence purified,
But its blue confirms it,
And His shadow unites
The rays of the soul take nourishment
His voice extracts fire

although invisible   to the eye,
as does   the host in heaven,
the mysterious pair   of fire and water.
   from the glow which   emanates from Him.
   from the abundance   of clouds.

And those who are related to Him
And in those who are aflame in Him
Those who know His word,
Human shoulders desire
Tired sighs would gladly choose

were encircled by   the holy spirit.
He fans   the ardent spirit.
live in it.   Take note:
   to bow   under His yoke,
   His roof   to flee to.

The steps of the angel
His wheels
His good treasures,
Rare works, whose
Clear miracles—they derive

can be heard at   the nape of the world,
set the course   featherlight,
they come close   to our place,
splendor and strength   come from Him,
from a higher source,   prophecy.

Awake! With shouts of holy
Create for yourselves
Hearts! Ascend the steps
Rewards those who protect
But those who scorn Him

become like   those above,
a share to inherit   in the kingdom.
to the Lord   of Lords!   Who richly
His honor as their   own standard.
He will never allow   to enter His Kingdom.

23] In Hebrew, the word *holy* originally meant something that is set apart. God's power is manifest as the quiet, almost inaudible activity of the first beginning. In this way, at first all remains as it is. Creation seems so ancient it almost could be "eternal" and the voice of conscience so unconditional it almost could be called "autonomous." And so orthodox Kantians probably can get the idea that it would not make much of a difference if one were to concede to the "religious point of view" that God is the originator of the starry firmament as well as of the conscience.

But one cannot claim this "point of view" so cheaply. God is not merely the One that was. He is not merely the foundation that supports both world and man. Indeed, this is an empty belief, a mere "concession," as long as it lacks the experience of God in the living present, as long as it is in fact not derived from that experience. Without the God who, powerfully efficacious, intervenes directly in the "day" of our present life, the Quiet and Inaudible One who created and maintains the world and our heart is turned into a fairy tale or worse into a dogma. It is the Holy One who sets Himself apart and everywhere engenders what is set apart, what is unheard of—election and holiness. Without these obvious miracles of the present day, the hidden miracles of any other day could not be seen, at least not seen as miracles. It is only the revelation of what is set apart that teaches us to revere the Creator even in what is "natural." Only the shudderings before holiness can hallow even the everydayness of the profane.

It is, therefore, essential for the miracle that it be conceived of as part of the living presence of holiness, hence also of hallowing: "Awake! With shouts of holy." It is sheer stupidity to ask why miracles no longer happen today the way they "once" used to happen. Miracles never "happened." The past is a murderous atmosphere for a miracle. The Bible itself gives a subsequent "natural" explanation for the miracle of the Sea of Reeds. Any miracle can be explained, after it has occurred—not because the miracle was no miracle, but because the explanation is an explanation. The setting of a miracle is always in the present, or possibly in the future. One

can pray for it and experience it; and as long as the experience of it is present to us, one also can be thankful for it. But once that presence has vanished, all one can still do is explain it. Any miracle is possible, even the most comical one—say, that an ax can swim[1]— and after it has occurred, one will not be at a loss to explain it. The only condition for the occurrence of a miracle is that one can pray for it; but this prayer must be a genuine one, one that is free of our will, not the manipulative prayer of a medicine man with his magical formulas nor the prayer of a young American lady with hers.

Only in this respect is there something like a difference between different times so that one person can pray for something that another cannot. But when genuine prayer is possible, the most impossible thing becomes possible. And when it is not possible, the most possible thing becomes impossible. Thus, it can be possible that the dead are resurrected but impossible that the sick get well. Nothing is impossible as such; but there is much that we consider to be so impossible that we are not capable of asking for it, while there are other things that we consider entirely possible, yet—for whatever reason—do not have the power to ask for.

There is really nothing miraculous about a miracle, except the time of its occurrence. The east wind has probably dried out the ford of the Red Sea hundreds of times, and it may do so hundreds of times again; but that it should do so precisely at the moment of the people's need, just when they enter that ford is the miracle. What had up to then been the prayed-for future now has become an event of the present. That present moment will be enhanced by a sense of the past, of its past, which will enable it to live on as a present rather than a past moment. Thus, it will be lifted out of the flow of all other moments yet remain part of them.

---

1. Ax miracle performed by Elisha, Kings II, 6:6: "And the man of God [Elisha] said, where did it [an ax] fall? And he showed him the place. And he cut down a stick, and threw it in there [the river Jordan]; and made the iron float."

It is in this way that the miracle becomes the germ cell of holiness. As such, and as long as it remains linked to its origin and therefore remains wonder-full, it keeps its inner force. The divisions man attempts to set up make Him, who brought forth but one creation, laugh. And so He lets them again and again be swept away by the reemerging original chaos. But the divisions set up by God Himself spread out over all creation, and growing toward one-ness and all-ness reveals the silent mystery of the one creation.

24. THE HELPER

Consolation comes   to the troubled heart   which already sees
                itself   decayed when il
  from Him,   the Lord of the hosts who says, "I, who rule, approach."
As He has the power   of death   in anger so that   we may perish,
  so He helps us   to life   in kindness—and   we live.
And so   the mouth   which once said   "let there be light"
  now calls   to the new light   —and   it is here.

24] This little poem is rather unusual not only because of its form—its peculiar meter which ends a heavily dragging line with a brisk double iamb—but even more so because of the way in which that form is filled. For it is in this double iamb that the point of the poet's thought is driven home in each of the three half and the three full verse-stops.

The poem deals first with the knowledge of God, the God who reveals Himself to us transitory beings as the One Who Forever Is, as the I of an eternally present activity—to us who are destined to passivity and to pass away. Second, it speaks with restrained jubilation of the fact that we have not passed away but are indeed alive. And third, it expresses the happy certainty of a moment to come, born of that first moment of the "And let there be light." "I, Who forever am," "We are indeed alive," "And there was light"—a threefold breakthrough from the heaviness of nocturnal affliction into the exhilarating light of [divine] help, each time increased in strength, because each time another line, still deeper inside the fortress which guards the treasure of help, is taken by storm.

The third time this onslaught is accompanied by a battlecry referring to the "new[ly-created] light." This word was used in exactly the same sense by the men who arranged the synagogue's liturgy, and who taught us to pray for a "new light" for Zion when they placed this prayer (recited every morning) directly before the one praising God, the Creator of the heavenly lights, who day after day renews the work of creation.[1] For man has a twofold certainty pertaining to God's help. One is the certainty of a person who once has already been helped. We know from Ibn Ezra that Yehuda Halevi once asked why God referred at Sinai to the liberation from Egypt rather than to the creation of the world; knowing Halevi's *Kuzari*,

---

1. "May you shine a new light on Zion, and may we all speedily merit its light. Blessed are you, Lord, who fashions the luminaries." The concluding two sentences of the second of the three blessings preceeding the morning recital of the Jewish declaration of faith, the *Shema*. Jewish commentators see in this new messianic light the same light God created on the first day of Creation.

we need not ascribe to him the foolish answer given by Ibn Ezra.[2] But there is also an affliction so deep that man's certainty fails him, suffocating even the memory of help once received. If what is closest to man is then taken from him, vanishing into the distance of incredulity, there remains only the help that comes to him from a distance still more remote. Then, and only then, the time has come for the ultimate call, the call to the Creator, not in a ritual prayer (where even in this situation different laws would apply) but in the fervent prayer of the heart. For in the depth of affliction there is nothing left of man but his creatureliness, so it is the Creator alone from whom he can learn once again to trust the Revealer, and to hope for the Redeemer.

---

2. Abraham Ibn Ezra (1080–1164) was a personal friend of Halevi, perhaps even becoming his son-in-law. In his commentary to Exodus 20:20, "I am the Lord thy God, who brought thee out of the land of Egypt, out of the house of bondage," with which the Ten Commandments begins, a question arises as to why God identifies Himself in terms of the exodus from Egypt rather than the creation of the universe. Ibn Ezra gives two answers: First, no one witnessed creation but all the Jews witnessed the miracles in Egypt. Second, while intellectuals (Hebrew: *maskilim*) can see by the natural light of reason that God is He who created the universe, all Jews, whether intellectual or not, witnessed and therefore know that God is He who brought the Jews out of Egypt. Though Rosenzweig impugns Ibn Exra in the name of Halevi's *Kuzari*, the latter's response to this question (see part 1, paragraphs 11–25) is for all intents and purposes the same as Ibn Ezra's. Both support the evidential superiority of personal experience and uninterrupted tradition over the conflicting arguments of the philosophers. That the interpretations of Ibn Ezra and Halevi are the same is the opinion of Stanley Abramovitch, Naphtali Ben-Menahem, and the editorial staff of the 1972 *Encyclopedia Judaica* (Vol. 8, p. 1163), among others.

SOUL

25. HERE I AM

How can I enter His service,
Happily I'll give up

    Yes, Lord and shepherd,
    This self untangled itself
    Whatever path I erred on,

You, oh remember,
Although it resembled the
    spider's web,

    Heart and soul
    But when I suffer,
    Both will stray again
May Your word enwrap me—
Look gently into me,

    Unlucky star!—when my
    What will be my lot,
    Oh God, heal me!
When someday strength is gone,
Do not destroy me,

    Shriveling and crushed
    Barefoot, dragging my bared
    Desecrated by great
Between us came
Woe, sensual glitter of the world—

    Oh bend my heart,
    What I consider play and fun!

    Oh quickly administer
If I could change your thoughts!
Help me escape from it!

to whom I owe my beginnings!
all others, if I only have His love.

    You envelop body and soul which are Your
    for You, You saw my inner being;
    walking, standing still—You helped,
        approached it critically.
when my foot dragged in exhaustion,

    You lifted me from its midst.

    yearn to rest, oh Lord, near You;
    my suffering takes them far from You,
    and forget to follow You—
Lead me high up to your battlement.
and absolve me from all sin.

    pride was high I grew slack for Your cause
    when someday old age reaches me?
    You, God, possess that which can heal.
and my chin trembles in a toothless face,
and do not break the reed that I am.

    I sit in eternal confinement,
    body where ridicule scorches me,
    sins, and many evil deeds—
jarringly my sinful spirit,
Your glow is pale before my inner spirit.

    to serve Your Kingdom, Lord.
    May it remove itself when I behold You
        Divine
Your balsam to my deepest pain.
Then you would not ignore my suffering!
Tell Your servant, "Here I am."

25] In the Jewish community of a village in the south of the Black Forest there was a man, Mendele, whom the community supported because he was a little feeble-minded. One day he was busy cutting wood in the square next to the synagogue. The little synagogue stood, as is only proper, on the highest spot of the village, close to the steep slope of the mountain at whose foot the village was located. Some young fellows, passing by on the path above that steep slope and looking for some fun, loudly called down: "Mendele!" Mendele looks up, but there was nothing to be seen. A little later there was another call, this time coming from another spot. "Mendele, Mendele!" Confused, he looked up again—and again, nothing. After a while, a third call comes: "Mendele, Mendele!" At this he throws down his axe, runs into the synagogue, up to its central platform from which the Torah is always read, and opening his arms wide he calls out in Hebrew the words once spoken by Abraham: "Here I am."[1]

Man can call out "Here I am" because the echo of these words comes back to him from the mouth of God. The divine "Here I am" is yearned, pleaded, atoned, and prayed for in this poem's twenty-three throbbing rhymes, until the twenty-fourth rhyme gives an answer to the yearning, pleading, atoning, and praying. And that answer is not merely yearned, pleaded, atoned, and prayed for. No, the plea to which a divine answer is expected must be couched in such human terms that there may actually come a moment in the poem where an answer is demanded in an almost threatening manner: ". . . but when I suffer. . . ."

The human heart has the inalienable right to deny over and over again the great truth of revelation that suffering is a gift from God—when it is made into a theological formula, as happens over and over again—and to reestablish in opposition to it the original state of nature in which suffering is suffering and nothing else. God answers only the word that arises from the depth of all human powers, those with which human beings were created as well as those which can be awakened in them.

---

1. Genesis 22:1, 22:11 (also said by Isaac, Jacob, Joseph, Moses, Samuel, David, (son of Ahirub) Ahimelech, an anonymous Amalekite, God himself through Isaiah, and Isaiah).

26. SOUL

Soul—
> most beautiful maiden, enjoying the love of her youthful lover,
Daily
>> she rejoices: my companion's song of his vineyard—oh
>> Song of Songs, of Solomon.

Soul—
> the maiden goes out to eagerly fetch the holy water,
She
>> brightly sings going and coming, her playmates with her:
>> If you pull us towards You, we will hurry.

Soul—
> and God's spirit awakens her: Don't be afraid!
Still you adorn yourself with drums
>> and join in the round of the happy ones and are mine—how proud you are!
>> Sweep down with me from Lebanon, oh bride, from Lebanon.

Soul—
> surrounded by envy, surrounded by enemies, she silently
Speaks:
>> He who is my friend—radiates white and red a thousandfold.
>> Great waters cannot extinguish our love.

Soul—
> she accuses herself today: woe, His anger has not yet abated!
Then she sings happily:
>> Look at me, I am a wall, a wall of precious stones!
>> Then I was in His eyes as one who has found peace.

26] This very tender, floating, ethereal fantasia on motifs from the Song of Songs (intended for the Sabbath service of Passover [*Oster*] week, in which the Song of Songs is read) is among the pieces composed in free verse. These represent a greater portion of the poet's entire work, especially when length is considered, than is apparent from my selections. This poem's content also is derived from its formal freedom; in its ephemeral mobility, it hardly could be imagined in a strict metrical form. It is intended as an introduction to the Sabbath and holiday prayer mentioned earlier,[1] "The soul of every living being. . . ." That prayer's first word, *soul*, used as a prelude to all five stanzas of this poem, appears here in the grammatical form that in Hebrew is possible only immediately before a genitive. But five times this genitive fails to materialize. Instead, it vanishes five times into the stanza, which is built on the bittersweet nonresolution of that diminished seventh chord, until the sixth time brings not a sixth stanza but the resolution: "The soul of every living being shall praise Thy name!"

---

1. See commentary to poem no. 7. The prayer is known as *Nishmas,* its first word, meaning "Soul." It is an expression of praise and gratitude to God. The Talmud (*Pesachim* 118a) calls this prayer the "Blessing of the Song" because it continues the theme of the Song of the Sea (*Exodus* 14:30–15:19).

27. SOUL IN EXILE

Oh, she who wailed near her father's house longingly
  and, to see it, dared to ascend to it in her dreams,
She who dared to ascend, to find consolation, but the dream
  cannot prevent the dissolution of the mirage, awakening tormented,
She was tormented unto sickness by day when she could no longer behold
                                               His smile,
  without whose glow she wilted and fretted.
She fretted! to new achievement! and worked hard, to victory!
  because she would not renounce the splendor because of the chaos.
As she renounced the splendor, she unlocked the source,
  whose depths she only sought heretofore,
She sought after the core—and the bonds of an oath tied her to
  you, wisdom, so long as there is daylight.

27] The overly artful form of this poem (which repeats each couplet's rhyming word in the first word of the following couplet, though in a shortened, two-syllable version that omits the silent *e* of the central syllable) is transformed by the poet from a technical tour de force into a spiritual vehicle for this small composition. Its rhyming line ends only seem to be ends. The identical words starting the next line reveal a new beginning that had already been hidden in them. This makes for a strange sense of suspension at the points joining the couplets, and it imbues the whole with a feeling of quiet breathing.

Yet the transition from the third to the fourth couplet turns into a powerful peripeteia. First, there was a mournful, pale backward glance, moving torturously from one couplet to another, toward the soul's bliss in God's paternal home, a bliss lost to the soul in its descent to earth. Then, after reaching its nadir, or, rather, immediately at this nadir, there comes an about-turn which moves in a logically incomprehensible yet absolutely believable mood swing form the despairing awareness of withering away to the wonderful certainty of a new blossoming—a certainty not in spite of but born out of that withering. And from this point onward, the tone changes, and the transitions between the couplets become proudly determined triumphant shouts of one who has conquered life.

This sudden move from the poem's first to its second half is shocking to "modern man" and his need for gradualism. Still, this powerfully ungrounded (because in the deepest sense it is powerfully grounded) "change of mood" is the same one that modern man could have encountered in the psalms, to the extent he has not encountered it in his own experience, if he did not prefer to cut these psalms up into two halves, assigning the halves to different authors and thereby protecting himself from the shattering experience of learning all that can take place in a human soul.

28. With You

I was with You, before the travails of earthly life—
   May I now harbor your spirit and increase it.
If I had strength to stand, would you disturb me?
   and power to walk, would you prevent it?
And my thoughts—remain Your thoughts.
   What I begin—how could I do without You.
You I seek at the time of grace—hear me;
   Equip me with the shield of Your grace.
Call me to service at Your gate,
   and awaken me to the honor of Your name.

28] The Jewish poet had no need of Platonism to tell him what Isaiah (45:4) and the Psalmist (103:14 and 139:1) already knew and what had been told to Jeremiah in so many words at the time of his calling (Jeremiah 1:5[1])—that even before a human being enters life, God already knows and loves him (the Hebrew language expresses both, untranslatably, in one word). Knowing this constitutes a foundation of our life, sustaining us even more than does the hope for what is awaiting us beyond the grave; for this hope is grounded only in that knowledge, which possesses an inner certainty proved in life itself. Every birthday confirms this certainty. Thus did my unforgettable teacher of Torah, Nehemia Nobel,[2] preach concerning the soul's awareness of its own descent from God in a sermon he delivered on his fiftieth and last birthday.

---

1. "Before I formed thee in the belly I knew thee, and before thou camest forth out of the womb I sanctified thee; I have appointed thee a prophet unto the nations."

2. Rabbi Nehemia Anton Nobel (1971–1922) was a German Orthodox rabbi and leader, as well as a Mizrachi Zionist leader. He was author of several exegetical works and known for his inspiring, erudite, and topical sermons. He studied at the Berlin-Seminary, as well as under Hermann Cohen at the University of Marburg. He was rabbi successively in Cologne, Köenigsberg (briefly), Leipzig, Hamburg, and finally Frankfort (1910–1922). Rosenzweig and Martin Buber published a jubilee book for him in 1921.

29. PRAYER

Oh God, You, when I beseech You,
  hear my voice, my cry, oh You God.
Oh God, You, show Your hand, reveal
  Your omnipotence and pardon me, oh You God.
Oh God, You, my heart beats wildly in my bosom,
  I wrap myself into my distress, oh You God.
Oh God, You, may my memory be pleasant to You,
  think of me and take care of me, oh You God.
Oh God, You, I always await Your help,
  may Your love be my consolation, oh You God.
Oh God, You, my creator You, my rock,
  who besides You is my helper, oh You God!
Oh God, You, may Your mercy envelop me,
  do not count the number of my sins, oh You God.
Oh God, You, my thinking desires only You,
  and my soul says: You are mine, oh You God.
Oh God, You, my fear envelops my heart,
  I pour out my soul to You, oh You God.
Oh God, You, hear me for Your sake
  and today accept my prayer, oh You God.

Oh God, You, see, my feeling is in Your hand,
  You know the secret of my heart, oh You God.
Oh God, You, bring healing to my pains,
  open Your eyes and see, oh You God.
Oh God, You, put my foot on the ground,
  I will affirm You before everyone, oh You God.

Oh God, You, see me waiting for Your help,
  until You look this way and turn, oh You God.
Oh God, You, lend an ear to my cry,
  be merciful and hear me, oh You God.

29] This litany—for that is what this piece is and intends to be—is meant for the soul-searching New Year's Day service. It was composed not to be read, but to be prayed. Whoever reads it as a poem will find it monotonous and lacking in a progression of ideas, and rightly so. Most of its lines could be arranged differently without causing a noticeable change. But this is not the way this litany wishes to be read. Rather, each line, cut off as it is from the others by its double invocation, [should be read] by itself. Each line is an entire prayer, simple and self-sufficient. And yet these almost uniform links are eventually arranged into a chain after all. This fact may not be understood by someone who thinks the soul should deliver lectures to God and who does not know that the soul always has only one thing to say but that this one thing must be said over and over again.

Still, the original text has an external (though not purely external) structure, but one that this translation was not permitted to replicate. Each line begins and ends with an invocation to God that has from antiquity on (even the Septuagint says "Lord") served as an appellation that veils the unutterable name of the God of revelation. This name, consisting of four silent consonants, has been worked secretly into the four stanzas. That is, the first word of each line that follows that appellation starts with a letter whose numerical value determines the number of lines—ten, five, six, and again five—that make up each stanza.[1]

But what does it really mean that God's name is unutterable? A college friend of mine, having just come back from visiting a well-known Humboldt scholar, told me in apparent horror: "And he refers to Frau von Homboldt as 'Li!'" Obviously, the case here is exactly the same as with all other genuine theological problems: they are not theological problems at all.

---

1. Because Hebrew letters have numerical values, so, too, do the four letters of the "unutterable" name of God—*yud*, ten; *hey*, five; *vuv*, six; *hey*, five. The initial letter of the first word in the verses within each of the four stanzas begin with these four letters respectively, and the number of verses in each stanza reflects its initial letter's numerical value. In non-Jewish English language Bible translations, the four-lettered name is often rendered "Jehovah" or more recently "Yahweh." When Jews pronounce this name in liturgy they use a substitute name, "Adonoy," which has in turn also become holy.

Oh God, You, and my God, I yearn for You,
　my heart, it desires Your salvation, oh You God.
Oh God, You, vouch for Your servant, to his good,
　do not look on the number of his sins, oh You God.
Oh God, You, will he who follows You be enmeshed
　in his sins much longer, oh You God?
Oh God, You, my thought advises my heart
　to dedicate itself to You in its distress, oh You God.

Oh God, You, yes—in You I rejoice,
　release the poor one from his pain, oh You God.
Oh God, You, Lord of the world, I yearn for You,
　as long as You love my yearning, oh You God.

Oh God, You, show Your patience to Your servant,
　who has turned to Your loving kindness, oh You God.
Oh God, You, see, I lay down my prayer,—
　before I call, You answer me, oh You God.
Oh God, You, make me strong through Your love,
　and balsam administer to my sick heart, oh You God.
Oh God, You, my sorrow made me ill,
　my soul is feverish day and night, oh You God.
Oh God, You, pull me from the abyss,
　and end Your servant's imprisonment, oh You God.

In general, names can be pronounced only under very special conditions. Take, for instance, a conversation among three persons, one of whom is essentially a listener. It is a violation of good manners and of one's natural feeling to pronounce that person's name. One will instead try to draw him into the conversation, at least for a moment, and then address him directly. That is to say, a person's name should be used in his presence only for addressing him directly. All names are originally vocatives. Any other grammatical case is applicable only once the name's bearer has left. To use a person's name in his presence, but without speaking to him directly, may make him feel excluded, if only at that moment. However, God, never leaves, so any attempts to pronounce His name could mean only that one wishes to exclude Him.

But that was in fact the real intent of certain scholars, at least with regard to that "old God of the Jews." Scholarship has seized upon the statement of a late Greek author concerning the "correct" way (among the Samaritans!) of pronouncing the four-consonant Name and has done so with an uncharacteristic enthusiasm and lack of scientific doubt. Otherwise, what scholarly Protestant theologian would still speak of Jesus and Mary (just to name the most obvious) instead of Yehoshua and Miriam—stressing the last syllables, of course. This is quite apart from the fact that during the time in which these scholars place the composition of the greater part of the Bible, the assumed name already had come into general usage in place of the real name. Assuming that they are correct in their belief about when the Bible was written, the favored reading of the divine name would be about as scientific as it would be to print the name *Goethe* instead of *Hafiz* throughout the *West-Ostlicher Diwan*.[2]

This stubbornness obviously has other reasons, and that learned donkey skin only serves to hide them. They would like to retire the old God of the Jews; they would like to make Him into a has-been, into a god as dead as Zeus and Apollo or Baal and Astarte are for today's world. This is totally different from the old Protestant naivite that pronounced the divine name with the vowels (which were never

---

2. Shams ud-din Mohammed Hafiz, fourteenth century, Persian lyric poet, mystic philosopher, expositor of Koran. His *Diwan* influenced Goethe.

meant as vowels of the divine name) of the traditional Hebrew text, when they sang—as Gellert and Klopstock did[3]—"To you, to you, Jehovah." That was genuine naivite, in that it wished not to objectify that name but rather to come face to face with it. But this is impossible in the same way as when a child, having somehow picked up his mother's first name, now tries to address her by it, though that name sounds impossible coming from him.

For indeed, the only real question is whether the name on my tongue is one used to address someone, and not merely one that is pronounced. If it is in danger of being used in the latter way, I must resort to a new name which, spoken only between me and the other, will serve as a cover for the old name. The first name, then, becomes unutterable for me, though it still shimmers through the second one and is spoken silently along with it. But that second one now becomes the proper name by which the One it means can be addressed. Anyone trying to revert artificially to the old name thereby excludes himself from the circle of the genuinely concerned.

One can, by rationalization after the fact, interpret all of this as magic tricks with names and the like. But this is indeed after the fact, even when such rationalizations originate with the name givers themselves. Anyone who is not overly concerned with distinguishing himself from Africans, as a German professor of philosophy probably feels he must, can discover in the names on his own tongue, the ones with which he addresses people close to him and those distant from him, all the primitive, numinous, and fascinating elements about which comparative religion teaches us.

But does God really have a name? Are not all names here simply attempts to name the Unnameable? May one therefore take any name, even the name *God* itself—since this is also a name, and today it is even the name—as seriously, that is, as being as real as a name that a man has?

But does a man really "have" his name? Is it not also something merely given to him? And does he have it anywhere but on

---

3. FR: Eighteenth-century German poets. [Christian Füchtegott Gellert (1715–1769), German poet and author of songs and fables; Friedrich Gottlieb Klopstock (1724–1803), German poet, author of *Messias* and *Hermanns* trilogy.]

the tongue of those who gave it to him? Does his name have any reality other than that he is called by it? When Yehuda Halevi, as well as Jews throughout the millennia, addressed God with the familiar name used in this poem, that name—through which the mysterious and unutterable name is still shining, just as it is clearly shining through in this poem—is the real name of God, that is if He is the living God and not a dead idol. And when Sabbatai Sevi[4] presumes to hasten the coming of the kingdom of heaven by pronouncing the Name according to its spelling, his failure becomes evident by the fact that he can pronounce only its vowels (which do not even serve to render the correct pronunciation). Thus, his attempt to leap over the end of Jewish history around the world had to fail, for exactly the same reason that the attempt of some today to use the alleged "scientific" pronunciation instead of saying "God" must fail. For they too are trying to leap out of the orbit of this Jewish world history that already has encircled them.

"But is the name of God, the God of the world and of world history, really the name by which Yehuda Halevi called him and you call him?"—"Is Frau von Humboldt's name really 'Li?'"

---

4. Sabbatai Sevi (1626–1676) was a relatively popular—among the Jews—false Messiah, who finally, under pain of death, converted to Islam.

30. Human Weakness

Why do you trust   in time, seeing that   there is no truth in it?
  Oh, how much   work there is! how quickly   my day passed!
Everyone warns   his brother, not   to sin:
  beware that that   which tempts you   does not overtake you!
If sin approaches,   say: "human hand—   what can it do!
  The human being   and his actions   are in the hand of the creator."

30] This short reflection, which is emotionally moving and also moves along quickly, changes from a mere soliloquy into drama, into two dramatized acts at that (and all of that in three couplets!) before it ends in a play on words (which, however, is more than just a play). For in Hebrew, the derivative of the root *to create* fully contains in its form both an active and a passive sense (Luther renders it as "mind" or "thought" [*Sinn, Gedankel*]; as "writing poetry" [*Dichten*]; as "hopes and endeavors" [*Dickten und Trachten*] but also as "creature"). In its ambiguous position midway between creature and creator, it designates in the most precise way imaginable the seat of our weakness, which consists precisely in the fact that we are strong but that this strength fails us just when it is called upon. In this desperate experience that our own essence again and again ceases to be ours, faithless Time, whom we must nevertheless trust again and again, precisely through its faithlessness, teaches us that our work belongs to us as little as does our day.

Man's strength and weakness dwell so close together that the question of premeditation really can be posed only in theory and only for the sake of making theoretical distinctions, thus in practice only when we seek to let life be governed by theory—in jurisprudence. A judge may try to analyze how much premeditation or how much mental incompetence is contained in a criminal deed. But whenever a deed is not analyzed after the fact, but rather functions in its present totality, this apparently meaningful distinction becomes meaningless.

First of all, it is meaningless with regard to the violated cosmic order, which demands to be restored by some healing "counter-deed"—though this always will retain a symbolic quality because there are only spontaneous deeds but no spontaneous "counter-deeds." But second, this distinction is also meaningless in view of God's mercy, which, according to a great Talmudic saying, turns premeditated acts into acts committed by an error of judgment.[1]

---

1. FR: Babylonian Talmud Yuoma, 36b: "Moses said before the Holy One, blessed be He: 'Lord of the Universe, when Israel sins before Thee, and then does penance, account their premeditated sins as errors.' "

And finally (and most amazingly), this distinction is meaningless even for the consciousness of the evil-doer himself. For when this consciousness confronts that deed, its own deed, it must not attempt to analyze it scientifically but instead must face it in its oppressive and unfinished presence, as an indivisible entity. It therefore cannot know where clear thinking stopped and his confusion began. And it must therefore reject any appeal based on his creatureliness, which his advocate may make on his behalf before the throne of God, disdaining it as an unworthy subterfuge—as does the author of this poem.

31. RETURN

Oh God, only You I desire,
  even if my lips never said so.
If I could only live a moment in Your grace
  how gladly I would then embrace death,
And lay my spirit's peace into Your hand
  and sleep gently with a smile on my face.
Removed from You—oh death in life's goblets!
  snuggled up to You—oh life in death's grip!
However, I do not know with what to approach You
  and which service, which deed could reach You.
Teach me Your ways, oh God,
  and free me from folly's compelling grip.
And teach me, so long as I have strength to repent,
  and do not disregard my penitent demeanor,
Before I become a burden to myself, before
  the joints of my bones bow to higher pressure
And I lie down unwillingly, and the moth
  gnaws at my bones, which have long been tired,
and I go to where the fathers went
  and find my final rest where they made a resting place.
A silent stranger on the earth's back
  in its belly I will shine as heir.
The young years produced only for themselves—
  when will I set down the poles of my tent?
He gave me the world into my heart—whose desires
  lulled me in a sleep that made me forget my end.
How can I serve my creator, when I,
  enmeshed in images, am a slave to desire.
Those who tomorrow are brothers to the worms,—can one imagine
  that today they vie for honor and for glory?
How happy my heart is on joyous days!
  Perhaps already tomorrow they may have passed.
Day and night, united tirelessly,
  attacked my flesh in order to kill it.
Strewn in the air, turned into dust—those two
  in the end satisfy their hatred.
What shall I say, I, who, since the days of my youth
  till they devour me, have been driven by hostile desires!

31] This poem, which in some communities has been made part of the morning liturgy for the Day of Atonement, does not look back to life's origin. Instead, it speaks from the middle of life, which here (as in the famous Latin hymn) is seen as already surrounded by death. Or, in the poet's own words: in the middle of life, there can be death. But also (and this is the particular turn that this poem gives the question): even in death, there can also be life.

What do I have on earth, if not Your grace?
    If I do not receive, You, what will I receive?
I am naked and bereft of all good deeds,
    Only Your Righteousness cloaks me.
Why do I move my tongue, why do I try—
    oh God, only You I desire.

This either/or of being removed from or nestled close to God focuses all energy on what lies between these two—penitence and return. Before our eyes there arise ever new images of the end. Man's youth is gone, and the power of his drives and of his worldly desires which, after all, God Himself has put into his heart, seems enormous and unconquerable (Ecclesiastes 3:11[1]). The mantle of his good works has slipped off him. Naked and exposed, man cannot cover himself with any righteousness other than God's own. And so the final word of his return will have to be the same as the one with which it began, that primal word that was the first to fall from his lips. For now his yearning has become fulfillment, while before it had been emptiness. Having to yearn turns into being allowed to yearn. To have found God is not an ending but a beginning. Here, searching and finding are not distinct from one another as present and perfect tenses; rather, both are future tenses, only one is temporal and the other eternal. The word of yearning is spoken by both.

---

1. "He hath made everything beautiful in its time; also He hath set the world in their heart, yet so that man cannot find out the work that God hath done from the beginning even to the end."

32. THE REWARD

Jewel, lodged in the body,
   a light, wedged in the dark—
She is tempted to flee to
   the workshop where her setting is crafted,
Fleeing there, where
   the desired fruit is distributed:
Original honey from Eden, heavenly nectar,
   and rich and finely detailed wisdom.
Then she sees the Creator walking,
   freed of all memory of her suffering,
Surrounded by all the souls
   who praise God in rhymes.

32] The third couplet of this little poem, proceeding from the soul's yearning to the reward awaiting it—the original text uses here the introductory words of the spies' report on the fruit they had found in the land (Numbers 13:27[1])—contains some thoughts that were as natural to the poet as they are strange to his present-day reader.

Even the basic premise that man may think of any reward while acting is considered obsolete by people today. Man's pride today is entrenched in the citadel built on the idea of the rewardless deed. From this vantage point, he looks contemptuously down on the "ethics of the Bible" (and that unfortunately means the New Testament no less than the Old), an ethics marching along the same road as the totally unethical morals of everyday living, which recommend being honest because "it pays in the long run," and warn against excess because it is "unhealthy." The relationship is undeniable.

When the discrepancy between biblical and philosophical ethics became too unbearable for some pious thinker, an attempt probably was made to remedy the situation by resorting to education. But from the strict ethical standpoint that refuses any reward, in which all that matters is one's conviction and not at all one's deed, such education could be only miseducation. But could one not possibly find some less elevated meeting ground for biblical ethics and the immorality of the everyday? What shall we call the plain, far below ethics' castle in the sky, where the two do meet?

The plain chosen by the Bible is that of experience. The warnings and advice offered by the common sense of a people's proverbs[2] are derived from nothing but experience. But it is exactly from those lowlands of experience that philosophical ethics flees into its own more rarefied heights. And it is exactly to those lowlands that the Bible descends. However, the experience to which

---

1. "And they told [Moses], and said: 'We came unto the land whither thou sentest us, and surely it floweth with milk and honey; and this is the fruit of it.'"

2. EJ: German proverbs have been omitted.

the Bible points does not indiscriminately embrace everything within life's horizon, as does the moral worldly experience of the popular proverb. Biblical experience embraces only a small, selected sector of life that, though, has a tendency to expand continuously until it reaches not the horizon, but the ends of the world. In other words, biblical experience is not simply the sum of human experience. It is the experience of endowment and promise, and it is given only to those who are aware of their endowment and determined to walk on the way toward that promise. But what to them is experience remains invisible to all others.

However, it is, highly significant that this experience is as brutally real as the experience of the everyday, so significant that it surely occurs only rarely. For the experience can be undergone only when a person is spread out between that certainty and this determination. This experience is not a matter of education. To gain it, one already must be educated, educated by life itself. Ask yourself whether it is really so easy to live with the certainty that every single deed will have its consequences—for its doer, not for "the world." Is that easier, truly easier, than to live with the certainty not that only that deed is permitted, but that only that deed will be considered to be good that is motivated by one's good will? What, actually, does this theory ask for other than to be accepted? Does it ask for deeds? Or does it not rather caution man to be wary of deeds—from Socrates' "Daimon" through the "Categorical Imperative" to the "Common Sense of the Real" to the "Pathos of Distance?"

The second premise, self-evident to the poet but not to the reader, is the total equality of "material" and "spiritual" rewards, the nectar of bliss and wisdom. The poet seems to see as small a distinction here as does the Bible, in which there is a hopeless intermingling of what today are called "this-worldly" and "other-worldly." Our ideas concerning the world of the beyond and of the here and now create a Platonic duality. They are much too static, making of this world and the next two entities existing side-by-side. And in practical terms, the major distinction between them is that we believe

in this world but not in the next. According to this sterile distinction, the next world, which is promised by God and hoped for by men, is both other-worldly and this-worldly: other-worldly, and entirely so, compared to our present world, this-worldly, and entirely so, for us who are awaiting it. This world will vanish once the next one appears; but we shall remain. Given that certainty, what sense does it make to ask whether our world is this-worldly or otherworldly, a question neither our prophets nor Christianity's apostles would even have understood. When you give a piece of bread to a hungry man, he will not ask whether it was baked of domestic or imported flour.

But it was out of this soil that the ultimate freedom could grow, a freedom that in the rapture—felt already in this world—of its love of God, disdains the bliss of the coming one, somewhat *toto coelo,* really for the sake of an entire heaven. This is completely different from the Kantian's stoical and haughty contempt for rewards. For here, the lover of God believes and knows that "one hour's bliss in the world to come is worth more than an entire life in this one."[3] Still, out of this highest abundance of love he prefers one hour's active nearness to God in this world to all of life in the next one. For him no future can supplant the completely fulfilling presence of that nearness.

However, there is, a boundary that prevents such an ultimate merging of the two worlds, and it is precisely at the point where people today would like to tear down that dividing wall: at death. This is the third of those premises contained in the poem's two lines. The day of the soul's "separation" from the body (and the original engages here in an even bolder play on words than does the translation) becomes the day when the soul feasts on "the fruit of her faith." This day does not cease being a day, nor is it superseded by "eternity within every moment." What may have kept the

---

3. Midrash Rabbah, Leviticus 111:1: "Better is one hour of repentance and good deeds in this world than the whole life of the world to come; and better is one hour of the even-tempered spirit of the world to come than all the life of this world" (Soncino translation).

poet from letting this "eternity within every moment"—of which he was as aware as are his modern readers and their representatives (as evidenced by many passages in these poems)—take the place of the "day of separation?"

True, eternity can break into any moment; but what it seizes is that moment alone. There are only a few moments that contain the whole of life in such a way that eternity can grasp it. There is the moment of birth, when all of life lies still ahead; in the course of one's life, there are one or two moments that may prove decisive for its future course; and then, there is the moment of death, when life is completed. Thus only in death is life a really existing whole. It is here alone that life has this worldly reality, and if one wanted to withdraw it from eternity's grasp, this would mean that life could never be a lived whole.

We do know something of the things that happen in life. Of death, we know both less and more, namely nothing as well as everything. We know everything that death is for us while we are alive and nothing that it will be for us once we are dead. This knowledge about death that we have in life is our most precious possession, and it grows along with any increase in genuine knowledge that we may gain. Whoever does not respect this mystery— that of our total lack of knowledge of death from the perspective of the next world—and who instead desecrates this mystery, together with the fools who exist at all times under various names, is punished by the loss of that genuine omniscience that is his possession.

There is surely a connection between that which, from the perspective of the here and now, can be completely familiar, far more familiar than anything else, precisely because it is completely unknown from the perspective of the other side. What we can see completely from here and not at all from there must be the same, for whatever is true here is also true there. Yet this certainty, which does not allow our foot to falter as it approaches the border between the all-known and the all-unknown, does not illumine for our eyes the darkness in which the unknown dwells.

33. THIS SOUL HERE

We strive to rhyme a song,
Him, who Himself has given

The loftier the thoughts,
   While I must remain earthbound,
   And yet: within the mind's limit—
   Because light sparks descended
Those who are within the reach
             of the light
Him,

   Here my Being frets in the
   What I took to be insignificant in
   Desire, the arch enemy,
   I anticipate with dread the day
Follow me into
But Him, who has given

   And the dust wanted to
   Though it only manages to pine
   Be quiet, heart! Silence your
             aspiration!
   Near You I would like to sleep!

Do not drive away
You, who Yourself have given

   In the heavens
   And she may not behold You
   She may behold You here:
   Thus, add the maid servant—to
They take shelter in You, oh Lord,
You, who Himself has given

   Extinguish the light, kindle
   That the night may dissolve,
   that the dismal wall of sin
   that the mild light of grace may
May You cast a protective glance
You, who Yourself have

to see His Glory,
us this soul here.

the farther away He flees,
He can ascend to great heights.
the heart finds Him
from the throne's canopy,

desire Him,
who has given us this soul here.

dark, my light dimmed.
my youth—convicts me.
seduces like a snake.
when my soul will not
   this ground here,—
   us this soul here.

consider itself equal to Him?
and to desire?

Fear for your life!
And when Your day of
            redemption comes,
   her who dwells here as Your servant,—
   us this soul here.

Your servant's soul seeks You.
if she looks left or right.
shatter the dark, oh wonder!
the women of Your covenant people,
   and behold Your Glory,—
   us this soul here.

it anew, wondrously.
in which Your anger is anchored,
may dissolve between us,
penetrate into anger's dark recesses!
   from the heavens onto the vine,—
   given us this soul here.

33] The soul is not a thing. All psychology from Aristotle and Thomas to Haeckel and Wundt has foundered on this truth. The appearance that the soul must be a thing, a substance, a "something," is engendered by the fact that it is "here," as all things are. But though things may indeed be "here," they can just as easily be "there." The soul, however, always can only "be here." A soul "there," a soul in the third person, does not exist. The soul is always present—my soul, your soul, our soul, and thus always: this soul here.

Our poem, a supplement to the hymn "The Soul of all the Living" from the Sabbath and Holiday morning prayer, focuses on that "hereness" with an intensity that goes beyond all artistic requirements. In three of six cases, the recurring phrase *this here* (*diese hier,* referring to the soul—Jeremiah 38:16[1]) is rhymed with the same phrase (*dieses hier*)[2] in another biblical passage, which, given our context, can also refer to the soul. Thus the figures of the biblical women Rachel and Hagar arise metaphorically to represent the pearl that sank down from the divine throne; even *metaphorically* is too strong a word for the singling out of the phrase *this here,* which eventually culminates in Psalm 80:15,[3] where the comparison of Israel to a vine is then applied to the soul.

---

1. "'As the Lord liveth, that made us this soul.'"

2. EJ: However, neither the poem's rhymes nor the biblical passages referred to by FR use the equivalent of his 'this here.'

3. "Look from heaven, and behold, and be mindful of this vine."

34. DELUSION AND TRUTH

Yes, expert of truth, you must destroy delusion;
    live here like those who live in the grave below the ground.
Elevate and beautify the service of God because you are alive,
    leave the beauty of the world to others.
May your labor affect the morning
    rather than the morning catch up with your sleep.
And learn about tomorrow from today, and happily
    leave the world to those who are fooled by it.
Better you serve before God's countenance,
    than that spectres claim you as servant.
Before God's countenance, His Being and His Name,
    praise every soul in exultation and in song.

34] Yet the soul does have a place, though it is no "there" to which our finger could point, but an "in-between." The soul moves, or it can move, between two poles: delusion and truth, world and service, masks and the face. These three designations in no way have "the same meaning"—this favorite category of scholarly as well as popular metaphysics offends not just a poet's, but any speaker's linguistic common sense. But for the soul that moves between them, these designations do share the same line of vision. While enmeshed in delusion, it also remains in the service of God, standing before His countenance. The soul's spiritual order, incarnate form, and mysterious vision are not one and the same; but they become one in the poet's own life, the unity of which is precisely a unity of that which, both "before" and "after," is all too often sundered, even in traditional Jewish life.

35. The World as Woman

This earth was a forbidden spouse to me,
  because my self was more precious than the universe to me.
Now she shares her splendor with others;
  seeing that I chose God as my portion.
Shall she choose me, her enemy unto death?
  Shall I choose her, who cause me to sin?
I, spouse of duty, despise her, she takes off my shoes,
  and spits into my face.

35] This little poem, loaded with some enormously explosive material, adopts the widely used medieval topos of "the world as woman." But the Jewish poet's relationship to both woman and world does not permit him to depict the one or the other simply as temptress, as did the medieval Christian masters of literature and painting. To make the image of either woman or world Jewishly authentic, he must add a number of specific features to both. The means for such specification is provided by the law.

It is not woman as temptress, but marital relations that constitute the subject matter of the poem's metaphors. The marital partners' disdain for each other, which in the middle of the poem finds expression in the general term for choosing a spouse (a word unencumbered by marriage law) is exposed in the framing couplets by two images drawn from circumstances particular to Jewish marital law. It speaks in words that sound like hammer blows of a woman's monthly period of impurity, during which even her husband is absolutely forbidden to touch her (Leviticus 15:15ff.). And the knifelike final couplet recounts the ceremony described in Deuteronomy (25:5ff.), in which the widow of a man whose brother refuses to marry her exposes him to public contempt as "that barefoot one."

Both rules are derived from a natural feeling, but the law vastly added to their impact. The one extended that prohibition of marital relations well beyond the naturally indicated time span, so that it came to affect half of married life; the other, having grown out of a natural reaction—now given legal status—to the refusal of what should have been a voluntary action, custom and law came to make by a mere gesture that, by now required as well as enforceable, would change a basically personal situation into a generally accepted norm. Both rules were meant to safeguard the sanctification of marriage within the framework of law and custom—an absolute sanctification, not merely one relative to "human weakness."

This characterizes precisely the Jewish attitude toward "the world." It is an attitude filled with asceticism, yet it is not at all ascetic. In principle, it is even totally unascetic. To the Jew, the

world is not a wanton seductress, tempting him to sin, but his con-
secrated wife. But the world has become "impure"; the law there-
fore extends the fence meant to guard him against serving false
gods, until finally half the world is forbidden to him. Yet whatever is
permitted to him he should not "have as if he did not have it." He
should indeed really "have" it. True, there are innumerable foods he
is forbidden to have. But he should enjoy those he may have; in fact,
he is even enjoined by law to savor a special Sabbath meal.

And now the opening image must be abandoned, since it does
not sufficiently convey the dramatic mutuality of disdain. And thus
it steers toward its concluding image: the world that scorns its
scorner. Suffering, which had originally been seen as a voluntary
and personal act—such as the prophet's martyrdom—becomes now
the entire people's dutifully accepted, routinely borne suffering,
the fate of the Jew. What originally had been suffering from a freely
chosen individual deed—the martyrdom of a prophet—has now
become routinely borne, fateful suffering from customary, dutiful
activity, Jewish destiny. But once it has become a habit, it is not
perceived as asceticism, but rather as the natural way of life, which
could not possibly be any different.

The Jew's knowledge that the world really belongs to him,
both for work and enjoyment is—despite all asceticism—not condu-
cive to the development of an ascetic mood. At most, it makes for
this poem's defiant battle hymn. By contrast, the medieval Christian's
consciousness is filled with asceticism; but for that very reason it
takes up very little space in his life, and that space is and must be
carefully delimited hierarchically.

36. Wise Teachings

Heart, beware! Can one have courage,
  whose heart lies on His scales?
Do not desire to see hidden things,
  so that the fire will not consume you.
Keep away from His work! He does not
  reveal the statutes of His might to you.
You are no angel. May your presumption
  not lead you to the place of the great.
In the upheaval of uncertain times,
  lay your well-being into His hand.
And be blessed not to be a troublemaker,
  do not fear the whip of unhappiness.
Do not listen to human beckoning,
  only listen to God's invitation.
Why do you serve earthly rulers?
  One kisses the knout of the other!
When in their favor—what uncertain luck,
  When in their wrath—what wild anger!
Be blessed, therefore, if you serve the Lord,
  whose power reigns absolute.
He gave you richly through His doorkeeper,
  and he never closed off His estate to You.
Wait for His advice and do not trust
  the academic wisdom of the scholars.
Then you will yourself see results and
  even someday your descendants in the future.
Build a penitential altar and thereupon
  bind the products of your sinful drive.
For He is kind to the one who is near; but also
  he who is distant shall hurry home lightfootedly.
Do not inquire into His deeds,
  remain quietly in the shadow of His courtyard.
He who, whether he takes or gives life,
  does what is good in His eyes.
He said: Let there be light—and it was;
  He commanded—and the earth obeyed.
And God beheld all that He made,
  and it was very good.

36] The "wisdom" to which the poet has dedicated himself is marked also by a certain casuistry, though its overall goal is the attainment of that moderation for which men—and particularly those of a passionate disposition—have always striven by a self-imposed discipline.

Behind the poet's sequence of wise sayings, one can sense the rich possibilities that Spain, with its countless princely courts, offered to the Jew of that time but also the dangers to which it exposed him. The formal appeal of this little didactic work lies in its quick rhythm, which, by means of the internal rhyme in the first line, gives heavy emphasis to the caesura right at the start, and thus this rhythm itself experiences an inner acceleration, so to speak. But the beauty of its content depends on the way in which the rules of moral wisdom are integrated into the trust in God that precedes all wisdom. In the last couplet, this trust sounds an infinitely moving and quiet final note with the simple literalness of its biblical quote[1] that, it would now appear, has from the very beginning lain dormant within the poem's rhythm.

---

1. Genesis 1:31.

37. SERVANTS

Servants of time   are servants of   servants;
  only God's   servant alone   is free.
Therefore, when every   human being   requests his portion;
  my heart says: May God Himself   be my share.

37] "For they are My servants," says the Torah in explanation of the general liberation of all servants in the fiftieth year and in order to set up certain norms for regulating the power a man may exercise over his brother (Leviticus 25:42 and 25:55). From this source, out of which has flowed a good part—the best part—of all world history since that time, the poet also has filled the cup of this epigram. It begins (quite epigrammatically) as a concentrated summary of all the widely disseminated moral wisdom that could ever be known and ends (quite lyrically) with the yearning call of Lamentations[1] for the God of man's heart.

---

1. Lamentations 3:24: "The Lord is my portion, says my soul, therefore will I hope in him."

38. WORLD

Oh heart, why do you pursue possessions and riches,
    and follow the cursed world which is crooked and never straight!
Observe: he who lengthens the train of his coat,
    easily stumbles over his own robe.
The deception of the world is obvious, but
    you nevertheless seek its glory. Oh, don't seek!

38] This little poem says in a few words what others say in many. The word that encapsulates the object of its negation, which I have rendered as "world," actually is *time*. There is a very peculiar reason why the poet does not say "world" (as does, for instance, Ghazzali,[1] who greatly influenced him): in the language of the Bible, the word which will later be used for "world" had the meaning "eternity." True, later on the language does distinguish between "this" and the "other" world. But the term *world* as such cannot convey a pessimistic feeling because it is too heavily loaded with the meaning of "eternity"; so the term *time*, which in the Bible has neither a positive nor a negative connotation, will have to do.

Scripture broke into the world as a differentiating force. But it is for that very reason that it did not yet contain the ultimate, the most fundamental distinction that was later to emanate from it. The cutting edge of a knife must have no nicks or cuts.[2] In the same way, Scripture does not itself contain the dichotomy between this world and the next, which everywhere would grow out of its aura, even within Judaism (though this dichotomy is entirely different from the Greek one between a "real" world and a world of appearance since in Judaism both worlds are known to be equally real). Thus Scripture is the warranty that this opposition, which it itself evoked originally, will not endure and that this world and the next are destined to come together again in that eternity out of which they had emerged as separate entities.

Yehuda Halevi's poem is medieval—neither biblical nor messianic. To assume, however, that these Middle Ages have today already been replaced by "modernity" would be a grave mistake. This kind of "Middle-Age" encompasses all of world history.

---

1. FR: Islamic religious thinker (1058–1111).
2. Rosenzweig here refers to the rules governing the qualities of a knife to be used in Kosher slaughtering.

39. THE SICK PHYSICIAN

If You heal me, my God, then I am whole.
  May the fire of Your anger not burn me.
Yours are spices and perfumes,—whether good
  or bad, whether strong or weak.
Because You are the one who chooses, You, not I, and Your
  omniscience guides and does not guide Your arrow to its goal.
I do not trust in my elixir,
  may I only partake of Your medicine.

39] Yehuda Halevi was a physician. He is therefore free of that belief in the miraculous power of the art of healing, to which even a person who never tires of ridiculing "those doctors" when he is healthy may fall hopelessly prey when he himself falls sick. Thus free of this superstition, the poet can sense so much more keenly the connection between healing [*Heilung*] and salvation [*Heil*], a connection already indicated in the German language and referred to in the words of Jeremiah (17:14).[1]

---

1. "Heal me, oh Lord, and I shall be healed; Save me, and I shall be saved."

40. To the Sabbath

Yes, to You I raise   my cup of love:
   Hail to You, hail,   my seventh day!

For six work days   I am committed to you,
Even if I get tired   of the work,
They seemed to me like   merely hours,
That's how I love You,   You my day of rest—
Hail to You, hail,   my seventh day!

When on the first day   I set out on worker's path,
For whom else but You, Shabbat,   do I prepare.
He who guides the heavens   blesses You.
You be my portion; whatever   else I do—
Hail to You, hail,   my seventh day!

Sacred light from   sacred source,
Sun and stars want to   bask in Your light.
On the second and third,   what did I gain!
Hidden in dark are the   lights of the fourth day—
Hail to You, hail,   my seventh day!

I hear the fifth day   prepare the happy tidings.
Oh soul, will you experience bliss   tomorrow night?
Though early in fetters, night   brings freedom's reign,
When my shepherd invites me to   His royal feast—
Hail to You, hail,   my seventh day!

Your morning dawns, sixth day   sure of my soul.
Does it already sense   a time that's worry-free?
Restlessly and fleetingly glimpsing   where it is safe;
At night it breathes freely: unrest and   haste disappear at once—
Hail to You, hail,   my seventh day!

Yes, delicious is to me   Your evening shadow,
Wherein I once more behold   my hallowed beloved.
Approach with apples,   come with heaping platters!
Oh sacred day, my friend,   beloved You—
Hail to You, hail,   my seventh day!

40] This Sabbath Song, which Nobel would sing at his dining table with a glorious melody he himself composed, belongs to the section with the title "Soul." To say that is to describe its singular character among other songs for the Sabbath, even Yehuda Halevi's own. For all of those could be included in the section entitled "People," or possibly the one called "God."

Jewish Sabbath poetry is of a magnificent objectivity. The subjective aspect of the Sabbath is self-evident. For the Sabbath, as our ancients already knew, is also "given to man"; it was not just that man was given to the Sabbath.* The Lurianic Kabbalah is the first to develop the forms in which the day's subjective aspect is objectively validated as well. However, Yehuda Halevi's hymn breaks a path for itself and out of itself. It treats of man and of his Sabbath. No, it does not treat of either. Instead, it speaks directly to the Sabbath, seizing upon the most simplistic, the most basic phenomenon about it: the fact that it is the seventh day. And instead of using this fact to polemicize against celebrating the week's first or sixth day, it simply takes a look at the seventh.

---

1. "The Sabbath is made for man, not man for the Sabbath," in Mark II, 27, and in the Mikilta *Ki Tissa,* said by Simeon ben Menasah.

So I sing songs of praise   to You, Shabbat,
That I pay homage   to Your grace.
    Day full of joy to me,   of three-fold meal,
Delightful banquet,   heavenly repose—
Hail to You, hail,   my seventh day.

Because the Sabbath is the seventh day, the week is organized around it; the days turn into "single hours," much as the seven years of the Patriarch Jacob's service to win Rachel turned into single days, "because he loved her so." Five of the poem's stanzas reflect this inner rhythm of the week in the mirror of the soul. The sixth stanza ends, then, in a wonderful comparison with the prescription for the "seven days of feasting," that seven-day wedding celebration during which the "seven blessings" of the wedding ceremony may be repeated as often as one sits down at one's table with new guests ("new faces," in the law's language), to say a blessing with them after a meal.[1] The Sabbath is received in the same nuptial manner as a "new face"; not as a guest, however, but as the ever-new bridegroom, the soul's beloved. And thus the poet toasts the Sabbath with the drink of love in this song, which maintains throughout the immediacy of personal address, of the I and the You.

---

1. In traditional Judaism, a marriage is followed by seven days of festive meals with friends and relatives, after each of which seven blessings are recited.

41. FREE

A servant who happily   awakens in the   morning
  in search of You,   and beseeches You   for freedom—
Today is the day of rest! Bestow the warmth of Your power onto the
  son of Your maid,   for he is blessed with   leisure time.
This is the day, on which song   strengthens   the soul
  and freely dedicates itself   to Your honor and to   Your call.

41] In spite of the fact that mystical thought was very late in picking it up, the Sabbath since its very origin has been the day of the soul. Even the introductory words, which celebrate the day (on the preceding evening within the congregation, on the following morning at home) as the sign of creation between God and Israel (Exodus 31:16f.[1]), use a strange word to describe the divine Creator's rest, a word which originally may have meant "a sigh of relief." But given a more mature feel for language, it denotes something that makes of the Sabbath a day on which man is at peace with his self, with his soul.

This triad of freedom, the sigh of relief, and the soul's fulfilling sense of being at peace with itself, sounds the basic note of this poem's three couplets and their three end rhymes. But this triadic chord, whose harmony would be destroyed if one of its components was missing, also sounds the basic notes of the Sabbath itself. The folly of playing off the "social" against the "religious" significance of the Sabbath law, emphasized respectively in Deuteronomy and Exodus, is demonstrated by our poem's linkage of its first and third couplets by that blissful word that, taken from the passage describing the Supreme Being's rest, is used here to describe the bondsman's sigh of relief (Exodus 23:12[2]).

Any separation of "the social" from "the religious," or vice versa, makes of the social an eternally open question and of the religious an eternally ready answer. Thus, it takes away from the question the healing power of its ability to be answered over and over again and takes away from the answer the test of its eternal questionability. The freedom of the bondsman is meaningless unless it is also the master's freedom; the freedom of the master is unreal, unless it is translated into the bondman's freedom. For every man is a master, and every man is a bondsman.

---

1. "Wherefore the children of Israel shall keep the Sabbath, to observe the Sabbath throughout their generations, for a perpetual covenant. It is a sign between me and the children of Israel forever, for in six days the Lord made the heaven and earth, and on the seventh day he rested, and was refreshed. . . ."

2. Six day thou shalt do they work, and on the seventh day thou shalt rest; that thy ox and thy ass may rest; and the son of thy handmaid, and the stranger, may be refreshed.

42. Sabbath Morning

Yes, You are beautiful,   only one,   when You are mine,   still more
                                                                          delightful
Today, when you stand   before the Lord,   whose Name is my
                                                          redeemer here.
And the repose which You   eagerly request   will be the reward
                                                            for your effort,
Therefore, be silent   and submit to and carry   the yoke,
You sense the   secret power   of time—open   Your heart's ear to it!
Learn to do good,   not evil!   Because such deeds—would
                                                  almost be madness.
Sanctify the Rock   —may every breath   praise Him,—   oh jewel
With joyous song,   and before Him,   the Name of the Lord,   rejoice!

42] This is a worshiper's soliloquy, directed at his "only one," as the psalmist calls his soul (Psalms 22:21 and 35:17), while he is meditating on the "mystery of time": the change from toil to tranquility, which the Sabbath brings to him in a seven-day rhythm, a change meant—and that is the mystery—to be more than a rhythm of the soul, namely a presage of the world to come.[1]

---

1. *"Vorzeichen des Weges der Welt."*

43. LIFE

"Rejoice, only one, in the one God of faith,
   with many fine melodies rejoice, with many songs.
Study His Law. And always
   feel free to pour out your tears of supplication.
Do not value earthly treasures, and do treasure
   the acquisition of wise deed and thought.
Leave the bad for the good, entire tribe:
   stupid people! You barely have any spirit.
Your existence, even if long,—leaves only a slight trace
   like a tiny moment in time."
She answers, "I soon understood,
   my friend, that all of this is true and pure.
Begin, a beggar before God,
   to unite the sounds of thanks and of rejoicing.
Even if you think that I am troubled, know:
   my heart is awake, even if I seem to sleep.
I left behind the hills, and am now in the valley of death,
   banned to the shadows and to the bones of the dead.
Before God counsels me to rest, and
   the bond of life is bound up in the coffin.
Because my redeemer lives, He will bless my
   memory of Him and take me into His fold,
'To life!' Souls still living in the bosom of life
   rejoice in His soul."

43] The "only one" proclaims the "One and Only." Hermann Cohen referred to this poem in his great apologia,[1] when he divulged to his students the insight of his old age: the need to take the step from "ethics" into "religion," in recognition of the fact that before God, the "One and Only," man too becomes an "only one," singular, a lonely being.

This poem is, once again, a man's soliloquy directed to his soul. Just as the leader of a prayer service knows that the congregation has authorized him to speak or to intercede for it (hence the designation "Authorizations" for the entire group of short, nonstrophic introductory poems to be recited by him) so, exactly so, should the soul intercede for man, speaking as the "only one" to the "Only One." And as a person who authorizes another to perform a certain task will first describe to him in lofty terms what it is all about, but then will get down to simpler language to speak of the particulars of the service to be rendered, so it is here, too. But this authorized one—the soul—evades the schoolmasterly demand with an easy motion. It does not need any authorization since it has authority. This authority has come to it from somewhere else—its home above, from which it has sunk down into this world of the body and death, an alien guest. Small wonder, then, that to an earthly eye it seems to be dreaming just when it is most awake.

"This world of death"—death and the brevity of earthly existence, facts cited by man as he admonishes the soul to do its duty, do not frighten it. For it is waiting only to be called away, to receive what to it is a call to return home. In life, it was fated to die. But on the stone under which its body, sheltered, will rest, will be written these words: "May the soul be bound up in the bond of life."

"The bond of life"—at this point, at the transition from the ninth to the tenth couplet—which in Hebrew is even more strongly accentuated by the opening acclamation of the acrostic that forms the poet's name and that, with its division of the poem into three

---

1. Hermann Cohen, *Die Religion der Vernunft aus den Quellen des Judentums* (1929); *Religion of Reason out of the Sources of Judaism,* translated by Simon Kaplan (New York: Ungar, 1972).

parts, can for once not be reproduced in translation—the soul's speech, which has been peculiarly alien from the start, begins to leave behind anything even resembling an answer. These last six lines convey a singular sense of floating away that has an immediate, one might say a musical, impact. With their repetitions of the same motif, chords that seem to follow each other ever more closely until, rapturously and ethereally ascending, they die away in the distance, these lines remind one of the floating away of the final chords in some of Beethoven's slow movements.

The constantly repeated motif is the word *life.* From its first appearance in the quote on the headstone to the end of the poem, the original has twenty-two words, of which six, that is, nearly every third one, refer to life—with ever intensifying, ever more exuberant, ever more serene certitude.

However, such certitude, which in earthly life is but a weak flickering little flame that threatens to go out at any moment, yet never does, nevertheless draws all its nourishment from this earthly life, from whatever in life is life. Because in the double meaning of this word, earth and heaven are touching; and because the original biblical passage (I Samuel 25:29) from which the headstone inscription full of other-worldly hope has been taken, is said in entirely worldly terms. Because not only am I alive here and now, "my Redeemer liveth" as well (Job 19:25), and because the soul knows that He is "mindful" of it (Psalm 115:12). Because of all this it also can be sure of His further blessing, today and always, here and there because He lives.

And so the call "Life!" "To Life!" or "Into Life!" with which we mean to hail earthly life (I Samuel 1:25–26) now hails the soul, as it hails Him, the One who lives now and forever, here and there. That call "Into Life!" then, becomes the password of admission into "the community of the souls of His righteous ones" who are "still alive" in life's mysterious womb. And with that, the poem, turning from the "Here and Now" to the "There and Forever," concludes by quoting one of Ecclesiastes' gloomy sayings, which "praises the dead and even the still unborn more than the living that are still alive" (Ecclesiastes 4:2). "Still."

44. THE DAY

My desire shall yearn   for the source of my life,
  before my days   turn into my grave.
If only the soul which   pursues air knew,
  that she alone   is my life in the world.
And if my heart would wake up   if it would think of my end,
  and of the day on which I will be laid to rest   and will arise again,
The day, on which my eye   will behold the work of my hands,
  the day when soul and spirit   enter into His storehouse.

44] A glance from our life in time into life eternal rebounds off the wall standing between the two: the day of death. Now poised here at this watershed it views both worlds through wide open eyes.

45. Turn Back, Turn Back!

Turn, oh heart, calm your storming!
Because God already granted it.

Jewel from among your Creator's treasures!
Rally! Do you wish to retire here?
Long is the way! Refresh yourself,—
The time has come! Do that which He can praise!

Here I am a settler like our forebears,
My years pass like a shadow—
Consider, if not now, when
Will you begin to create eternal life?

And if you are eager to seek Him,
And if you have renounced all that is common—
Bravely dare to come to Him!
Your deeds accompany you.

You haughty one, know your path!
Do not get lost in the sphere of dreams!
Short is your day and long your journey—
Consider what you will say when all is said and done!

Did your eye suffer from thirst for heaven?
Will your step always hesitate before Him?
Turn back, turn back, oh Shulamit,
Home to your Father in Heaven!

45] Using the seventh verse of Psalm 116[1] as this poem's preface, Yehuda Halevi was able not merely to give it the form of a rhymed couplet but also to develop from it the recurring rhyme of the poem's five stanzas, its overall rhythm, and even its content.

The injunction to return, and to enter into the peaceful certainty that God already has granted to man what his heart is still raging for, recalls the image of a life's journey, which now becomes a journey home.

As were the patriarchs, so is the soul but a stranger and sojourner on earth. Yet it has been promised a home. And the end of the last stanza, with its reinterpretation of the wedding guests' rhythmic call to the dancing bride in the Song of Songs (7:1)[2] ("Shulamite," the "one who found peace," Song of Songs 8:10) is that celebrating soul, as a call to the soul to return and turn inward, takes up once more in its first word—Return!—the first word of the psalm verse of the introduction, as if to announce its fulfillment.

---

1. "Return, oh my soul, unto they rest."
2. "Return, return, oh Shulamite; return, return, that we may look upon thee."

46. THE ASCENT

Return, you unique one,   to your place,   oh return!
   always desire   to sit by   God's throne!
Thrones of the world—   give them up!   for you know: you
   rose up high, you achieved   the splendor of victory,   exalted one.
Bow   and give praise to God   and glory,
   where God's people   live, honor Him   with song.

46] "Return"—that word so pregnant with meaning—opens this little poem, too, but in the key that the great preceding one used only at the end. Here, the soul is no restless wanderer, not even at first. Rather, it is right away the ascending, indeed the already risen victress, the daughter of God, worshiping among His sons.

47. BREATH OF ALL LIFE

To God I sacrifice the vapor of our thanks,
To Him, in whose hand rests the breath of all life.

He is the beginning of all cause and effect:
God in the highest, beyond all measure.
The eye strains heavily to behold Him.
Known to the heart that overcame the limitations of the flesh.
Someday I shall also behold Him, free of the body—
Him, in whose hand rests the breath of all life.

He embedded the soul into the
Earthling: to be wise and clever, He
Lent it the reflection of the heavenly light—see:
Even the reflection renders it lovely and pure,
May it avail itself of my years!—
He, in whose hand rests the breath of all life.

And it consumes itself upward to the
Source, awaiting the day when it will be free of the body.
While it dwells in me, it demands
that I praise its Creator, that
He receive praise like buds on a bush—
He, in whose hand rests the breath of life.

His works testify that He is at all times and always unique:
Even as humans pass away and fade,
He alone remains. Pronouncing judgment,
He frowns on the secretiveness of the senses.
He sees whether a person is pious or a fool—
He, in whose hand rests the breath of life.

Bow to the son of the maid, your servant,
When he stands before your people!
When I enter into your chain of inheritance:
I will teach my brothers, "Praise, praise to Him!"
So that I enter into Your covenant—
You, in whose hand rests the breath of all living.

47] This great hymn, a composition meant, once again, as a complement to the prayer "Soul of all the Living," the opening words of which are repeated almost literally in its refrain, can conclude these Songs of the Soul. For it contains nearly everything the individual poems of this section have sung about: the soul's yearning for a vision of God while it is still dwelling in a body and its certitude concerning the day of separation from that body; the soul's heavenly origin and its longing to return home; and the soul's submission of its furtive thoughts to the Judgment of the Judge. Finally, it contains the moved and moving words with which the poet—humbly, yet without denying his right to it— hands over to his people the special position conferred upon him as a poet, as he wraps himself into the finality of the covenant that enfolds him and all of them like a prayer shawl.

What follows now are the Songs of the People.

PEOPLE

48. In Eternity

Sun, moon, the two eternally   keep watch;
    Day and night, their rhythm never   is disrupted.
As symbol they are   assigned to Jacob's seed,
    His people will exist forever   and will never be destroyed.
If God's left hand pushes them away,   the right hand brings them near.
    Even in dire times   they never think of blasphemy.
No, they firmly trust that   they will exist forever, and
    that their end will not come   so long as there are day and night.

48]

Thus saith the Lord,

Who giveth the sun for a light by day,

And the ordinances of the moon and the stars for a light by night,

Who stirreth up the sea, that the waves thereof roar,

The Lord of hosts is His name:

If these ordinances depart from before Me,

Saith the Lord,

Then the seed of Israel shall also cease

From being a nation before Me forever.

Thus saith the Lord:

If heaven above can be measured,

And the foundations of the earth searched out beneath,

Then will I also cast off all the seed of Israel

For all they have done, saith the Lord.

(Jeremiah 31:35–38)

49. GOD SPEAKS

May hope remain young!   May your heart remain   strong in hope!
  why do you calculate   the end of misery,   almost listlessly?
Stand up and speak,   and lyrics   compose anew!
  Your sullied name   still says: My   tent is in you.
And ignore him   who blasphemes, even if   he shouts loudly!
  Gently you lead the herd,   —you are the last one   to come home.
Your Dearest One tortures you,   But He, He also   gives you joy.
  Your ailing part is He.   He is also   your elixir.
Your loving is most beautiful   while you await Him who   will redeem you.
  Do not rush! You will yet see   the glory and grace   of my deed.
When they boast   of their king,   you boast:
  He, Jacob's saint,   is my King,   my savior.

49] The power that eternally sustains life is hope. In this poem, which could not be part of the Bible for it is filled with the kind of certitude that only an exile of a thousand years could ripen, God Himself calls upon Israel to have hope. Now hope has become "the greatest" of all; it has absorbed the forces of love. The poem flatly states that it is Judaism's secret to transmute love into hope for redemption: "Your loving is most beautiful while you await Him who will redeem you."

This is a hope not because but in spite of everything. It is a hope that is not allowed to calculate deadlines since all of them have elapsed. It is a hope that, even in the prophet's prophecy of shame (Ezekiel 23), can hear the proud claim "my tent is in her" contained in the name Oholigah,[1] the female figure who symbolizes Israel's depravity. It is a hope that, in Jacob's answer to his rash brother (Genesis 33:14[2]), can sense, as does the Midrash, the world historical irony of him who, though walking slowly, eventually will reach his goal. It is a hope that is as well aware of its bearer's frailty as of the undying forces of renewal inhering in that very frailty. And it is a hope that has the courage to set over against all the kings of the earth the King of Heaven.

---

1. Rosenzweig is referring to the literal meaning of this Hebrew name.

2. Jacob to Esau: "Let my lord, I beg you, pass over before his servant, and I will lead on slowly, according to the pace of the cattle that goes before me and the children are able to endure, until I come to my lord to Seir."

50. FESTIVAL OF LIGHTS

Always through Your light, bright Lord, do we see light.

Hope—pointing the way for the people
Throughout the night, how long will its beam shine
and sin follow it?
Oh may it be crowned with light,   like fire and light!

Encircle the bare head with sacred ornament,
The torn robe—replace it
With priestly robes, allow the seed of the first light
To blossom anew, as in "let there be light"   and there was light.

May Your sign strengthen shaking knees,
Let the angel precede them,
And may soon the day dawn
When salvation envelops the pious and humiliation those   who   despise
                                                                      the light!

He who, as a servant, yearns for shade,
Surround him with the light of Your salvation,
And call to him: "Where there is dark,
How long will you remain there? Come, be cheerful!   There was light!"

"Grace, grace"—exclaim! Make palm trees
Grow in rows of two, so that
In the Temple the oil will flow.
To light lights for Him, who is bright,   to His glory!

50] This song is dedicated to the Sabbath of the winter Festival of Lights.[1] It takes from that day's prophetic portion (Zechariah 2:14–4:7) the images of the soiled priest who is clothed once more in clean garments, of the Lord's call of grace, and of the two olive trees. From the breadth of Scripture it takes the symbolism of light— the light of God and the light of man, of primeval creation and of final redemption. And from the depths of the people's consciousness it takes this fusion of the world-encompassing symbolism of light with the national liberation and purification that this holiday celebrates. For the lights, whose fuel seemed almost exhausted and nevertheless miraculously sufficed, these lights around which the holiday's customs are centered—during these eight days they are rightfully permitted to signify to the people the divine light of the Psalms (36:10[2]), in which they may glimpse the light of their own life and destiny.

---

1. Chanukah is also known as the "Festival of Lights."
2. "For with Thee is the fountain of life; in Thy light do we see light."

51. MORNING SERVICE

All morning stars   sing up to You,
  For their luminosity   arises from You.
And the rungs of God,   fixed on their post,
  Night and day spread the overflow   of Your praise.
And the members of the community   learned it from them,
  When happily they bring the morning light   into Your house.

52. LIGHT

By day and by night songs shall   surround Him youthfully,
  He allowed the fire of His eye   to pour into mine.
He chases away the night   by lighting a high bright light,
  he courageously tore   a window into my clouds.
And he presented me   with His own beam,
  His spirit became word for me   through the efforts of the saintly ones.
The original light   paved the way for me,
  Shining from Seir,   from the Sinai,—
I imbibed the nectar   from His word and rejoiced:
  Oh come and see   my eye spew forth light!

51] This is one of the small poems meant to be recited by the leader of the congregation's daily service as an introduction to the regular morning prayer, something like Bach's preludes, played by the organist before the chorale.

In the early dawn, stillness surrounds the small praying congregation. But at a global distance there are two vast circles surrounding them: the circle of stars and the circle of angels. And from all three there arises the same song of praise: Israel is the lonely center of the world, whose sound is echoed by the heavens.

52] Israel can be the center of the universe because the line of world time runs through its center. In the poem before us, this center is also located precisely—in the peculiar verse in which the poet answers God's devastating question to Job: "By what way is the light parted . . . upon earth?" (Job 38:24), not with a devastated "I do not know," but with a humbly audacious trusting reply that dissolves the mystery of creation into the commandment of revelation: "The mysterious way of the primeval light is none other than the one You commanded me to take."

In these ten lines, through which flashes all the light of heaven and earth, a line can be drawn from the glowing of the divine countenance into the reflection of this glow in the human face, a line that leads from the primeval light of creation and the created lights, across the lightning of Sinai, into the eyes of the worshiper at the Feast of Revelation,[1] for which this poem was composed— One light.

---

1. The Jewish holiday of Shavvot or "weeks," (Pentecost).

53. Conquered Darkness

Did they hunt you, little dove, until
Hurt penetrated even the cry of sorrow—
Raise the banners of your fighting forces
Around Him, who, sure in His heart!
Also for You set aside a day—
  He creates light and He creates darkness.

Loudly resounded his creative Yes,
Momentarily everything was created.
The world saw that He was powerful
and did not wish the return of chaos,
From the East He summoned
  His light, and banished darkness.

A host of clouds heard the word
"Let there be light." A stony refuge
was—recognized at once,
It tore asunder; and in its place
The foundation sank. It became known:
  Light triumphs over darkness.

May His light enter into my darkness!
May He send him, who will raise me up,
so that my people may break through to the light,
And that my treasure may be surrounded by glory—
He is the rock, whose glory I praise,
  In the darkness.

53] The connection between the creation of light and the re-kindling of the people's extinguished light—the light of the people whose sanctuary stands on the world's foundation stone—is an inexhaustible theme. Here the point of departure is the concept and the rhyme of darkness. For this poem is meant, as are most of its kind, to complement the morning prayer, which also includes Isaiah's great words about the God who creates both light and darkness (Isaiah 45:7[1]). It is this "and" around which the poems revolves.

---

1. "I form the light, and create darkness; I make peace, and create evil; I am the Lord, that doeth all these things."

54. THE DAY AT THE SEA OF REEDS

May they rejoice brightly in the morning sun   on the festival   of Your might,
The multitudes who are dedicated to you, and shielded   and protected
                                                    by You.
Here they stand, poor in Your world,   before You   in supplication,
And they bring before Your throne   the heavy weight   of words.
Those whom You chose   for eternal glory   go the narrow path,
Your Law as a guide post, so   their ear receives   Your word.
Help Your messiah, You!   Come, shield,   take your watch!
Remember all of the world's days   when Israel   bore your yoke.
Allow Your Redeemer arm,   which once fought   Your battle,
To shine as then, retrieve   the banner   from the night!
The human breast is filled with Your breath,   all are united   in Your might,
May it sing of Your splendor   in the morning star's   jubilation.

54] Light, the light of the sunrise and that of the morning stars' jubilation at creation (Job 38:7[1]), surges around this poem, too. It belongs in the liturgy for that day of the Passover [*Oster*] holiday on which the scriptural portion is read recounting the drowning of the Egyptian pursuers in the Sea of Reeds and Israel's song of triumph. But the poem's central lines are taken up entirely by the present-day supplications of the flock of Israel, for whose sake the miracle happened in those days.

They know that they are in the shadow of this miracle and are its eternal possession and yet that in its transitory world, they are the poor and wretched ones. They also know that the synagogue, with its divine law and divine word, is the legitimate place holder for the former and future sanctuary and that it is that "Little Temple" mentioned in connection with the Talmudic interpretation of a passage in Ezekiel (11:16[2]).

But that is not all: they know that in oppression and seclusion they are the promised Messiah, Isaiah's "servant of God" whose world-expiating suffering and world-redeeming majesty the poet understood to be Israel's destiny. This view also is expressed in Halevi's philosophical work, as in the work of so many others throughout the ages, up to Hermann Cohen. And because in this knowledge the flock preserves its connection with the millenia, so it may await the final miracle, for which it prays, quite simply as a metaphor of the first, the primal miracle, which the present day and every day recalls to mind. For the ultimate miracle will surely be greater than the first, but no different. The God of the world's renewal is the old God of Israel.

---

1. "When the morning stars sang together, and all the sons of God shouted for joy?"

2. "Therefore say: Thus saith the Lord God: 'Although I have removed them far off among the nations, and although I have scattered them among countries, yet have I been to them as a little sanctuary in the countries where they are come.'" FR: The Aramaic translation of the Old Testament (by Onkolos, about second century) already renders 'a little sanctuary' as 'synagogue.' And in Tractate Megilla, 29a, of the Babylonian Talmud, where among other topics the synagogue's role in the life of the Jewish people is discussed, Rabbi Yitzchak "the blacksmith" explains that "a little sanctuary" refers to Babylon's synagogue. Rabbi Yitzchak lived in Palestine at the beginning of the fourth century.

55. MY KING

May my prince shine youthfully
  May the banner flow
  May mockery end,
May he hear:

    everywhere,
to the sound of marching,
and he who killed, be killed,
  Prepare the universe for God!

He brought down the city
  Listen! the horn of the guard:
  The anger rises,
The corn stands ripe—

    on high.
run, bloody fountain!
the grass wilts,
  sickles mow it down!

And with the speed of lightning
  to you, city, saying:
  Sing hymns,
Arise, be happy!

    the good tidings spread
"Stand straight, stand up!
the Messiah is coming!
  See the prince, the powerful
             forces."

For the son he chose a path
  He raised the veil of sin
  Until he who had lost
And the king entered Gilgal

    of crystal,
and opened the gate of the eye,
him committed himself anew,
  before Him.

His word resounded:
  He creates a window:
  Covered by stars, witness
Moon and sun circle

    it encircles the globe.
Valley and mountain,
the pure light of the spirit.
  the spheres.

55] But since God is to rejuvenate the world, He Himself is the One who is forever young. Thus, the people see Him in Scripture and its interpretation "in black curls on the day of the battle." Thus, the poet sings in the jubilant flourish of this hymn, in four-syllable lines, with a five-syllable fanfare ending each stanza, of the appearance and manifestation of his King's beauty.

For both the source and outlet of all Jewish messianic faith is the belief that God Himself will finally be the Redeemer: "He Himself and no other."[1] Even if the river of this hope may—between its source and debouchment—carry the Davidian king or even, in its final extension, the entire people on its waves, in its suffering and in its glorification. All of this still might be nothing but a mythology, one which, because it is future-oriented, may be less easy to examine but is by no means better than a mythology that remains bound to the past—were it not for the fact that this people has never forgotten to transfer all its messianic expectations to the only true "King, Savior, Helper and Shield."[2]

It is He Himself who will now raise the flag of redemption (first stanza); who will carry out the punishment for Babel, as foretold by the prophets (second stanza); and who will send a messenger with the glad tidings of approaching salvation to the other city, to Jerusalem (third stanza). It is He too who in the original gift of light and of the heavenly lights gave to His creation signs and an assurance of all future redemption (final stanza), a gift that is hailed in the morning prayer's "Songs of Light." The words "Arise, for thy light is come" (Isaiah 60:1), for the messianic glad tidings, become a renewal of those words of the first creation: "Let there be light."

In between God's calling forth the light at the beginning of days and at their end stands man. He is not forgotten despite all of God's might. Indeed, the fact that man is not forgotten constitutes

---

1. A phrase found in the Passover *Hagadah,* the service Jews read at home during the Passover meal.

2. Concluding words of the penultimate sentence of the first of the benedictions said in the central Jewish prayer known as the "Eighteen Benedictions."

the very essence of messianic faith. For the Messiah whose royal entry march, surrounded by his hosts, the messenger of glad tidings asks us to envisage, is totally human. Indeed, he is so human—even though he is also God's "son, this day begotten" (Psalms 2:7)—that the "path of light" espied for him by his Father can only be a path toward the light. And so the life of David (II Samuel 1:11–19) becomes exemplary for the King Messiah precisely because of his entirely human turn from guilt, moral blindness, and wantonness. As a divinely imposed penance, David's turn leads through the most painful fights within his household and for his throne, up to that decisive day at Gilgal with its recrossing of the Jordan (II Samuel 19:41) that brings to the humiliated human being, who just then is for the first and only time in his life addressed as "Messiah" (II Samuel 19:22[3]) the realization that he is finally and in truth "king over Israel" (II Samuel 19:23). And from this awareness of divine forgiveness, he derives the strength to forgive his greatest enemy, in whose curses he had seen the embodiment of the divine curse directed at himself.

For whether he comes riding on a donkey or arrives with the clouds of heaven, and whether he awaits his hour as an unknown beggar or in the cave guarded by Elijah himself—come he will! And this insight, certain beyond all prophecy and interpretation, leads to another: that man with, as well as out of, his sinfulness, and in no other way, is called to be a co-worker of God and that God Himself is the true and the only Redeemer.

---

3. "The Lord's annointed."

56. OUT OF MY STRAITS

May Your source give me blessing,
   just as Your anger produced a rain of fire!
Should my sin come forever
   between us?
Did I not seek You for a long time, but
   You never met my efforts?
Residing below the wings of cherubs
   that surround Your sacred place,
Why do You allow strangers to enslave me, instead
   of caring for Your plantling Yourself?
Get up, my redeemer, to set me free,
   see, You who travel the paths of the stars!

56] This people's singularity, which whenever one tries to shove it out the front door of reason, insists obstinately on re-admission through the back door of feeling in the paroxysms of anti-Semitism (which has never taken more absurd forms than in the last one hundred and twenty years, during which the attempt was made to show that the Jew is quite normal)—this singularity consists in the fact that the people sees itself exactly as it is seen from the outside. An entire world calls the Jewish Tribe both rejected and chosen, and the tribe itself confirms these words of others, instead of countering them with words of its own. It is only that the thing as perceived from the outside assumes the form of an external connection, of a historical sequence, while on the inside it is experienced as intrinsically inseparable, meaning that the vessels of curse and of blessing are so interconnected that the one can run over only when the other is also filled to the brim.

57. TO THE REDEEMER

Young dove—You carried her   on eagles' wings,
   She nested in Your lap   feeling safe and secure,—
Why did you chastise her, now   she had to flee through the forest
Where trappers lurked   everywhere in droves,
Tempting her to foreign altars,   the barbarians.
But she—weeps clear tears for Him   and her young years.
   When the smooth tongue of the   enemy had already enmeshed her,—
   Her dull eye asked: where is my true beloved?
Why do You leave my soul   to the grave?
I know that besides You   I have no redeemer.

Fair one, is your veil   torn forever?
   Is he robber and blasphemer   crow and vulture?
The son of the maid, now the groom,—   woe, the gruesome groom!
He is all strength without blessing,   he flexes the bow.
My tent is the place of celebration,   therein shrills the litany of words!
I ask where is my refuge in this world!   Is He still with me?
   No more miracles, no signs.   Vision and pale dreams.
   And when I ask: when do we reach   the day of all days—
Alas, the prophets evade the answer: stop your queries!
I know that besides   You I have no redeemer.

And the slender daughters   are dragged from the city limits,
   From the clean linens   and the fine arbor,
They limp toward the nations   who lack insight,
Toward the scorn of the barbarians   and the bickering of foreign tongues,
But faithful to the thought   which sustains them,
They never bent the knee   before the colorful plaques of the horror picture!
   Since He, the meek one,   who is my shield
   now withdrew into the clouds,   the wild one chases me!
Until the end of all days   dig, question, oh dig!
I know that besides You   I have no redeemer.

The armor of unity   fled from me,
   And the heavy step of haughtiness   rests on my neck.
I am exposed to chastisement,   in the lap of cruelty,
Banishment and chains are my lot,   I am miserable and sullen.
No general, no clatter of swords,   no king, no one who is great.

57] In the countries that follow the Polish rite, this gloomy song, a hymn of redemption, was made part of the liturgy for the last Sabbath of the mourning period between the festivals of liberation and revelation. It was included because of its refrain, which was taken verbatim, though with a shift in meaning, from the Book of Ruth (4:4[1]), which is read on the festival immediately following this Sabbath. One should probably not even call it a shift in meaning, for the people's cry of distress for its one and only Redeemer is surely no less serious, urgent, and genuine than the word that Boaz addresses to Ruth's closest relative, who is duty-bound to "redeem" her. The seriousness and weightiness of that legal concept also characterizes the Jewish concept of redemption, which does not have anything blue-sky about it, except maybe the blue of a beautiful summer day's sky arching over the green earth.

In its form, it belongs to the hymns in free verse; but because most of the half-verses consist of only two words, hence of two stressed main syllables, the original does achieve a certain formal cohesion. Another cohesive effect is achieved by the way in which the rhymes are arranged, though this too is not carried out as strictly as elsewhere. Plays on words and far-fetched biblical references link the externally loose form from within. What finally emerges is a certain approximation of the "piyutim," that other branch—older as well as more recent—of our poetry, the poetry of the Italian-Polish-German school, which originated with the great Kallir.[2] In any event, poems of this kind seem less strange to a Jew today who is at home in his tradition than do the metrically

---

1. Boaz to Ruth's closest kin: "And I thought I would tell you of it [Elimolich's parcel of land], Buy it in the presence of the inhabitants, and in the presence of the elders of my people. If you will redeem it, redeem it; but if you will not redeem it, then tell me, that I may know; for there is none to redeem it besides you; and I come after you. And he said, I will redeem it." (Boaz actually redeems the land.)

2. Eleazar Kallir was, according to the *Encyclopedia Judaica* (1972; Vol. 10, pp. 713–715), "the greatest and most prolific of the early *paytanim,* and one of the most influential liturgical poets. . . . From a linguistic point of view it would seem that Kallir lived in Erez Isael at the end of the sixth century."

The tough one approaches me!   I lost my refuge!
  In anger's ecstasy destroy the place   where he walked,
  Set fire through the blazing anger   to the beams and the foundation,
Whose furor causes   fire which burns to the end—
I know that besides You   I have no redeemer.

Oh, will He forever   avoid me angrily?
  Visions—can   they not vouch for the goal?
Arise, God! to refresh   me and to destroy those who envy me!
May You dwell anew   behind the silky curtains.
Show Yourself as You did at Sinai   to the two eyes in splendor.
And give the heathens   the reward of my suffering.
  Cover him whom fear destroys   with a dew-like blanket of grace.
  Topple the son of the maid, the scoundrel,   from the throne into purgatory.
Soon! so that I shall not   meet death in misery.
I know that besides You   I have no redeemer.

strict compositions of the Spanish school for which it is actually renowned.

This poem's dark tone is determined in large part by the fact that the biblical phrase with which each stanza closes, and with which the refrain thus rhymes, gets this rhyme either from the word for 'grave' and 'underworld,' or from forms of the verb for 'to ask for,' which sound the same as this word. Thus the cry for redemption here arises truly from the depths of the grave.

58. Excursus: A Linguistic Stunt

You shall request from your ardent heart
That Salem shall be called holy.

  For years I cried and suffered
  Between the poison of snakes and deceit.
  I did not find grazing nor did I
Find a bed. Lend me your compassion,
Take away my suffering quietly like a dream.

  Lord, steady my gait,
  Build my fortress anew,
  Smite the enemy nation, You
Avenger, may it be your abode
And my treasure, my new one.

  And in banishment, in night and in gray
  I fear my persecutors, I shudder.
  Correct him who trusts graven images!
Toss that which makes him strong
Into the red-hot flames.

  Tear Your people from the gate of death.
  They do not ask, like fools,
  When the day of salvation will come, whose glory
Will satiate the hungry heart with delight.
Don't cast them away because of their sin.

  Carry Your salvation as our banner,
  Forever after—ingather Your people,
  So that He may come again,
Who attacks the enemy in the dark,
And plants a new shoot on Zion.

58] This piece is totally dominated by something that appears in many of these poems, very prominently in the preceding hymn "To the Redeemer": the delight in word play, more precisely in words that sound alike but have different meanings. It is amazing that such affectation did not produce even more odious results. Indeed, one cannot deny that this poem has a certain grace and at some points even a certain beauty. But just because this poem displays in concentrated form a phenomenon that appears in less concentrated form everywhere in the poetry of Yehuda Halevi and the other Spaniards, let us raise the question: what is the relationship of these poets to language, on which this (to our ears) so unpoetic practice is based?

The Spaniards' poetry is essentially what is called "classicist." At its cradle sat grammar. In contrast to Kallir's poetry, that of the Spaniards' had to wait for the creation of a scholarly grammar of the Hebrew language before it could be created. This poetry subjects itself to the law of linguistic correctness. It has nothing of Kallir's stormily baroque treatment of the possibilities of language, or of his bold creativity in which anything linguistically possible is permitted. The Spaniards' poetry permits itself only what already exists in language and has a scriptural source that can be cited. However, both the former's creativity and the latter's classicism are, quite different from what they would be in a living spoken language. For here the norm is set by the *written* word, not the *spoken* word. And that norm is as audaciously leapt over by the one as it is reverently adhered to by the other. Thus, the boundaries that are either violated or respected are rigid ones, not elastic as would be the case with a spoken language.

The very rigidity of these boundaries produces a much more baroque baroqueness and a much more classicist classicism than would be possible in a living language, where every daring formulation has occasional precedents and where the reverent poet still has a practically unlimited field of possibilities available to him. Anyone as determined as are the Spaniards to remain reverently within set boundaries will plow through the limited area he calls his

own, until there is not the smallest spot of unproductive soil left. And the means for doing so is the young science of grammar.

Grammar and what we would call "lexicography" are at first not separated. Indeed, during its early years grammar considers itself an auxiliary science to lexicography, intent on finding out the meaning of every word in Scripture. And the amazing phenomenon—amazing, to be sure, only for a rationalistic concept of language that regards it as a medium and thus sees words as signs (but all primitive philology is in this sense rationalistic)—the amazing phenomenon that words that sound alike can (most awkwardly!) have different meanings, is at least partly elucidated by grammar. So the vocabulary of Scripture is unfolded and thus spread out for the first time before the eye of the observer.

But now the poets go about appropriating this wealth in innovative ways, for instance, by using a word freely that appears only once in Scripture and thus is "hardly known." The entire wealth of this treasure of language, contained in the twenty-four books that are all that remain of ancient Hebrew literature, first became the people's conscious possession by way of this body of Spanish poetry. And this treasure is still available today for anyone who entrusts himself to the guidance of those masters through the museum of the Bible, as they constantly re-arrange the precious objects, moving one and then another into the proper light, and thus saving the whole from seeming like a museum. This, then, is the national-historical significance of the admittedly childish game played by this poem.

59. Upward Gaze

Stretch out Your arm, Your powerful right hand,
　　come to the aid of Your remnant in battle!
Does not Your arm have the strength to redeem?
　　Does time and fate affect You like the human race.
And yet—the heavenly lights surround You,
　　and are servants of Your mouth and Your word.
Your word, the multitudes in the heavens await it quietly;
　　the starlight testifies to the truth of Your treasure.
Their brilliance alights from Your splendor,
　　their light from the circle of Your clusters of stars.

59] It has been asked often how the Jewish people preserved itself through all its troubles, and there have been a number of more or less clever, or to put it another way, more or less stupid answers offered in reply. This poem can teach us the one true reason that excludes all other "reasons."

The poem begins with a cry from an abyss of anguish so deep that the One to whom it is directed can at first be only screamed at, doubted, and blasphemed. And in this cry, full of doubt and blasphemy that surpass all biblical precedents since they are nourished by the poisonous juices of a skeptical and blasphemous philosophy—almost before the cry has ceased, the eye discerns in the One to whom the cry is directed, that being around whom the stars revolve, and the mouth, breathing a sigh of relief, acknowledges the power of Him who commands the hosts of heaven, and the heart sinks in rapture into the contemplation of divine glory and forgets all its trouble.

60. MAIDEN ISRAEL'S SABBATH

Jewel of a day, surrounded
By peace and life,—
You hallowed it, so that it separated
Israel and the heathens.

They would like—by a twist of a phrase!—
A day like my holy day:
Rome had the first one of old,
And Arabia the sixth most recently.
Their scorn—as if it
Could be mistaken for the truth!
Can sullied clothes and silky jewels
And death and life not be separated?

And my neighbors would love to
Ascend to the royal throne
Of peace for God and humanity,
To which He accorded the reward of salvation,
Celebration's first call here and now,
From the days of creation—
Your word sows pastures of life:
Thereupon we live among the heathens.

To be Your priestess—is her proud lot!
Your Name is her float in the rush of waters!
She pours out her suffering in Your lap,
She rejoices only at Your table,
Manna satiates her, free from suffering,
A measure remained the size of a small jug,
Far-off islands envy her,
Her fame reaches as far as the heathens.

Stretch out again, oh Lord, Your arm,
Take renewed mercy in Your old kingdom.
Even if Your people lives in deep suffering,
Dispersed in warm and cold regions:
How poor are Arabia and Greece,
When You lead home Aaron's host of priests!
In the camp of the Levites You will be
Praised, You, blessing of the heathens.

60] Here on earth, the Sabbath erects a wall that encloses the "covenant of peace and life," into whose sacred realm the people of Israel escapes from the world of the nations. The separation that in the last minute of the day of rest is proclaimed to be that day's essence is the same as that that the first morning of creation brought into the world—the separation between light and darkness, which was then renewed and deepened by revelation to become a separation between the holy and the profane, between Israel and the nations.[1] The Sabbath song immerses itself in this separation—with all the fire, all the passion, but with all the jealousy as well, that are part of all love, especially a love so mocked and reviled as this.

In this song, it almost seems as if the Sabbath signified not the covenant of peace and life, but rather the separation, derived from this covenant, between Israel and the nations. This attitude has been described as resentment, but that is not the case. It would be characteristic of resentment that rejection would be its central feature, rather than merely a peripheral—truly peripheral!—consequence. It is the inward joy in possessing the truth, in having a claim on the kingly blessing of that day that God commanded before all other festive convocations for blessedness, as it is said in a borrowing from the great Sabbath eve blessing (Leviticus 23:3[2]), and that has its origin in creation itself; and finally, it is the joy in being part of those whose obligation it is to be "a kingdom of priests, a holy nation" (Exodus 19:6)—it is all of this that adds up to an internal wealth so great and fulfilling that no outward thorniness can ever be as sharp as that blissfulness is blissful.

And in any case, if my daring translation of the last line is correct—based on a reading arrived at by disregarding both the

---

1. Rosenzweig if referring to the blessing that concludes the Sabbath: "Blessed are You, Lord our God, King of the universe, who separates between holy and profane, between light and darkness, between Israel and the nations, between the seventh day and the six days of labor. Blessed are You, Lord, who separates between holy and profane."

2. "Six days shall work be done; but the seventh day is the Sabbath of rest, a holy gathering; you shall do no work in it; it is the Sabbath of the Lord in all your dwellings."

Ezekiel passage (36:23[3]) on which that line is based, and the psalmist's summons to "all pagans" to "praise the Lord" (Psalm 117:1), as well as passages such as Malachi 1:11[4]—then here too the way is clear for that perspective opened up by the other prayer for the end of the Sabbath, a prayer that in contrast to the one cited at the beginning is intended to separate, not the Sabbath from the workday, but the consecration of the Sabbath from the lesser consecration of holidays. There, too, all the distinctions that are usually referred to at the end of the Sabbath are enumerated: between sacred and profane, light and darkness, Sabbath and workday. But then the final passage, which places a seal upon the whole, praises the God who separates the sacred from the sacred.

For the poem's final lines have come to us in the following form: "Be, then, sanctified in the camp of the Levites, You, whom the pagans revile." In and of itself, this text seems unproblematic. It is based on the passage from Ezekiel mentioned above, and it is consistent with the rest of the poem. The version on which this translation is based is nothing more than a possibility. But that it surely is. The two versions differ, after all, in only one letter, and that is the letter most easily mistaken for another.

This minor divergence from the scriptural passage may have held a particular charm for the poet. To prove that something like this is possible, let me cite the relation of the twentieth couplet in Gabirol's[5] poem (no. 57 in Bialik's edition) to Judges 1:1, whose word play actually involves the same word roots as here. And it goes without saying that in the author of the *Kuzari* there

---

3. "'And I will sanctify My great name, which has been profaned among the nations, which ye have profaned in the midst of them; and the nations shall know that I am the Lord,' saith the Lord God, 'when I shall be sanctified in you before their eyes.'"

4. "'My name is great among the nations; and in every place offerings are presented unto My name, even pure obligations; for My name is great among the nations,' saith the Lord of hosts."

5. Solomon ben Judah ibn Gabirol (c.1020–c.1057), Spanish poet and philosopher.

is an inner disposition in favor of drawing the Gentiles into the community. The *Kuzari*, though definitely holding fast to its belief in the preeminence of Judaism even in the future, is nevertheless in its content a missionary work. But being a Jewish one, it knows as little of an internal *coge intrare*[6] as of an external one. Instead, without compelling anyone to enter, it simply opens the door to anyone who knocks, motivated by world-historical considerations of their own. It does not really give an answer to their questioning, not even "that's the way we are," but rather it points and says, "look here."

---

6. 'Coge intrare,' literally "compel to enter," is taken from the Vulgate translation of Luke 14:23, which reads: "Then the master said to the servant: 'Go out into the highways and hedges and compel them to come in that my house may be filled.'"

61. HOME

The host which wanders in the
        enemy's fold—   let it go
Home, where Your Promised One will
        take charge of   their fate.

Someday the desire for salvation will be
        pronounced   in the exile,
And the messenger will point the sinners   to the nearing of the end.
He, whom time did not gently envelop,   may he play happily—
And he, who still dares to tempt,   may he flee.
Allow him who was made to suffer from
        the plague   relief.

Listen! the enemy orders,   "may the axe cut off the
        rump!"
His diligence plans that   my hoop encircle his head,
He boasts: "Now no more green   will sprout from Jesse's root."
Let us beseech You that   the dry stick my sprout,
Be kind, and may   the scales of fate turn.

Lead us whom You freed from
        exploitation   and from bondage,
From now on, stand watch   on Zion's hilltops Yourself,
Then Your people will live under   the tent of the Almighty—
Allow the flood of evil   to disperse,
Allow rest to the wild wailing   of the lakes.

The crying of the persecuted, may it   ascend to You,
The lamb among the lions—save it   from bloody fangs,
Shepherd! May Your heart tremble
        compassionately   for Your animal—
Do not desert Your herd,   faint of yearning,
Light of salvation, nearly extinguished,
        shine anew,—   let us see it.

Now that the night is torn asunder,   the seedlings of the light sprout.
You solve Your firstborn's   troubles
Blessed be he whose conscience is   influenced by Your light!
Then You will reign. And on that day   Your grace will
Spread far and wide. And let all my
        sorrow—disperse   like a dream.

61] The last hour of the Sabbath is the critical hour of Jewish existence. Whatever this life can know or anticipate of perfection has been crowded into the Sabbath. Now there threatens an immediate and precipitous fall, from the height reached in a twenty-five-hour ascent into the abyss of the workday. Thus, those last hours with their "third meal" are filled with an excitement sustained in equal measure by messianic longing and the despair of exile. And Elijah the prophet, whose return as the herald of the Messiah has been foretold in the last words of biblical prophecy (Malachi 3:23[1]), is present in these hours—as someone absent is yet present to a group whose every thought and word revolves around him.

That mood is intensified in this song, though the end of the Sabbath as such is not mentioned at all, and Elijah and the Messiah are each mentioned only once at the beginning. This intensification is evident already in the rhythm of each individual line as it flows from a broad, as it were, visual first half into the short groan of the second half. It becomes even more evient in the form this rhythm assumes in the recurring lines, where the second half turns not only rhythmically but also in its linguistic content into a monotonously imploring urgent cry: "Let, oh let, oh let. . . ."

---

1. "Behold, I will send you Elijah the prophet before the coming of the great and terrible day of the Lord."

62. ELIJAH'S MIRACLES

We miss his miracles every day—
Oh, where is he, God of Eliyahu?

His seed listens to his words,
And cries for fear when enemies come,
And says: where is the rock and His name?
For thousands of years already he forgets us!

Because of the horrors of the northern kingdom
Elijah closed the doors of heaven;
Fire and water descended
By His word.

Thus he spoke to jar and bowl,
Blessing them to abundance,
Tears the child from the valley of death—
Did anyone you know see and hear it?

He burns up generals and armies,
Fasting forty days and nights;
Ravens came, so that one might think:
He attracted them,—now he eats their bread.

When he rose up in thunder and lightning,
In the fiery trembling of the fiery wagon,
Elisha stayed behind, crying bitterly:
Father, father! but he received no answer.

The waters of the Jordan river receded,
So that they did not even cover the ankles,
Also for Elisha they stood,
Those who saw it were amazed.

Those who hope for prophetic signs,
When will they see them full of miracles?
When will he do the same for them
And raise the flag of God!

62] This is the kind of Elijah song that is recited during the last hour of the Sabbath, a folksy and simple enumeration of the miraculous deeds of the great "Tishbite" (I Kings 17:11ff.). Again and again it recalls, through its rhyme alone, the lamenting question of the poem's beginning, which is transposed from the passage relating Elisha's bold assumption of the prophet's mantle (II Kings 2:14[1]). This question is the source of the rhyme, which in the original is Elisha's name itself. At the end, the despairing "where" of the beginning is transformed into a hopeful "when"— both of them questions, but the former is an uncertain groping in the dark, while the latter is a hurrying toward the distant yet certain light.

For miracles do not ever happen when they are sought by a "Where." They wish to be conjured up with a "When."

---

1. "And he took the mantle of Elijah that fell from him, and smote the waters, and said: 'Where is the Lord, the God of Elijah?'"

63. THE JEW

Because of You those who wander through the nights despise me,
  the servants of cast-iron figments of the imagination,
I responded: to serve God is the right thing to do.
  What did they achieve that He couldn't do?
When He is angry with me, I am the servant of the servants,
  When He favors me, I am all-powerful.

63] This is an echo of the prophets' polemic. The eternal existence of this people is manifest also in the fact that nothing that was once important ever loses its importance. The eternal people immortalizes even its adversaries.

64. THE PROMISE

"Young doves, which are suddenly transplanted
    into a wild land of much wind,
Arise! since you have no rest here,
    and the glow of home now pales.
Home! where you are refreshed
    and fanned by gentle air—
May God find it within Himself
    to grant you rest!"

"Lord! since we left Salem,
    and the daughters who surrounded it,
And moved away from Zion,
    whose meadows are buried in desert,
We—the path leading towards night!
    The Land—needing a jubilee year of rest!
We sincerely hope that
    the sound of prayer will never leave Him.

"And who gives me dove-like wings!
    I would fly up, gliding toward home.
I would ride on the horses of south and north,
    asking only for a wind to Zion.
The end and the beginning of time are the same,
    Shepherds and royal steps approach
And the blows of the sword numb to pain
    will come from the avenging sword, the avenging sword.'

"To You who walk on the hills of hope,
    the distant shimmer does not lie.
The reigns of harmony created the hope,
    but there is no harmony for me.
A beautiful daughter returns on wings
    of youth to my room.
From the salvation angel who swims through the air
    I receive an intimation of where you find rest.

64] This is a conversation between God and His frightened doves, as Israel is named in connection with passages such as Psalms 68:14, Isaiah 60:8, Ezekiel 7:16, and Hosea 7:11.[1] Here as elsewhere we are faced with a name rather than something that actually exists, if only as a metaphor. The metaphor dissolves, as it were, in the poet's hands; for at the start of the third stanza the people break into the psalm's cry of longing (Psalm 55:7[2]), which could not possibly come from a dove. From that point onward, the metaphor is abandoned.

This is due not to a lack of poetic talent, though such talent might have manifested itself by holding onto that metaphor. Rather, it is due to a will that is unpoetic and super-poetic at the same time. This will confronts each metaphor that the imagistic tendency of language places in the speaker's mouth and tries to break through the metaphor into the imageless truth of prose. The style of the Bible is only involuntarily poetic. To regard, say, the Psalms as poetry is the most inadequate way of reading them for it creates an atmosphere that lacks that element that all art, even the most "genuine," the most religiously oriented, needs to have: the pleasure in games or, more precisely, in masks. It is bad enough that the word as such always has something masklike about it already since it not only is the word of a particular moment but also bears in its face traces of earlier destinies. Thus, the speaker, concerned with the word's veracity, will not limit himself to any one word but will, as soon as he has uttered it, say it in yet another way—and in the same way the poet of this circle will not limit himself to one single image.

There is one apparent exception. The images of kingship and those of filial, betrothed, or marital love are not subject to this law of abandoning images. The reason for this is that although these too are images, they are not copies but rather prototypes. What is a copy here is the inner-wordly reality of those relationships that we know only in combinations and distortions and whose pure form is manifest only in the relationship between God and humanity. Pure

---

1. EJ: Rosenzweig also refers to Job 2, 14:5, 2:5, 12:6, 9, and Psalm 56:1, but these citations have no apparent connection to doves.

2. "Oh, that I had wings like a dove! Then I would fly away and be at rest."

Beware!—May you be consoled,
    as if with dew in a dry year.
Replant empty places.
    May the town be erected on ruins.
He awakens, like warriors,
    love from the depth of the heart,
He makes the barren one
    into the mother happily surrounded by children."

homage kneels before God alone; pure yearning longs for God alone; and pure gratitude thanks God alone.

The metaphor of the dove arises here because the keynote of the entire poem, and the source for its recurring rhymes, is the promise of "peace," peace in the homeland, which according to Moses' prophecy now "lieth desolate" to make up for those Sabbath years when its inhabitants neglected to provide for it (Leviticus 26:34 and 26:43). It is this land over whose restored soil one day the "seven shepherds and eight princes" will tread. Their return is foretold by the prophet Micah (Micah 5:4[3]) and is expected by the people in accordance with the Talmudic interpretation of the prophet's words.[4] Of this rest the exiles have made themselves worthy not through their conduct toward one another but, as it is said with deep insight into the essence of Judaism, through their conduct toward God—through the untiring protection of hope, which one day must surely re-awaken the now hidden love of the Father for His children and bring it anew to stormy power.

The third exile gathered within itself the sufferings of the first two, the Egyptian and the Babylonian. But the divine promise, too, gathers within itself the power of the law and of the prophets. The power of the last stanzas surpasses even that of the biblical word, much as any suffering endured in the present surpasses all past suffering, if only because it occurs in the present. For biblical promises are all future-oriented, and they have as their foil an implicit threat. They speak in one voice—the divine—and contain the always two-voiced present only in the form of a condition: "If you . . ., then. á . á . ." But here we have the fully two-voiced, the divine-human reality, and the promise shines not as a conditional "either-or," but as a radiant "yes" into the night of lament, repentance, and return, uttered in the present, and in the other voice. And so the moment has come close.

---

3. "And this shall be peace: when the Assyrian shall come into our land, and when he shall tread in our palaces, then shall we raise up against him seven shepherds, and eight princes among men."

4. *Sukkah* 52b: "Who are the 'seven shepherds'?—David in the middle, Adam, Seth and Methuselah on his right, and Abraham, Jacob and Moses on his left. And who are the 'eight princes among men'?—Jesse, Saul, Samuel, Amos, Zephaniah, Zedekiah, the Messiah, and Elijah."

65. Loving One's Enemies

Of old you've been the heavenly vest of love,
    my loving settled with you in the nest.
Angry words of my enemy, I enjoy them, for Your sake;
    Leave him—he will pressure him whom You have long pressured.
Your enemy learned Your anger: that's why I love him;
    for his fist meets Your blow head on.
  If You would cast me away, on that day I would cast myself away,
    how could I wish the best for him, whom You cast away!
  Until some day Your anger disappears and You send salvation
    to the remnant of the heirs redeemed by You.

65] One does as little justice to the dictum "Love your en-
emies," from the Sermon on the Mount, as one does to other
great realities if one views it as an ethical demand and thus from
the point of view of unreality. The Christian's love for his en-
emies is a reality—wherever it cannot be anything else. And it
enters this state of not being able to be anything else wherever
the church or an individual obeys Christianity's original com-
mand: to missionize. Loving one's enemies here becomes the
most powerful weapon for world conquest: the enemy is loved as
a future brother.

So Jewish love for an enemy must be something totally differ-
ent if it is to be real. For here the reality is a community that has
been granted not the blessings of victory but instead those of
defeat. Thus love for one's enemies arises here at the point that
Yehuda Halevi reveals in this poem. For what we have here is truly
a revealing. The real is rarely that which is spontaneously ex-
pressed, and a word easily falls into unreality when it attempts to
become objective. But what is here revealed is the objective truth,
precisely because it is expressed in an entirely subjective manner.
The Jew loves in his enemy, the executor of divine judgment, a
judgment he accepts. In contrast to all other people, he has no
other choice since he alone does not have at his disposal the Jews
whose fault it is—and therefore makes his own. A man's love for
God becomes the law of life for all the love with which he can love
other people, even, to take it to the extreme (but is there an
extreme for love?), his enemies. "Of old you've been the heavenly
vest of love."

66. MIRACLE OF LOVE

Once you looked benevolently on the ornaments
   of my song and praise?
Gem of my heart, who fled far from me
   because of the mad drive of my wickedness!
If I could only hold His hem,
   oh what wonderous strength would I retain!
Your name would be reward enough for me,
   Even if my work would exhaust me.
If You increase the sorrow—I will love even more!
   The miracle of my life is Your love.

66] This poem (as, by the way, the last one, too) could, despite its concluding line, make one wonder whether it is rightfully included in this section or whether it should not have been made part of the preceding one. But the longing for suffering is expressed here in terms so utterly personal that one will find it difficult to assume that it is the people whom Yehuda Halevi allows to speak here, despite the powerful third couplet, which testifies to the people's abiding consciousness of having been chosen in spite of its depravity.

But in this formulation one already can find the whole mistake. The poet does not allow anyone to speak. He speaks himself. And he speaks not from behind the mask of the people but from the very midst of the people of whom he is a member. Only as a member of this people does he know at first what it is he knows. But—and in this "but" comes now the excuse for that mistake, and at the same time its whole mistakenness—what he has experienced originally as a member of the people, he can now experience personally on account of his own soul. In genuine experiences there is a power of propagation and transference. Not in the sense that one's first experience becomes a symbol for others, rather precisely because the first experience is not a symbol, it can leap over walls, while a symbol must remain within its own sphere. Where the Jewish people has turned into a symbol, as it has in the Christian world, it reaches through its symbolizing power only the nations. For the Jew himself, however, the Jewish people never becomes a symbol. Therefore everything that he has learned as part of the people is transposed for him even into the inner life of his soul.

In exactly the same way, the love of God leaps over to become the love of man. Whoever has understood these things will become very cautious about engaging in constructions of religious history and will no longer dare, based on findings of literary scholarship ("Literature is the fragment of fragments") to ascribe to Jeremiah a "personal piety" that Isaiah, whose "religiosity was entirely political," did not "yet" possess. Nor will he set up a prize competition for the best essay on "The 'I' in the Psalms," even if he is a member of the theological faculty of a Prussian university.

67. IRATE LOVE

Dearest, how could You ever forget   the resting place at this breast?
   and sell me just like that   to my destroyers?
Did I hesitate then to follow You   to a desolate land?
   You mountains, oh Sinai, testify   with your perception,
You were rich in my love   and I was full of Your grace,
   oh, that I now have to share   the glory with others.
Those whom I sent to Edom,   sent away to Hagar's tribe,
   Suppressed under the Persian yoke,   tested in the furnace of Hellenization,
Oh, aren't You the only God?   Is there another awaiting You?
   Oh, give me Your strength! And   I will dedicate my love anew to you.

67] The reality of the love between God and Israel, as the Prophets, the Song of Songs, and the Midrash all testify, is evident in the fact that this love did not end in being expressed, as a "poet's love"[1] ends in the poem that testifies to it. Instead, this love proceeds throughout time, inexhaustible in its reality. Thus, in this poem for the morning service of the Feast of Liberation, which is accompanied by the Song of Songs, we are swept away to face an outburst from the abandoned beloved who has been exiled to a strange land and forced to live in misery for a millenium. The classical testimonies to this love do not contain any such terrifying outburst, simply because at that time, at the beginning of the millennium, there did not yet exist any reason for it. There is no tone of repentance in these words, only righteous indignation at the faithlessness of the beloved, to whom Israel has sacrificed everything. The history of two millenia, from Sinai through the Persians, Greeks, and Romans, and up to the Islam of the poet's day, is gathered in the witness stand of the three middle couplets with their reproaches. And then comes the outcry, at which one hardly dares to believe one's ears, in which Israel, as one human standing erect before the one God, ties her omnipotence to the redemption that He owes to Israel. For there is no one else waiting for Him. There must be no one else for the power of love tolerates nothing "outside." Whatever exists is within her. Whatever is not within her does not exist.

If this Jewish? No, for all love forgets—in its love—that there exists still something beyond love, an It besides Me and You. Is it Jewish? Oh yes, for the power of expressing this truth has been given to mankind only since and because there have been Jews.

---

1. TK: *Dichterliebe,* a reference to the famous cycle of poems by Heinrich Heine (see note 1 on commentary no. 86 in this volume), set to music by Robert Schumann.

68. DREAM VISION

My meadows are bathed in starlight.
  Does now my Fall harvest return anew?
A delightful meadow, a vineyard for me,
  mine is the drum, mine is the mouth of the flute.
The ring returns on my arm,
  a golden ring in my nose.
And his palace and my abode
  face each other threshold to threshold.
Then I returned for their unification,
  heart and senses all united.
May it intoxicate the soul,
  may the tongue announce the union joyously.

68] A dream vision of the daughter of Zion, forever young, never old, whose youth was already a fruit-rich autumn and to whom renewal may therefore approach at all times in the form of a return. A return of youthful autumn, of youthful appearance, of the youthful union with her lover, which occurred at the same time with him and within herself. But the former implies a return to her, while the latter—even in her dream—implies a return that is incumbent upon her.

69. FAITHFULNESS

"Beloved, year after year You
        Banned me miserably to jail
      to snake bite and to scorpion sting—
  Have mercy   have mercy!

  My heart hopes to exhaustion! In the morning
  of every day the goal seems equally far.
  Dearest, what shall I still say, since
Edom stole itself into my room as the owner,
        Arabs, Normans rule over me,
     Together with the pack of dogs that
  encircled   my herd.

  And the sweet melody of my name
  Was spat at me as curse from alien mouth,
  Opposing me!—Every ruffian of a people brags with prophecy,
      Unaware of their fate,
     He pushed and shoved me,
    That I resorted   to lies!"

  You! Let us wander through the garden air,
  And taste the smell of nards and roses,
  What shall the mountain goat do in the fox's den!
Wake up my harp, my bell,
        Drink my wine and harvest my fruit!
     Open my paradise,
    Whose glory grew   faint for me!"

"'Hold out! No matter how many years.
I did not betroth myself to another people.
You chose Me, so I chose you.
Where would there be a tribe, in which universe,
        which resembled my son, the sacrifice, the first born,
     Whom I could call friend,—
    And where is there   a God like Me.'"

69] The primal Jewish word, from which the world has drawn its belief, actually means "fidelity"; this word implies mutuality. This mutuality always has hovered over the Jewish perception of the divine-human relationship, and it has assumed forms that are totally inconceivable to anyone looking at it from the outside. Old Eisenmenger,[1] for instance, who in contrast to his modern successors and copyists at least made an honest effort to investigate the subject matter he set out to "expose," collected a great number of quotes from the *Haggadah*[2] (each more splendid than the preceding one), with which he filled many pages under the heading "The Jews' Monstrous and Heretical Notions of God the Father."

The poet may well have had one of those quotes in mind when he wrote the powerful conclusion of this dialogue, whose lament is almost hidden under the pride of a people justified in feeling superior to its enemies, of whose eventual destruction it has, moreover, been assured by the angel's conversation in Daniel (8:13ff.). In addition, there is the sweetness of the Song of Songs; and there is the Talmud's famous question about the contents of God's tefillin[3] since God too dons tefillin, much as man does to show his love of God. (In the "Book of Love" from his great *Code*,[4] Maimonides lists all the prescriptions for how they should be made and how they should be put on.)

---

1. Johann Andreas Eisenmenger (1654–1704), lecturer at Heidelberg University, studied Talmud and Midrash for nineteen years under Jewish guidance, pretending to want to convert. In 1699 he completed a massive two-volume "scholarly" anti-Semitic work in German, *Judaism Unmasked (Entedecktes Judenthum)*, which appeared in English translation in 1732–33. Supporting his theses by manipulating source material, often presented in erroneous and distorted translation, Eisenmenger denounced Judaism as morally inferior to Christianity, charging Jews with well poisoning and blood libel.

2. Primarily a narrative of the exodus from Egypt, the *Haggadah* is recited at the dinner services that begin the Passover holiday.

3. Teffilin are small square prayer boxes Jewish men traditionally wear on the left arm and forehead for morning prayers. According to Tractate *Berachot* 7, God Himself wears teffilin, as Moses saw when God passed before him on Mount Sinai, as related in Exodus 33:23 ("and thou shalt see My back,").

4. The fourteen Hebrew volumes that make up the *Mishne Torah* (1180), the "Second Torah" (the *Yad ha-Hazakah*, "Strong Hand"), by Moses Maimonides (1135–1204), reorganized and presented all prior authoritative Jewish legal conclusions.

Man's tefillin contain the proclamation of God's Oneness and the subsequent commandment to love Him (Deuteronomy 6:4ff.). But what is contained in the ones that God "puts on"? "And who is like Thy people Israel, a unique nation on earth?" (I Chronicles 17:21). Man's acknowledgment of the one God is echoed by God's acknowledgment of the one people, the people whose three-thousand-year-old countenance bears the traces of the patriarchs' destinies— Isaac's willingness to be sacrificed, Jacob's ruses and the suffering connected with his birthright, and the friendship between God and Abraham.

70. CONSOLING LOVE

"Why, sister, are you counting
        the days that you are in confinement?

   Do you, dove, dash about aimlessly,
   Lonely from roof to roof,
   Do you ask: 'When will you come, my day?'—
   Take courage, heart, bursting with fear,
The testimony of hope did not lie,
        keep hoping—the sap already rises."

   "Could I still hope for the elixir
   For my illness, since I was ill
   From your anger. My image sank
   In darkness because of the inconstancy of my deeds.
I dwell in the fiery pain of widowhood,
        the night has stolen my happiness.

   And enemies speak: 'She lost
   salvation! It is of long duration.
   Her savior lives? why doesn't he come?
   Her judgment fell into our hands.
To be sure, prophecy deceived her,
        and what you prophets see is false.'"

   "Beloved! This shall suffice:
   I shall raise my banner anew.
   I shall cleanse the realm of your inheritance.
   I shall spread my name. I shall
Redeem my tribal inheritance
        and revive those whom the sleep of death exhausts.

   My heart rallies when I think of
   The love of old.
   The word can no longer express it.
   It burns like a coal fire.
A storm of passion blows through me:
        the power of love is strong as death."

70] This is a conversation between God and Israel, the "sister-bride" of the Song of Songs (4:9, 4:11, 4:12, 5:1, 5:2). From the beginning, the poem's recurring rhymes point toward the famous words about the love that "is strong as death" (Song of Songs 8:6).[1] The poem begins with consolation, which is answered in the second and third stanzas by inconsolable despair, to which consolation replies in more forceful tones, speaking in the fourth stanza in a very godly way and in the fifth in a very human way, and thus culminating in the most human and the most divine of all sayings.

---

1. Rosenzweig had previously analyzed these words in *The Star of Redemption*, Part Two, Book Two.

71. FINDING EACH OTHER AGAIN

"How can I make it up to my
        Beloved?—woe, he vanished!
Oh, if he would only flourish for me anew
        from the Orient!"

"Maiden, mild like a dove,
        when they bring you to me,
Gird yourself with colorful embroidery,—
        for my eye's enjoyment!
Then I will outfit myself with weapons of
        wild, vengeful desire.
Still in the dust? Behold:
        budding redemption already hails:
The sons are loyal to Him
        whom my command sent forth."

"Beloved, I called to you
        from the deluge of water,
Hear the echo of my
        melodies which rises to Heaven.
When do my sinful deeds reach
        the degree of punishment prophecied—
Did you already record the upwelling of sin
        in the book;
Shower your grace on it,
        and delete it with a benevolent hand.

Oh bestow on me unhappy, lonely one,
        the hour of grace!
Graze the remnant of your herds
        on your pasture!
How long shall the poison of
        scorn affect me?
Ishmael and Edom
        imprison me,
The consecrated head that fears the knife
        looses its token of consecration."

71] This sweetly human love dialogue, in which the beloved is called by the pet-name of secular love poetry (the first lines could be translated as "How can I make it up to my sweetie?"), anticipates, dreamlike, the moment in the future when the lovers will find one another again. Everything that today is past, everything that today is present, everything that today still lies in the future is united into the single level of the past, and as such it is made present once more by the love dialogue with its familiar: "Do you remember?" "Can't you recall?" "A year ago around this time. . . . " Everything, including the love of Abraham; Israel's psalm-songs; Isaiah's promise of redemption after Israel's guilt is paid off, "that she hath received . . . double for all her sins" (Isaiah 40:2); the book of divine judgment; the scorn and profanation of the troubled present; the promise that "a remnant shall return" (Isaiah 10:21f.); the assurance of help for him whose victory will come "in stillness and in staying quiet" (Isaiah 30:15); God's revulsion, expressed through the mouth of the prophet, caused by Israel's celebratory sacrifice (Isaiah 1:14); and finally, in the Song of Songs (5:1), the bridegroom's delight as he enters his garden, and the call of his bride who had seen him flee like a hart (Song of Songs 8:14)—all this and more—becomes an enchanting present in the exchange between the lovers who have found each other again, swelling from the trembling of the first joyful anticipation to the jubilation of the ultimate consummation.

"Be grateful! It happened for the sake of the remnant,
that I did not cast away.
Your salvation—now it is near.
Who prophesied it?
He who remained silent, he saw it.
Come! those whom I never abandoned.
Your sacrificial fire smells
like the flowing of myrrh,
May I enjoy your feast
which once caused me horror.

Awaken, oh you my treasure,
You who are still surrounded by grief.
He who harvests fruit
came to your garden's steps.
Your light, ready to dim,
flares up! Get up, be bright!
Your friend, who escaped you
quick as a deer
Is coming! The blue of God's heavens
envelops you."

ZION

72. UP

Sleepyhead, the heart's awake,
Full of fire and thunder,—
Get up! Leave sleep behind,
   Enter into the light of my eye!

Happily begin your journey!
Your star has risen.
He who was believed to be dead,
   Climbed up to Sinai.

One day silence those who
Rejoice: "A mountain of sin
Burdens Zion!"—see, and still
   I do not turn heart or eye from them.

I open and close myself,
Anger burns and mercy flows:
How could I leave
   them, my children, them!

72] Unlike the last poems of the preceding section, this one is not a dialogue. There is only one who speaks here, the One. Thus, what is represented here is no longer the present but the future, no longer a drama but a vision. Lament, which is always an expression of the present, has fallen silent, and so have consolation, promise, and hope; all of them silently look toward the future, though from out of the present. Only the future, which is entirely present, now speaks—sounding that appeal, that admonition to "be ready" for the hour that now, finally, has come. And it speaks out of the mouth of the One who has brought it about, the One who in all the contradictions of His nature and the ebb and flow of our destiny has maintained His love for those He calls His own—the Lord of the future.

73. GLAD TIDINGS

Distant young dove,   sing your   most beautiful song—
  Offer to Him, who calls you,   what is sweet   in you.
It is Him, Your God   Himself, who calls you: hurry,
  Bow down   deep to the earth! Present   your offering.
Toward Your nest   ascend, on the way   to Your tent,
  To Zion,—put   markers for   the way.
First friend, who sent you   away, because your   actions proved evil,
  He Himself will   redeem you today. Praise—   where did it begin?
You are getting ready for   the return to the   many-splendored beautiful land;
  the empire of Arabia,   of Edom,—oh,   may they lie in the dust!
All who once   subdued you,   smite their house,
  and may love   encircle the house   of your friend.

73] This poem, not very significant in itself, nevertheless belongs here because of the circumstances that gave rise to it. The assumption of its publisher, Luzzato, may well have been correct—and I fail to be convinced by the counterarguments of Geiger[1] and others—that it was composed under the immediate impact of some reports concerning the appearance of a messianic pretender, a number of which are recorded during that century. It is not Yehuda Halevi's way to fabricate the situations that motivated him to write certain poems. When they are based on a dream or some vision, he says so. Hence, it was probably an actual report that made him write this poem, however long or short the time in which he believed this report.

Thus, we may surmise that Yehuda Halevi "paid a customs duty" to his faith. For the expectation of the Messiah, by which and for the sake of which Judaism lives, would be an empty theologumenon, a mere "idea," empty talk, had it not been for the appearance of some "false Messiah" that again and again would actualize and frustrate that idea, raise and disappoint that hope. The false Messiah is as old as is the hope for the true one. He is the ever-changing form of that abiding hope. He divides every Jewish generation into those whose strength of faith allows them to be deceived and those whose strength of hope does not allow them to be deceived. The former are the better ones; the latter are the stronger ones. The former bleed as sacrifices on the altar of the people's eternity; the latter serve as priests before that altar. One day it will be the reverse, with the faith of the faithful becoming the truth and that of the hopeful made into a lie. Then—and no one knows whether this "then" may not come even today—the task of the hopeful will be at an end. When the dawn of this "today" has arrived, anyone who is still among the hopers and not among the believers must risk becoming an outcast. This is the threat that hangs over the seemingly less dangerous life of the one who hopes.

---

1. Abraham Geiger (1810–1874), rabbi in Wiesbaden, Breslau, Frankfurt, and Berlin; a German Jewish advocate of modernism.

Once, when Hermann Cohen was already past seventy, he said to me: "I am hoping still to see the beginning of the messianic era." What he meant—he, a believer in the false Messiah of the nineteenth century—was the conversion of Christians to the "pure monotheism" of his Judaism, something he believed was taking shape in the liberal Protestant theology of his day. I was startled at the force of this assertion "soon, in our days" and I did not dare to tell him that to me *these* signs were no signs at all. Instead, I replied merely that I did not think that I would live to see that time. Whereupon he asked: "But when do you think it will arrive?" I did not have the heart to give him no date, so I replied: "Well, probably only after hundreds of years." However, he must have thought I said "only after a hundred years," and he cried out: "Oh, please say 'fifty!'"

74. CALCULATING SALVATION

Distant young dove,   she flew away   into the forest;
  she fell: she seems to be lacking   the strength   to lift herself up.
She flew there,   she turned there,   she pulled there,
  around her friend   she creates   a whirlwind.
And she calculates   the period of   one thousand years,
  but every number   gets her deeper   into debt.
It is the fault   of the friend   who has been torturing her
  for "eight! eight! more years,"   that she lives at the edge   of the grave.
When she called out: "I no longer think   the name":
  it flared up—   and she was   deeply shaken.
Are you alive, to be   her enemy? and she—   strives,
  thirsting for   your grace's   late rain.
How firm her heart!   It does not waver   at his name,
  proudly rising up,   she is glued to the dust   around him.
Come soon,   you strength of God,   do not be silent,
  and, flashes of lightning   and thunder   surround her!

74] So the attempt is made, again and again, to calculate the date when redemption will come. And yet every calculation collapses, so that even in the Talmud it is said that all the deadlines have passed and all that is left is the power to return.[1] Yehuda Halevi's lifetime falls precisely in such an epoch, that is, one in which a deadline had passed. For people had hoped that redemption would come in the one thousandth year of the exile, which according to the historical chronology of that day would have been the year 1068 of the Christian era. By now, sixty-four years—the poet transposes that number, based on the dove metaphor, into the numerical value of the Hebrew equivalent for "floating away into the air," something the translation obviously can approximate only loosely—sixty-four years have once again passed by in misery. The years past are counted, but calculation no longer dares to predict the future. "No longer dares?" But just out of this despair at the futility of all calculation, there arises—as it once did for the prophet (Jeremiah 20:9[2]) in his desperate attempt no longer to "make mention of Him"[3]—the flame of faith, with the utmost force carrying heavenwards the Psalm's (50:3) words "let our God come," which, it now appears, from the start had been anticipating His resurrection in the seemingly so artificial rhythm of the poem.

---

1. FR: Babylonian Talmud, Tractate *Sanhedrin*, 97b: "Rab said: 'All predestined dates have passed, and the matter now depends on repentance and good deeds.'"

2. "Then I said, I will not make mention of him, nor speak any more in his name. But his word was in my heart like a burning fire shut up in my bones, and I was weary with restraining myself, and I could not."

3. JK: The German is *gedenken*, which means to "recall" or "remember," but the translation follows Jeremiah 20:9.

75. IN THE SANCTUARY

My God, how heavenly is the place of Your abode!
   to behold You closely and not only in stories!
A dream transported me to God's sacred place,
   I was allowed to immerse my gaze into its works:
The burnt offering as well as meal offering and libation
   and all around dense clouds of smoke.
And I was blessed to hear the Levites' song
   in their circle, grouped by rank.
I awakened, and was still with You, God!
   and thanked You—You, full of grace!

75] The Jewish people's yearning for Zion has never been merely the longing of the tormented for surcease; it has always also implied a desire to move out of a diminished life into a higher one. Thus, even if the daily prayer's petition that God may blow His mighty trumpet to mark our liberation[1] is omitted on the Sabbath and festivals since on those days all requests stemming from worldly neediness should fall silent, the prayer for the re-institution of the sacrificial cult is said just the same:

Be gracious, oh you our God, to your people Israel and to its
    pleading
And grant new holy custom to the cell of your house.
And blazing flame and prayers of love, accept them graciously,
    oh God,
And at all times may the brightness of your mercies illumine
    Israel's service.
And may our eyes see
How You return home to Zion, mild in mercy.
Now praise, yes praise them, oh God who lets his light dwell
    anew in Zion.

Yehuda's dream places him, the Levite, in the midst of his brethren as they perform the sacrificial service. He revels in the sight of the sacrificial rites, which represent for him the re-established immediacy of God's proximity. In the same century, Maimonides, who in his *Code* had given a detailed account of the laws for the sacrificial cult that would be in force after the rebuilding of the Temple, spoke of those laws in his philosophical work as a mere pedagogical concession by Moses (following Leviticus 17:7[2]). Today that legislation and the prayers for its re-institution have become an embarrassment, one that is generally recognized by the liberals and unacknowledged by the orthodox.

---

1. The tenth benediction of the central prayer known as the "Eighteen Benedictions," reads: "Sound the great shofar for our freedom, raise the banner to gather our exiles and gather us together from the four corners of the earth. Blessed are you, Lord, who gathers in the dispersed of His people Israel."

2. "And they shall no more sacrifice their sacrifices unto the satyrs, after whom they go astray."

The reasons usually given for this negative attitude are so unconvincing that they obviously cannot be the real ones. For the horror at the "murder of innocent animals" expressed by active nonvegetarians is too comical to be taken seriously. And any argument going beyond this one could equally be used against any other visible and fixed cultic act that helps to make the relationship between the natural need for food and the provider of that food more easily perceptible, which is most likely the intent.

Still, even for someone who sees all of this quite clearly, there exists an emotional difference. For him, too, it is difficult to pray for the re-institution of sacrificial rites. But then it should be difficult for what is involved here is the difference between prescribed and spontaneous prayer. The latter is uttered out of some acute need, while the former is meant to make the worshiper feel a need of which he would otherwise not be aware.

This holds particularly true for prayers meant to hasten the coming of the messianic era, to the extent that they do not ask merely for deliverance from present-day pressures. Man is rooted so deeply in his life, even the hardest, that he has every reason to be afraid of any radical change, despite his constant wish for this or that partial change. The messianic time represents such a radical change. In fact, it represents *the* radical change, which would, to be sure, put an end to the hell of world history but also to its ambiguities and its apparent irresponsibilities. Then all will become transparently clear. But it is just this all-pervasive clarity, and the clear-cut responsibility that goes with it, from which man shrinks—as he shrinks from God's nearness at death, for which he may likewise yearn without being able to extricate himself from his love of life, even a deficient or sinful life. The change is simply too radical. Nevertheless, he should learn to pray for radical change, even though he will find this prayer difficult until that change has occurred. The awareness that God is close to man even in the present world of half-truths, entanglements, and weird happenings, or rather that man can come close to Him, that he can find this way to Him, becomes clear to Yehuda Halevi as he awakens from his dream and reenters this world.

It would be a lie if yearning should forget what it already possesses. But it would be death if possession should forget to yearn.

76. CARPETS OF SOLOMON

"You carpets of Solomon
     in the tent of the desert dweller
Alas! Your glamour is distorted
     and your texture!"
""The great people
     who resided among us has vanished,
leaving us ravished and empty—
     how can we be compensated for the loss?
And when the sacred vessels
     went into exile and became common,
Did you expect roses to be pure
     when they are mixed with thistles?""
"Every one desires them, near and far,
     ask only your own master,
who calls each one by name
     —no one is lost from His world,
He will weave their harvest wreath
     from the springlike splendor of blossoms,
so that light like the light of creation
     brightens their dark luminaries."

76] This poem, which some communities have made part of the liturgy for the summer period of mourning for Jerusalem's destruction,[1] reaches the heart by a detour over the largest possible distance, that of objectivity. It does not speak directly of the fate that has befallen the victims. Instead, it dramatizes that fate, presenting it as a dialogue between "Solomon's carpets" and a wanderer who had seen them in their former splendor and now happens upon them again in the Bedouin tent of an Ishmaelite. The poem's lament is therefore put into the mouths of the carpets, while both mourning and hope, along with the awareness of Israel's closeness to God—which, in a bold figure of speech, is compared to that of the stars (Isaiah 40:26[2])—are put into the mouth of the wanderer. Mourning, lament, awareness, and hope return from this alienation with even greater passion into the worshiper's breast.

---

1. Rosenzweig is referring, again, to the fast day, *Tish B-Av,* commemorating the destruction of the first and second temples in Jerusalem, and the three week mourning period preceeding it.

2. "Lift up your eyes on high, and see: who hath created these? He that bringeth out their host by number, He calleth them all by name; by the greatness of His might, and for that he is strong in power, not one faileth."

77. NOCTURNAL TEAR

Jerusalem, wail,
   shed the tear, Zion!
The eye of your sons cannot stop weeping
   when it remembers you.
Forget me, oh hand, if I forget you
   City of psalms!
Cleave tongue, to my mouth, if I am
     ever happy!

If my sins
   drove me from my mother's teaching,
If my father's punishment would await me
   because of the weight of my sins,
And if my brother and the son
   of my servant maid took first-born's honor,—
If the soul could
   lay all of this before God!

And turn the cheek to lashes,
   Do not hide your face from spitting,
After such chastisement
   The burden of guilt will be easy,
And live, where hyenas cry,
   with ostriches in desert eggs,
And walk with a heavy heart
   robed in blackish disgust.

But be silent to Him, who does
   not forever forget the poor soul,
Who does not totally destroy!
   No, who turns and takes pity,
Until it will be Israel's day,
   to embrace them in Zion's redemption,
Until He will pull you from the prison of misery
   on robes of love.

77] The lament for Zion, to which three weeks in the summer are dedicated, does not fall silent throughout the rest of the year either; it combines with all the other laments. Thus, it laments also in the nocturnal lamentations during the period preceding the great Days of Judgment and Repentance in the fall, when a tear for Zion is mingled with the confession of sin, and the hope for Zion with a plea for forgiveness.

Oh God, do not be too angry,
   don't remember the guilt forever.
Be zealous for Zion! Do not trade away
   Your remnant in the future.
Speak to Your heir's heart,
   do not steep it deeper into sorrow—
And in the morning there will be jubilation,
   where tears still gushed at night.

78. THE CITY ON HIGH

You sit up high and shine on the world
    You city, throne of the Lord of the world.
  For you my heart yearns from
    the world's western wall.
My insides well up hotly,
    when I recall how it once was,
the glory, now in shambles,
    the abode, now scorned.
And if I could fly on the wings
    of the eagle, I would soon mix
my ears with your dust,
    until it would be malleable like clay.
I seek you, even though your Lord
  is far removed and even
    though in Gilead, Your consolation,
    there now are viper and scorpion.
To caress and to kiss
    your stones I desire,
  and the taste of your soil would
    be for me a reward sweet as honey.

78] In this poem, which begins with the psalmist's vision of the city built on high (Psalm 48:3[1]), certain notes are sounded that appear again and again in the poems of yearning and of travel, up to the great "Zionide." Here, though, they might still be poetic turns of speech, growing from living writings and meant to be used during the summer weeks' liturgy, of which it actually has become a part, if the last line did not contain an almost bashfully hidden allusion from which one can sense that the poet was quite in earnest, as were many thousands in later centuries, when he expressed the wish to die in Jerusalem. For this is the hidden meaning of the concluding double line and not, as might be assumed, a mere spinning out of the preceding one. That last line, using the Hebrew term for a "clod" of soil, alludes to one of the only two scriptural passages in which this word appears but avoids making the allusion obvious by adding the rest of the same verse, in which Job remarks that to the dead, "[t]he clods of the valley are sweet" (Job 21:33).

---

1. "Fair in situation, the joy of the whole earth, even Mount Zion, the uttermost parts of the north, the city of the great King."

79. Between East and West

My heart is in the East, and I   myself am on the western edge.
How could I enjoy drink and food! how   could I ever enjoy it?
Alas, how do I fulfill my promise?   my sacred vow? since
Zion is still in Roman bondage,   and I in Arabic bonds.
All goods of Spain are   chaff to my eye, but
The dust on which once stood   the tabernacle is gold to my eye!

79] Yehuda Halevi's yearning for Zion and his sense of being torn between East and West—which he himself increased by taking the vow that could be fulfilled only in Zion—mark a turning point in the history of the Jewish exile. For a millennium, after the heroic convulsions in Babylon's academies during the first centuries had subsided, the longing for Zion has remained a lifeless possession—"religion." But during the following millennium, at whose start Yehuda Halevi was born, Jewish life begins to flow back into the ancient land. Historically speaking, this flow becomes a broader stream only a century later with the emigration of the French scholars. But the lonely yearning of Halevi's soul is the first beacon of the new movement, a movement that carries into the present day, with only a single fortifying pause for breath during the century following Moses Mendelssohn, during which the leading voices of Western Jewry sought radically to deny this connection.

80. REPLY

Your word—it is steeped in the aroma of myrrh,
  and wrested from the rocks of myrrh mountains;
Any praise can only weakly
  reach for the values of your and your father's house.
You approached me with flattering words,
  but they contained a hostile hidden purpose;
And behind the guise of gentle speech—hid bees,
  and thorns under a mountain of honey.
Shall we not seek the bliss of Salem,
  because today the blind and the lame live there?
So we should seek the welfare of our God's Temple
  for the sake of our brothers, our next of kin.
If what you say were true, see: then it would be sinful
  to bow in the direction of Jerusalem,
And the fathers who lived there as strangers
  would merely have received the right to bury their dead.
And the burial of the embalmed remains of their dead
  would have been an abomination.
And see: the land for which they sighed,
  was caught in the grip of a bad people.
The altars which they built there were for naught!
  Pointless that sacrificial vapors rose to heaven!
The dead shall be remembered—and the ark,
  the tablets shall be devoured by oblivion?
We travel to the place of death and of the worm—but not to the source,
  from which the waters of eternal life sprang forth.
Can we still expect an inheritance besides God's consecration?
  Could we forget the memory?
Do we find, in the East or West,
  a place of hope with assurances of life?
Only the land full of gates
  before which the gates of heaven opened:
Mt. Sinai, Carmel, Bethel, and the
  prophets' houses surrounded by the glory of a Divine mission,
The thrones of the priests of God's throne
  and those of the annointed kings.
And He preserves it for us and for our children,
  even if the desert birds would attack it!

80] The famous man's decision to set out for Zion becomes known, and he receives some advice in the form of a poetic epistle urging him to reconsider. We can only infer the content of this epistle from Halevi's reply, which shows in any event how outrageous his decision must have seemed at the time.

The epistle's author is unknown, but he seems so familiar to us that we could call him by name, not just in one but in a hundred different forms. After all, the assimilationist is an eternal figure among Jews. And his arguments, too, have remained the same—shall one say, appallingly so? Jerusalem, it is said, is no longer of concern to us today, because it is once again inhabited by "the blind and the lame" (II Samuel 5:6,[1] 5:8[2]), by foreign nations, just as it was when David conquered it. And this unhistorical historical argument is linked, then as now, with an unphilosophical philosophical one, with only the unpolitical political one missing, which would be inapplicable in the case of a single individual, anyhow. And philosophy, called upon to provide some relief for the people's forgetfulness, is, then as now, the offspring of Greek thought, which can conceive only of an eternity without beginning or end, but not of an Eternal One who determines the beginning as well as the end.

With its quote from Psalms 122:8ff.,[3] Halevi's reply likewise immediately strikes the immortal double chord of the love of Zion: God and His people. For the sake of the Temple and for the sake of our brethren, Jerusalem remains for us what it always has been. The argument then deals in some detail and at some length with the "historical" objection of the "no longer," refuting it with references

---

1. "And the king and his men went to Jerusalem against the Jebusites, the inhabitants of the land, who spoke unto David saying: 'Except thou take away the blind and the lame, thou shalt not come in hither'; thinking: 'David cannot come hither.'"

2. "And David said on that day: 'Whosoever smiteth the Jebusites, and getteth up to the aqueduct, and taketh away the lame and the blind (that are hateth of David's soul)—.' Wherefore they say: 'The blind and the lame cannot come into the house.'"

3. "For my brethren and companions' sakes, I will now say: 'Peace be within thee.' For the sake of the house of the Lord our God I will seek thy good."

Did not once the fathers receive a field
    fertilized only by thorns and thistles?
And they walked through the length and breadth of it,
    as one strolls through the flowering of a garden,
And they were strangers, sojourners only, asking for hospitality
    and grave site as their ultimate wish.
So they strolled there before the face of God,
    on paths which constantly transform towards the goal.
It is also said that there the dead will rise,
    from the graves' shrouds which envelop them tightly,
That the bodies rejoice there and that
    the souls enter into eternal peace.
Oh see, see my dear, and understand,
    avoid the net and rope which hang all around.
And do not be led astray by the wisdom of the Greeks,
    which never bore fruit, only blossoms.
And their fruit never was to create the world,
    to spread the tent of heaven,
They had no first beginning with first laws,
    no goal for the new month.
Listen to the misguided words of their most wise,
    where night and chaos are the suppositions.
You return home, empty-hearted and confused,
    full of words and distant ideas.
Would it therefore be alright if I had strayed
    from the original path, seeking alternate paths??

to a situation that corresponds to our own, the "not yet"—namely, the time of the patriarchs, to whom the land was holy even though it was just as little their possession as it is ours. In between, the reply points to the orgies with which piety celebrates the dead, thus freeing itself from the burden of genuine future-laden making present of that which is alive. And it praises the land as the only secure place of refuge and as the place of both historical memories and eschatological hopes. And the argument knows it is on the right track, compared to which all the twists and turns of the other's words are merely winding by-paths.

Those words have been forgotten. The reply has remained.

81. The Pilgrim

Yearning for Him, the only one free of death
    drove me to the Temple mount,
Until it no longer allowed me to kiss the children
    in the house and the next generation,
I do not bemoan the garden that I planted
    and watered, whose plantlings happily grow,
And I no longer think of Judah and of Azarel
    who are my flowerbed's most precious flowers,
And the fruit of my sun, the growth of my moons,
    of Isaac, who stood by me like a son.
And I nearly forgot the house of prayer, whose
    classroom was available for care-free hours,
Forgot the joy of my Shabbat days,
    the splendor of the festivals, the proud Passover time [*Osterzeiten*]
And give away my honors to others
    and leave my fame to gentiles.
The shade of brush I trade for my rooms,
    Thorns for the safety of a latch,
And my soul, tired of cultured smells,
    enjoys the smell of cut wild wood,
And I stop walking on the prepared path
    and set my course through oceans wide
To the footstool of my God,
    in order to lay down my senses and my soul,
And I want to go to His holy mountain
    through the gates opposite the gates of clouds,
And allow my nards to flower anew in the Jordan,
    and bathe my flowers in the waters of the Siloa.
God is with me—why should I be afraid,
    since His angels of grace accompany me.
I bring praise to His Name because I live,
    and thanks in the eternity of all eternities.

81] Emigration was no easy matter for Yehuda Halevi; this poem shows how much he had to give up. And just as everything one must leave behind seems to come together at moments of parting, and just as one can fully grasp what one has possessed only at the time of its loss, so the poet, too, traces here in fourteen lines the outline of the life he had lived and loved for all those years: family, friends, a circle of students, some of whose names he memorializes, the synagogue to which he dedicated his poetry, and the school to which he dedicated his thought, the rhythm of the Jewish year with its sabbaths and festivals, and his fame as a poet, which was spread throughout the land.

He speaks only briefly of hardships of the pilgrimage to which he is submitting himself. But these hardships are swallowed up immediately by the dream image, conveyed in all the sweetness of his language, of that which beckons to him at the end of his journey. One senses that it is truly that "yearning for the living God" that allows him to give up the world he knew uncomplainingly, or almost uncomplainingly. "Almost uncomplainingly," for the soft sounds of the regret still resonating within him are preserved in this poem.

82. ALL OF THIS MEANS LITTLE

This heart is Yours, in trust and in fear,
  bending the knee, with boundless gratitude.
I will rejoice in You, then, restlessly and hurriedly,
  I call You when flight and unrest threaten to devour me.
When my ship sets its sails on the dark seas,
  like the wings of storks over the cypress trees,
And when below me the depths roar,
  —do they learn it from my heart or from whom?
And when the flood bubbles like a boiler
  —turning the sea into a boiling brew—
When the West's ship enters the sea of the Phillistines,
  And of the Hittites who contemplate piracy,
And when the wild water animal of the small vessel
  and the ocean dragon sneers, hoping for a meal,
If distress exists as in a first-time mother,
  —the children mature, powerless the waves of birth pangs.
Your name shall be food in my mouth,
  for which I gladly forego drink and food,
And I will not worry about winnings and loss,
  and not about market and fairs,
I will leave them, creations of my loins,
  sister of my soul, only one.
I will forget her son, arrow in my heart,
  whose image fills me instead of mind games,
Fruit of my womb, child of my joys,
  Yehuda, can he ever forget Yehuda?
All of this means little compared to Your love,
  gratefully I approach Your fiery furnace
And live there and bind my heart onto
  the altar, more delicious than animal offering,
And I will have my final resting place in Your land,
  so that it shall bear witness to all this.

82] This poem has not only the same meter as the previous poem but also the same subject matter. Yet one barely notices this similarity, because of the difference in their mood. Here, the poet's imagination, anticipating the future, flies ahead of the slow course of events. What is anticipated is that passionate, God-enthralled "I am Yours" of the pilgrimage and the artfully described terror of the sea journey on a Christian vessel through Islamic waters. Also anticipated is the entirely present subject of the previous poem—pain at all that he leaves behind. But even this pain is described here as something he is going to feel rather than something he is feeling today. Thus, instead of mentioning, as the preceding poem does, the names of many people, and the things that had enriched his life, and bathing it all in the golden glow of the hour of parting, this poem singles out only the two persons closest to his innermost heart, the wound that no passage of time will ever allow to heal: his only child (and he divulges at this place and at this moment of unabashed pain how much she has meant to him) and her son, the evidently still young grandson who bears his name. Then comes the only sentence in the poem not written in the future tense: "All of this matters little, compared to Your love." It is the line that designates that point in the present, this present filled with longing for God, from which all his anticipation arose. From here, too, will arise the last anticipation, that of the fulfillment, the goal, when he shall present his heart as a burnt-offering at the sacred place. The offering of the poet's heart means to him, who dreams of a restoration of visible sacrifices, not a substitute for these, but, just as in the quarrel among the prophets and psalmists concerning the sacrifices, a supplement to them and an elevation of them. And then comes the very last anticipation of all, that of the final fulfillment and the final goal, his grave in the sacred ground, bearing witness to the greatest deed of his life.

For this is how the poet, who had lived so rich a life, saw the end of his life. And it is thus that he interpreted it in anticipation at the conclusion of the *Kuzari*, which is the most paradoxial, hence most true-to-life and most moving, of all endings of philosophical works. It ranks along with—no, it is superior to—Plato's *Phaedo*, because there is no Plato standing between the Socrates of the dialogue and the man dying in reality.

83. A COMPELLING FORCE

Already my heart rose   to the house   of the Lord,
  but I still   dreaded home-   lessness.
Then He, who is rich   in wisdom, created a reason   for me to be homeless;
  thus He provided   for me   the meaning.
Therefore at   every resting place   I prostrate myself,
  and thank Him   for every step   that I advance.

83] And yet, despite all his yearning to undertake that pilgrimage, the fear of having to give up the life in which he had felt rooted and at home for more than fifty years and the horror at the thought of homelessness prove to be stronger. But something happens that gives him that which he still lacks: compulsion. Now he goes willingly.

The poet does not divulge what it is that happened. We do not know what event made leaving home appealing to him, or made it actually necessary. The fact that he tells us even this much is almost amazing. For this is something people usually do not talk about, though perhaps everyone experiences it at some time for it deeply hurts their pride.

Man seeks honor through the deed. But in every deed there is a moment when man loses his courage, precisely because he has expended it fully. If at this point a compulsion did not come that helped give birth to this deed, it would never see the light of day. But this compulsion does come. Man has a right to it, and this right is recognized by God. All praying is ultimately a praying for this compulsion; all thanking a thanking for having received it. Yet the shame surrounding the prayer has its basis in this need.

84. SUPPLICATION

Oh God, may the wave always rock me to sleep
   and do not order the ocean bottom to dry up,
Until I thank You for Your grace, and thank
   the flood for its welling up and the West for its flight.
They bring me closer to the place of Your loving yoke,
   No longer do I have to submit to the Arab yoke.
And how did my wishes come true!
   I trust in You—Your surety is real.

85. THE FLOOD

Did the flood come anew which buried land and sea?
   So that we can no longer see the boundaries of solid earth,
Not human being, animal or bird—has it all
   ended? did it retreat to the land of the shadows?
If I could see mountains and cliffs—what relief!
   My heart yearns for desert thorns.
I look to all sides—not a soul.
   Only water, heavens, and the planks of the ark.
And Leviathan,—ashen grey the abyss,
   when he beats on the depths with his sides.
The ocean's heart would gladly hide the small vessel,
   as if a thief's bounty in its clutches.
Thus the ocean roars. My heart rejoices, for soon
   it may thank God in the sanctuary.

84] How strange is this little prayer spoken during the sea voyage, which regards waves and wind and God's mercy only as vehicles for the poet's yearning! Once this yearning is stilled, the waves may rest and the sea may dry up. World, do not perish, sky, do not collapse, before I may be with my beloved!

85] This is probably the most beautiful of the poems written on that sea voyage. It keeps an equal distance from the cheap bombast and the equally cheap moralizing to which its subject matter could easily lead, and it remains within the sphere of the most immediate facts. To this sphere belongs, for the poet, the biblical memory that must necessarily become present to him due to the solitude of the high seas: the Flood. He expresses the most natural sentiment of a sea traveler: a terror that has not yet been robbed of its good conscience by any sentimentality about nature. And it is from the very absence of any ambivalent feelings that he elicits what is at the same time the simplest and the most powerful word and image. And he finds in just this purity of vision the courage for the grand ending, which dares—and which may dare—to contrast the roaring of the vast sea with the exultation of his own heart, which is on its way to its goal.

86. Excursus: Storm

1.[1]

Yes, He plans and works
even enshrouded in clouds,
—far from the ocean
takes place His Judgment.

Human deed is praiseworthy?
Without His counsel
it is a vain possession,
effort without importance.

From the grip of the land
the heroic strength
happily takes off to the sea,
it blazes a trail.

But sin turns the
wheel; the journey goes
to the West, and see,
how it pulls to the East.

Until he realizes:
no steering, no learning
makes a safe journey,
and does not set the direction.

In reflection he
recognizes humbly,
what his despair expresses
while he is in exile:

Where do I go
before Your spirit
and oh, where do I flee
from Your countenance!

---

1. Numbers have been added to aid the reader in following Rosenzweig's commentary.

86] Since its discovery and publication by Luzatto, this has been perhaps Yehuda Halevi's most celebrated poem, next to the "Zionide." It may owe its fame, at least in part, to the surprise that he was, or even that "people at that time," "were able to produce something like that." Heine's[1] "North Sea Pictures," and probably the tendencies toward worldliness of modern Hebrew poetry as well, were the forces behind the enthusiasm expressed for this poem in the nineteenth century, and they also haunt the numerous translations of this work.

Actually, it is a brilliant showpiece; today, one might call it a piece for recitation. Poetically, it ranks far below the little poem "The Flood," just to mention something related in content. But just because of this, it may perhaps lend itself to a study of Yehuda Halevi's art, of his *techne.*

The poem displays a monumental objectivity. In view of the compass points mentioned in the fourth quatrain of its first stanza,[2] one might even question whether it really owes its creation to the poet's journey to Zion, if it were not for the fact that this abstraction from the reality he himself experienced was not so typical of this poem, which does not mention with a single word the goal of the poet's voyage. In short, it is a very generalized "I" that speaks here; and at the poem's beginning, it is not even that.

---

1. Heinrich Heine (1797–1856), born Jewish, chose baptism; he was a poet, essayist, critic, wit and a famous member of postemancipatory German Jewish intelligentsia.

2. TK: Rosenzweig uses the word *Stropehn*, "stanzas," to refer to sections of the poem, each of which contains several quatrains.

2.

The oceans broil
in chaos
and they roll
without rhyme or reason.

In the dark night
the noise of the waters crashes down,
hell's depth awakens
with a deep roar.

The kettle of waters sighs
the ocean roars
but oh, who soothes
the noisy horror.

But the energy consumes
itself: The wall of water disperses!
It half sinks, half lifts itself
up high like a mountain

The small vessel shoots
upward, and down! the eye
hesitates, and the crew
queries whether the body will hold up.

My heart petrifies like stone
I wait: does someone relieve the pain
as Moses once did that of
his brothers and sisters?

I would like to cry
to the Lord loudly
but do not sins
block the way?

3.

And all around waves encircle
and the noise from the East
breaks up the vessel's screeching and tosses
the spray all around

The first stanza is purely gnomic. In the most general way, it anticipates the content of the whole work, which is structured with most conscious artistry. In the same way, within this stanza it is the first quatrain that presents the theological basis for its moral content. That stanza's subject is "the man"—the man who sets out, full of self-confidence, and by means of the sea voyage is led to repentance and a recognition of divine judgment, so that he learns to pronounce the words of the psalmist (Psalms 139:7[3]) in awareness of their truth. Then the actual content of the poem begins.

This is distributed over the four stanzas in such a way that the second and third portray the storm, the fourth and fifth the rescue. The depiction of the storm, with the exception of one passage, which will be discussed presently, maintains the objectivity of the third person, without a lyrical "I," matter-of-fact. In the depiction of the rescue, the first person—the I of the speaker—dominates in the fourth stanza, whereas in the fifth the personal third person of the blessing wish dominates, as it were, borne by the address to God. These two parts are now meshed by the same device that also rivets together the two just-described halves of the second part, a device that, were it not the product of consummate and conscious artistry, could only be called bungling. It could easily have been avoided. And as if that were not enough, this bungling is distributed over the whole poem in strict symmetry.

---

3. "Whither shall I go from Thy spirit? Or whither shall I flee from Thy presence?"

The vessel's bow shoots forth
  and its foredeck shudders,
  the vessel's mast no longer
is flanked by a pair of wings.

There it boils without fire;
  courage demands a high price;
  the steering wheel refuses
to obey the captain

The vessel's master is meek and silent,
  and the vessel's servant paralyzed and bowed
  and the vessel's man sad and stupefied,
and the vessel's bridge empty.

And the small vessel—wobbles and stomps
  as if enveloped in a stupor,
  the fist lets go
resignedly that which is too hard

And Leviathan, hero
  on ocean's floor, invites
  as guests into the
wedding tent his entire host.

And the hand of prince ocean
  holds fast to its token—
  there is no refuge,
and no light of hope!

4.

The eyes look up to you,
  to the Lord, far away,
  yes I gladly sacrifice to you
all our supplications.

I tremble within
  and stand here fearfully,
  and submit to You my pain
as Jonah once did.

The first quatrain of the third and fourth stanzas and the last quatrain of the fifth one—that is, the center of the first and the cornerstone of the second part—are linked together by the same rhyme, in part even by the same rhyming words. One of them, the divine and gracious name *Lord,* appears in all three stanzas and only in those three. No other name for God appears in the poem. The first of these three passages, which are distributed through the poem like the rhyming link between two stanzas in *terza rima,* inserts the I of the poem and the name of God into the raging of the abandoned, truly godless, and impersonal elements. This name is still in the third person, and the I is still hesitant in its awareness of sin, not yet raising itself to cry out to God. The whole second half of the storm section must first pass by, and the autonomy of the elements must increase to the terrors of mythic personification— in the two final quatrains of the third stanza—before man in his utmost fear overcomes his fear of crying out to God. The opening quatrain of the fourth stanza marks the moment of this outcry. And this stanza, which is the first half of the second part, spins this

When I remember
the Sea of Reeds—
do I merely desire
to recall it in song?

That the waters of the
Jordan receded, gives
me paradise-like joy,
revealed to Him.

He who sweetens bitter waters,
that the day turns friendly,
which at first was
angry and bad, a day of wrath.

The two eyes flee
upward to seek Him,
paths crisscross
the dangerous waters.

The earth's fire—
results from its anger;
it flows and see: all
around there are flakes

5.

He turned the wrath
from the servant, so that
he took courage anew, he
does not rest in the night

The word descended from the heights,
and resounded peacefully
in hell's anger—
then the battle ceased.

And the storm's frenzy
became smooth like cream,
fear disappeared
and confidence awakened.

outcry further, giving, as it were, the sketch of a poem of supplication amid a watery catastrophe. But since the destiny of Jonah is the only parallel case in the Bible, the poet must resort to other cases that manifest God's power over the watery element, such as the miracles at the Sea of Reeds (Exodus 14) and at the Jordan (Joshua 3), the sweetening of the bitter waters (Exodus 15:22–25) and the gushing forth of the waters at Massah and Maribah (Exodus 17:1–7). Finally, after Isaiah's words about the God who "maketh a way in the sea, and a path in the mighty waters" (Isaiah 43:16), the prayer ends in the simple acknowledgment of God's omnipotence and His power over wind and water. And here, from the final quatrain of the fourth stanza to the opening quatrain of the fifth, there occurs that other, previously mentioned, equating of rhymes and near equating of rhyming words, by means of which the beginning of the fulfillment becomes the rhyme to the end of the supplication.

The ear of the oppressed host
listened to the heavens,
and heard the
chorus of Grace approach.

May salvation's message
reach the people in need,
whom prison exhausted
and despot and pressure paralyzed.

Those who experience storm and suffering
like the vessel, may they
soon rejoice
in psalms of gratitude:

Emerge, oh faith, from a
starless dark night,
because the glory of the Lord
surrounds you anew!

And now the fulfillment is complete, and the waters have once again transformed themselves, like the testing drink of jealousy (Numbers 5), which according to the Talmud did not kill but instead made fruitful the body of a woman who is unjustly suspected.[4] Thus, the poem sees in what has happened a metaphor for the "storm-tossed, tormented" (Isaiah 54:11) Maiden Israel. The name of God is now given and used as a rhyme, for the third time; but now again it is used no longer as an address, not out of timidity like the first time, but out of certainty. And with the calling of the divine name, it calls down blessings upon those it now addresses: the people.

---

4. I am not certain of Rosenzweig's reference, but perhaps it is to the Midrash, *Numbers Rabbah* 9:15 where the ashes of the "bitter waters" are likened to Abraham's "I am but dust and ashes" (Genesis 18:27), indicating that a worthy woman—one who passes "the testing drink of jealousy"—will bear a son like Abraham.

87. SPOKEN TO THE HEART

I speak from the heart   of the waters   to the heart
  that shudders and trembles,   when their anger   resounds:
When you trust in   God, who created   the waters,
  in the Name, in   whom rests an eternity   and a world,
Then you will not tremble,   even if the waters   build up,
  because He   who stays the waters   is with you.

88. CALM AFTER THE STORM
(Fragment)

Night arrived! The sun is gone,—the multitudes
  of the heavens are in place, and he is the general of the brothers.
Like a Moorish woman decked out in gold,
  like purple surrounded by precious stones.
And stars, who wander through the center of the ocean
  like heavenly rungs which have been displaced.
According to their model they light up the ocean's heart,
  as if fire workers played a joke.
The surface of the waters and the heavens—far
  and deep they rest, clear, as if cast in stone.
The ocean parallels the heavens: the two now
  are two oceans, which flowed together.
And between them a third ocean: my heart,
  the waves of its new songs rise up high.

87] The substance of the great hymn discussed in the preceding excursus is given here in six epigrammatic lines. Yet this is no epigram. Instead, in the sublimity of the rhythm, with the alternately thunderous and jubilant gravity of the bisyllabic line ends, this is a true lyric poem, more so that the ambitious hymn.

88] These lines form the conclusion of a long poem in which the poet admonishes himself to give up the pleasures of his familiar surroundings and to make up his mind to leave for his pilgrimage. The anticipatory account of the discomforts of the voyage, particularly of a storm on the high seas, then takes up the greater part of the poem. In its technical mastery and facility, it is strongly reminiscent of the poem discussed in "Excursus: Storm."[1] There, too, one could not quite get rid of what is at least a suspicion that it may have been written before that voyage. But then we come to the concluding lines, which, whether they were written afterward, under the actual impression of the voyage, or beforehand in brilliant anticipation, are among the greatest of Yehuda Halevi's poetry. This is totally objective poetry, metaphor following metaphor, vision following vision. But each vision expands fully within itself; in all the fullness there is no crowding of visions. Instead, there arises from all these images only one image, that of the nocturnally calm sea.

---

1. Poem number 86 above.

89. To the West Wind

It is Your wind, West!   Its wingbeat   is as mild
  as the smell of nards   and apples!   In the
Grocer's pantry   with spices   is your origin,
  not in the hamper,   where the winds   are kept.
Swing yourself up herald-like,   little swallow   I, like the nectar of myrrh,
  from the swallow-like whiff   that escapes   the bouquet.
How do those yearn   for you who sit   backwards on
  the ocean's back and   on the back   of the plank!
Oh, do not remove   your hand   from the vessel,
  whether the day   is light or   looses its sight.
Master the abyss of the depths,   split the heart   of the oceans,
  before you go   to rest, hurry to the   holy mountain.
And scold the East [wind]   which stirs up   the ocean, so it
  resembles a pot which   the servants put   on the stove.
What shall one do,   tied to a creature,   which soon
  sits like an old man,   and soon plays freely,   like a child!
But the secret of   my pleading   rests with Him,
  who forms the   mountains and created   the winds.

89] Among Yehuda Halevi's poems there is also one called "To Zephyr"—not among the love songs but among the songs of his pilgrimage, which after all are likewise songs expressing a kind of love. "To the West Wind" is equal in its sweetness to any of the famous west wind poems in world literature. It sings the praises of the moist pinions that bear the ship to the place of his yoke of love. In Hebrew, the rhyming word for wind[1] has in itself a melting sweetness, just as its corresponding German word[2] has a gentle softness. Out of this mood, engendered by swaying and fragrance, but without destroying it, the poet can say everything—as demanded by his high office, which he shares with children and fools. Immediately following the humorous shoulder shrugging of the next-to-last couplet, which smiles at the creature's bond to a "creature," he can pass on to the humbly serious sublimity of the last couplet, looking up to the One who, in the words of the prophet, "created the wind" (Amos 4:13).

---

1. *Ruach,* also translated as "breath" and "spirit."
2. *Wind.*

90. In the Harbor

Be silent, roar of the ocean! Until the vessel's bow
  approaches for the disciple to kiss the master's
Clever eyes and hands, master Aharon,
  whose staff greened again and again.
He teaches—never telling his mouth: enough!
  he gives—never telling his hand: enough!
Today I thank the East wind for its soft breeze,
  but tomorrow I will curse the west wind's rush.
How could he leave the balsam of Gilead
  in whose flesh the plough of a snake's fang sunk itself?
How could one exchange the shelter of thick leaves
  for heat and frost and the lies of an illusion?
I choose the home of the Almighty over flimsy huts!
  My roof is the city in which He dwelled!

90] A constant east wind deflects the ship from its course, forcing it to land in an Egyptian harbor. From the open sea, whose roaring had filled the poet's ears for weeks, it steers into the port of Alexandria. And what happens then is what we would least have expected: while thinking of the friend he plans to visit there, the memory of his old life's sweet routine, which he will find again among Egypt's fortunate and cultured Jews, regains its hold on the weak human heart of the poet and pilgrim, who thought he had left all earthly ties behind. Even in this first moment, he feels this with such force that at the mere thought of a familiar roof, he remembers with a cry—to be sure, a cry of jubilation, but nevertheless one that is shattering in its shrill suddenness—that his roof will be in a place where no more roofs are standing. So this cry at the moment of landing calls the life-addicted soul of the one landing, who after all thinks he will be traveling on "tomorrow," back to the self-imposed discipline of his lofty goal. And nevertheless this "tomorrow" will turn into months.

91. On Egyptian Soil

See the cities, open the mind to the places
    in which the people Israel lived,
And honor Egypt, step on the soil
    gingerly and do not walk with self-confidence.
The streets here—God walked on them, looking
    for doorposts that testify to the blood bond,
The fiery column and the pillar of clouds
    everyone's eyes hope for and see.
Here the keepers of the covenant despaired,
    the quarters of the eternal people are here!

92. The River

God, Your miracles are told truthfully from generation
    to generation, from father to son.
The river Nile which You turned to blood testifies
    —not to work of necromants and mystagogues,
Only to Your Name, through Moses and through Aharon,
    the staff, first turned into a snake,
Helps Your faithful servant who has come
    to see the places of Your miracles.

91] As he thus travels throughout the land, everywhere a guest of the luminaries of the Jewish community, everywhere celebrated, everywhere lovingly urged to stay, he can nevertheless justify his delay to himself with the reflection that this too is historic ground and that the honor he pays to Egypt is intended for the land as the stage of Jewish history. To such an extent is the tone of this poem one of self-justification that it has even been suspected that this is not the poet's voice speaking but instead the admonition of one of his Egyptian friends to leave off his strange and perverse plan of a pilgrimage and to remain in their midst. But such a distribution of voices among different persons is hardly necessary, for the following poem, whose ending is certain proof of Yehuda Halevi's authorship, shows how he himself had been seized by the magic of that historical soil. Therefore, it is within himself that those cautionary voices now speak, asking him whether he had not tried to be "too righteous," and whether what is enough for others should not suffice for him, too.

92] Historical memories still cling to rivers in a different way from how they cling to solid land. For centuries past have altered the land in many ways, although—no, because—it is solid. But the river flowing through that land is the same today as it was millennia ago, just because it never, not even for one moment, remained the same. Thus, it still bears more immediate witness to that which happened by it and with it than does the land surrounding it.

93. HITHER . . .

Oh waters, carry me to Zoan,
     to the Sea of Reeds, to Horeb, waters,
Then I shall turn to Shiloh
        where the sacred place is buried under rubble,
And I shall follow the ways of
        the sacred ark of the covenant, until I
Have tasted the dust of its grave,
        which is sweeter than honey,
Have seen the abodes of the fair one
     who forgets her nest,
From which doves were exiled,
        now the brood of ravens lives in it.

93] But the river awakens also the old tones of yearning. For its network of waterways could carry the vessel that could take the poet from the northeastern "Tanitic" arm of the Nile Delta (according to the Septuagint, "Tanis" is the biblical "Zoan"[1]) on one of its narrow corss-connections over to the lakes of the Isthmus of Suez, and from there into the Red Sea—it could.

So he loses himself completely in his longing and forgets for once his inner conflict. Or might those concluding verses—which, along with the rest of the poem, were in several communities made part of the liturgy of the midsummer weeks of mourning for the fall of Jerusalem—be genuine? Earlier publishers rejected them, due to their metric deviation from the preceding verses; but those deviations actually speak for their authenticity, or at least for their author's familiarity with the subtleties of Arabic metrics.

> Thus does this greatly pain
> My heart, which fears
> Tomorrow will become night through
> My sinful flesh and blood.
> My bosom perishes quite
> And languishes at the mountain of myrrh
> Thus does life desire
> To be housed in the care of the body.

If this is so, then the poet's conflicted consciousness of delay for which he himself is responsible would hammer away even in this poem, with its spondaic displacement of the iambic rhythm of the longing motif.

---

1. Zoan is mentioned at *Numbers* 13:22; *Isaiah* 19:11, 19:13, 30:4; *Ezekial* 30:14; *Psalms* 78:12, 78:43.

94. PRESENTIMENT

Your heart— does it want that   my will   be done,
   allow me   to see   the face   of my Lord.
For I do not   find rest   for these   two feet,
   until I   shall dwell   where He   dwells.
My step,   do not   detain it   from leaving,
   for I fear   that before then   I will experience   my sorrow.
My prayer: below the splendor   of the wings   a place
   so that I   may rest   where   our fathers lie!

94] Out of all this tangle of feelings, the simple word of truth, his heart's truth, breaks through once again—and it cannot be otherwise. This poem is part of a poetic epistle, one of several written during those Egyptian months that have been preserved. But the letter part preceding it is lost, and the part following it does not refer to it. Even so, its meaning is clear. The poet implores his Egyptian friends, in the name of their friendship, to let him go. This time, there is no weighing of the advantages of the Holy Land against the reluctantly admitted advantages of Egypt. There is no arguing, nor are there any poetic courtesies. There are only very quiet words, but they are spoken from the heart. And the longing for a grave in holy ground, which again and again causes him to shudder, is now combined with the fearful premonition that his fate might overtake him, were he to hesitate any longer. Supplication, unrest, and premonition are joined in the quiet prayer at the end. Anyone who prays in this way has found himself again, at least in that moment.

But how was it possible for him to lose himself? Anyone who would ask this question does not know how narrow is the space allotted to man and his freedom just in making ultimate decisions. If ever an entire life went into ripening the fruit of a single deed, it was this one. And yet it took a compelling force before the deed could really begin to be carried out. And as if there were a danger that this deed might even then become arrogant and might forget to render the thanks that had been promised at every step granted to it, its strength fails once more just before its final realization. The waters of earthly life threaten anew to engulf the swimmer, and in and from his distress he must again learn how to pray—the prayer of anguish, quite sudden, immediate, astonishing even to the one praying himself—and out of his plea to his friends, there breaks forth the restlessness of his feet, the trembling of his heart, hardly in the form of a prayer, only the thought of a prayer, a wanting to pray.

God gives man the freedom to make the ultimate decision— indeed just this and only this decision. But in giving this, He never-

theless retains the strength for its realization in His own treasury, and he makes gifts from it just to him who has made a decision and only when called on over and over again to do so. For He does not wish to make Himself superfluous by that gift of freedom; on the contrary, He wishes to be highly necessary. He loans to man a Today, and thus He makes Himself the Lord of Tomorrow. Therefore, man must tremble for his Today, as long as a Tomorrow may still be coming. And if at the beginning of his hopes' realization there stood that God-sent compelling force, there stands at the end, just before the goal, the driving force of fear, of God-induced fear that no more Tomorrows will follow this Today. But then, out of this fear the deed is finally born, raising his Today into an eternal Tomorrow.

95. TO ZION

Zion! You do not inquire about those who carry Your yoke,
  Your remnant, who asks for You alone?
West, east, north, and southwind,—oh allow them to bring
  You greetings from him who is far and near, everywhere.
Greetings from him who yearns, whose tear is like [Mt.] Hermon's dew;
  Oh, if it could only sink to Your mountain meadows.
When I weep about Your sorrow, I turn into a wolf; when I dream of You,
                                                                freed,
  I become a harp that accompanies Your song.
My heart years for Machanajim, for Bethel, for Pniel,
  And wherever Your people worship You.
Here the Almighty descended to You, and He who created You,
  Created Your gates parallel to the gates of heaven.
And God's brightness surrounded You,—how could
  You see the lights of the sun and moon and stars?
How could I hesitate to pour out the soul, where God's spirit
  Poured itself out onto Your great ones.
You, Royal palace, throne of God, how dare the
  Grandchildren of your servant sit on the throne of your leaders.
Oh if my foot would only take me to where God answered
  The questions of Your messengers and prophets.
If I had wings, how would I fly to You,
  To hide my torn heart in Your crevices.
I would fall on my face, on Your ground, and I
  Would caress Your rocks and touch Your dust sorrowfully;
And if I could stand before our ancestors' graves deeply moved,
  In Hebron before Your proudest sarcophagus
If I could stroll through Your woods, the vineyards, and if in the south
  I could stand before Your border mountains full of fear,
Where Hor and Abarim, Your great twin stars,
  Your two luminaries and teachers, once lay in death.
Life of the soul, Your air! Your dust is filled with the spicy myrrh of the
  Fragrance, honey drips from the arriving wave.
To wander barefoot and bare through the desolation
  where once stood Your Temple—where could one find equal joy.
There where Your cherubim lived in the innermost room,
  There where he lived who escaped from the confines of the inner sanctum.
I shave, discarding the adornment of the head; my curse may accuse the time
  Which cast off anointed ones to an unclean land.

95] This dirge is chanted in synagogues all over the world every year on the Ninth of Av, the day on which the first and the second temples were burned. It is only one among a great many "siblings," quite a few of which are direct imitations of this one, down to the meter, rhyme, and opening words. For Yehuda Halevi created this genre. He was the first to adopt that meter of Arabic poetry whose effect, due to alternating lines of thirteen and fourteen syllables, strangely resembles the elegiac meter used by the ancients—a resemblance that disappears again, due to the enormous, dragging weight of the concluding line's three-stress ending. By the rhyme he chose here (but which he also used elsewhere, for instance in some love poems—it is the feminine possessive pronoun in the second person) he gave, maybe unconsciously, to that meter a sound reminiscent of the "Alas!"[1] at the beginning of the Lamentations of Jeremiah, which are read on that day. That sound, as has been noted, and probably correctly, may have contributed to making this rhyme the classical one for that day's Lamentations. But all of this is merely what is most obvious. The poem's impact is due to something else: the actuality of its address, something for which all poetry constantly strives, but which it very rarely achieves; in short, to the truth of its first word, *Zion.*

Zion is the addressee.[2] Yet it is by no means "personified." To be personified, something of its existence preceding that address would have to resonate still. But that is not the case. Zion exists only in that address, only as an addressee. All else—with the sole exception of the poet who addresses it—sinks back into the third person, coming alive only to the extent that it is taken up in the word *your,* which is repeated more than sixty times as an end rhyme and within the line. It is not only the people that loses whatever existence it has other than that implied in this "your," but the One who is usually the most addressed, who is the Addressee as such, God Himself, is perceived exclusively as the One whose spirit flowed into "your great ones," as "your Creator," "your Light," as the One who "revealed Himself to your prophets and seers," as the One who—in the most powerful formulation—"desires to make you His home."

---

1. Hebrew: *"Eicha"*; German: *"Ach."*
2. TK: Rosenzweig uses the feminine form, *die Angeredete,* whereas the German noun *Zion* normally would be either masculine or neuter.

How could I enjoy food and drink at an hour when
   Packs of dogs harass Your lions.
Or how could my eyes enjoy the light of the day,
   When I have to see crows feed on Your eagles' flesh.
Cast off the cups of suffering! Grant a small rest!
   For my heart has long been heavy from Your poison, and my stomach
                                                    full of gall.
I empty You from froth to yeast, when I
   See Shomron and the fate of Salem in prophetic garb.
Zion, You jewel, long embedded in grace and love,
   See how Your faithful surround themselves with You like a wall.
Those who celebrate Your well-being, and suffer
   The agony of Your desolation, and decry the woe of Your demise;
They bow wherever they are, turned to the direction of Your gate,
   And they flee from prisons to You on the chariots of yearnings.
Flock of Your exiled herds, straying from mountains to valleys.
   Yet it never forgot the time spent in Your walls.
Those who grasp the hem of Your train, those who would like to swing
   Onto Your palm trees, into Your branches.
Euphrates and Nile valley—how small they are before You with all their glory!
   Their knowledge became wind when Your justice, Your light prophesied.
Where did Your king, Your prophet, where Your priest
   And bard find tribes and armies?
Change and transformation threaten each heathen kingdom;
   Your treasure stands, Your crowns reach upward, eternally young.
Your God Himself desired You as His abode—And blessed is the being
   Who may settle near Him on Your rocky estates.
Blessed is he who persists and experiences, and sees the rising of Your light,
   Whose beams lighten up the nightly shadows.
To see Your chosen in happiness, to rejoice with You,
   Who shines youthfully as once in the days of yore.

This flame of immediacy, burning with undiminished intensity throughout thirty-four couplets with only two interruptions (the first of which is hardly noticeable) could not have been powered by the poet, not as a poet. It is the millenia of this people, those past as well as those still to come, from which the power of this immediacy flows to the poet, a power that is so great that even if its sources may vanish from his sight, it still flows back, year after year in an uninterrupted stream, into the sources from which it arose.

The two interruptions in the flame of the "You," which are mentioned above, divide the poem's otherwise continuous flow of lamentation. *Longing* is the dominant word in its first third, up to the fifteenth couplet, a longing that penetrates questions, wishes, the price, and the dreaming anticipation of fulfillment until in the sixteenth couplet it breaks into a jubilant cry of rapture in which even longing is forgotten. It is through just this jubilant cry that the longing is awakened from its dream of fulfillment to an awareness of suffering and of the self, in the seventeenth through the twenty-first couplets. This awakening is sufficiently abrupt to do what the rapturous dream of the sixteenth couplet could not do: break for a moment through the magic circle of the I and You, even linguistically. In the twenty-second couplet, the I, now torn out of the previous context, no longer speaks with Zion, but apostrophizes its own suffering for two couplets: "Cups of suffering! Grant . . ." But it is just in this apostrophe that Jerusalem's lot intrudes, and in the twenty-fourth couplet, Zion is once again addressed in a renewed apostrophe that continues to the end: "Zion, You jewel . . ."

And now it is no longer dreamy longing, but neither is it awakened despair, but rather lucid, manly consciousness, clear, enthusiastic vision, knowledge of Israel's suffering and Israel's greatness, and knowledge that they are both destined to crown Zion with an eternal crown. Thus, the two last couplets may forget all lamentation and jubilantly anticipate the jubilation that is to come: "Blessed is he who persists and experiences, and sees."

It is customary to dismiss as a legend the story that Yehuda Halevi, a song on his lips as he saw the holy city at the end of his pilgrimage, was murdered by an Arab. No doubt it is a legend. But there is even less doubt that the real story cannot have been much different. The man who wrote this poem must have had it with him in the hour of his death. It left no room for anything else.

SELECTED BIBLIOGRAPHY

Selected Works of Rosenzweig

Hegel und der Staat, 2 volumes. Munchen und Berlin: R. Oldenbourg, 1920; one-volume edition, Aalen: Scienta Verlag, 1962.

Der Stern der Erlosung. Frankfort on the Main, 1921; second edition, Frankfort, 1930; Heidelberg, 1954; The Hague, 1976. *The Star of Redemption.* Translation (of second edition, 1930) by William W. Hallo. New York: Holt, Rinehart, and Winston, 1964, 1970, 1971; Boston: Beacon Press, 1972; Notre Dame: Notre Dame Press, 1985.

Sechzig Hymnen und Gedichte des Jehuda Halevi, deutsch. Translation and commentary by Franz Rosenzweig. Konstanz, 1924.

Briefe. Edited by Edith Rosenzweig and Ernst Simon. Berlin: Schocken Verlag, 1935.

Kleinere Schriften. Berlin: Schocken Verlag, 1937.

Franz Rosenzweig: Der Mench und sein Werk. Gesammelte Schriften, three volumes. Edited by Rachel Rosenzweig and Edith Rosenzweig-Scheidmann, with Bernhard Casper. The Hague: Martinus Nijhoff, 1979.

Judaism Despite Christianity: The "Letters on Christianity and Judaism" between Eugen Rosenstock-Huessy and Franz Rosenzweig. Edited by Eugen Rosenstock-Huessy. Translated by Dorethy Emett. Tuscaloosa: University of Alabama Press, 1969; New York: Schocken Books, 1971.

Von gesunden und kranken Menschenverstand (1921, unpublished). Dusseldorf: Joseph Melzer Verlag, 1963. *Understanding the Sick and the Healthy: A View of World, Man, and God.* Translated by Nahum N. Glatzer and T. Luckman. Edited by Nahum N. Glatzer. New York: Noonday Press, 1954. Cambridge, MA: Harvard University Press, 1999.

On Jewish Learning. Edited by Nahum N. Glatzer. Translated by Nahum N. Glatzer and William Wolf. New York: Schocken Books, 1955, 1989.

Franz Rosenzweig: His Life and Thought. Presented by Nahum N. Glatzer. New York: Schocken Books, 1953; second revised edition, 1961, 1967, 1972.

(With Martin Buber) *Scripture and Translation.* Translated by Lawrence Rosenwald with Everett Fox (Bloomington: Indiana University Press, 1994).

God, Man, and the World: Lectures and Essays. Edited and translated by Barbara Galli. Syracuse: Syracuse University Press, 1998.

Franz Rosenzweig's 'The New Thinking.' Edited and translated by Barbara Galli and Alan Udoff. Syracuse: Syracuse University Press, 1999.

Philosophical and Theological Writings. Translated by Paul W. Franks and Michael Morgan. New York: Hackett Publishing Company, 1999.

Selected Secondary Works on Rosenzweig in English

Cohen, Richard A. *Elevations: The Height of the Good in Rosenzweig and Levinas.* Chicago: University of Chicago Press, 1994.

Freund, Else-Rahel. *Franz Rosenzweig's Philosophy of Existence: An Analysis of "The Star of Redemption."* Translated by Stephen L. Weinstein and Robert Israel, edited by Paul Mendes-Flohr. The Hague, Martinus Nijhoff, 1979.

Gibbs, Robert. *Correlations in Rosenzweig and Levinas.* Princeton: Princeton University Press, 1992.

Miller, Ronald H. *The Challenge of Dialogue: The Contribution of Franz Rosenzweig to Jewish-Christian Understanding.* Washington, D.C.: University Press of America, 1992.

Moses, Stephane. *System and Revelation: The Philosophy of Franz Rosenzweig.* Translated by Catherine Tihanyi. Detroit: Wayne State University Press, 1992.

The Philosophy of Franz Rosenzweig. Edited by Paul Mendes-Flohr. Hanover: University Press of New England, 1988.

Rubinstein, Ernest, *An Episode of Jewish Romanticism: Franz Rosenzweig's 'The Star of Redemption.'* Albany: State University of New York Press, 1999.

Schwarzchild, Steven S. *Franz Rosenzweig (1886–1929): Guide of Reversioners.* London: Education Committee of the Hillel Foundation, 1960.

INDEX OF INTRODUCTIONS AND COMMENTARIES